Interpr

The New D(

INTERPRETING AMERICAN HISTORY SERIES

Brian D. McKnight and James S. Humphreys, series editors

THE AGE OF ANDREW JACKSON
Edited by Brian D. McKnight and James S. Humphreys

THE NEW DEAL AND THE GREAT DEPRESSION
Edited by Aaron D. Purcell

INTERPRETING AMERICAN HISTORY

THE NEW DEAL

and the

GREAT DEPRESSION

Edited by

AARON D. PURCELL

The Kent State University Press

Kent, Ohio

Library of Congress Catalog Card Number 2013043542
ISBN 978-1-60635-220-5
Manufactured in the United States of America

LIBRARY OF CONGRESS CATALOGING-IN-PUBLICATION DATA
The New Deal and the Great Depression / edited by Aaron D. Purcell.
    p. cm. — (Interpreting American history)
  Includes bibliographical references and index.
  ISBN 978-1-60635-220-5 (pbk.) ∞
  1. New Deal, 1933–1939. 2. Depressions—1929—United States. 3. United
States—Economic conditions—1918–1945. 4. United States—Politics and
government—1933–1945. I. Purcell, Aaron D., 1972- author, editor of
compilation.
  E806.N4146 2014
  973.917—dc23

                             2013043542

18 17 16 15 14   5 4 3 2 1

For Caroline Marie

Contents

PART III: LEGACIES AND OUTCOMES

Foreword

Interpreting American History Series

Of all the history courses taught on college campuses, historiography is one of the most challenging. The historiographic essays most often available are frequently too specialized for broad teaching and sometimes too rigorous for the average undergraduate student. Every day, frustrated scholars and students search for writings that offer both breadth and depth in their approach to the historiography of different eras and movements. As young scholars grow more intellectually mature, they search for literature, sometimes in vain, that will clarify historiographical points. As graduate students prepare for seminar presentations, comprehensive examinations, and dissertation work, they continue to search for works that will help to place their work within the broader study. Then, when they complete their studies and enter the professoriat, they find themselves less intellectually connected to the ideas that they once showed a mastery of, and they again ask about the lack of meaningful and succinct studies of historiography . . . and the circle continues.

Within the pages of this series, innovative young scholars discuss the different interpretations of the important eras and events of history, focusing not only on the intellectual shifts that have taken place but also on the various catalysts that drove these shifts. It is the hope of the series editors that these volumes fill the aforementioned intellectual voids and speak to young scholars in a way that will supplement their other learning, that the same pages that speak to undergraduate students will also remind the established scholar of his or her historiographic roots, that a difficult subject will be made more accessible to curious minds, and that these ideas are not lost among the details offered within the classroom.

BRIAN D. MCKNIGHT, University of Virginia's College at Wise
JAMES S. HUMPHREYS, Murray State University

Introduction

"So what was the New Deal, and why should we care?" Twenty years ago, a high school student challenged me with this question on a Friday afternoon—a question I had every assurance I could answer. Instead of rattling off a fast response, I paused and decided to reward the entire class with a weekend activity. I assigned all the students in the class to pose that very question to their grandparents or someone they knew who would have remembered the 1930s. The sudden assignment made my popularity ranking fall even further, but the results the following Monday were worth it.

For the students who accepted my challenge—I found that high school students considered my outside-of-class assignments optional—most had been regaled with stories of hard luck, heartaches, and hard times during one of the worst decades in American history. Suddenly, the New Deal and Great Depression mattered to this small class of eighteen-year-olds. Although I steered my career away from high school teaching and headed to graduate school to study the 1930s, the experiences and results of that exercise stayed with me.

The passage of time has made it difficult to repeat this exercise—literally fewer and fewer people of that era are available to share their memories. However, the relevance of the New Deal and the Great Depression is even greater for today's students than it was for those who graduated from college a decade ago. Today's popular media compare the political, economic, and social climate of the 2010s (now being referred to as the Great Recession) to the dark days of the 1930s. The New Deal as a real or imaginary solution to the Great Depression is discussed and debated by conservatives, liberals, independents, pundits, and apolitical Americans alike.

But what is missing from these frequent discussions and our common understanding of the period, is the fuller story of how the New Deal has been judged, criticized, applauded, remembered, and interpreted since the 1930s. That larger viewpoint is most accessible through analyzing the past work of scholars and historians. Their interpretations were shaped by the times in which they lived and worked, but those perspectives are part of history, which we must understand, interpret, and learn from. Finally, as I reminded my high school students and now tell the college students who visit my special collections department, history is not static, it is an active part of all of our lives. We are all part of the story and have the ability to add new chapters to our shared history.

The essays in this volume constitute the most recent chapters in our understanding and interpretation of the New Deal and the Great Depression. The period is generally defined as beginning with the October 1929 stock market crash and ending in 1940, when overseas events and the mobilization of American industry for military preparedness fully intersected. The book begins with a review of the largest threads in the historiography of the New Deal and the Great Depression. That chapter is designed to give readers a brief overview of the period, what historians have written about the decade, and generally how those interpretations have changed during the past eighty years. The subsequent chapters in the book are written by subject experts, newer scholars with only a few years separating them from graduate school. These authors address specific topics and events of the New Deal and the Great Depression, and how historians have interpreted those particular subjects.

The book is arranged by three general themes. The first section includes essays related to Franklin D. Roosevelt's New Deal programs and how his first two terms as president changed the economic, political, and cultural landscape of the United States. The essays analyze how the programs, policies, and personalities of the New Deal affected politics, agriculture, the environment, the economy, social programs, and the arts. The second section examines the fringes of the New Deal and the uneven nature of reform. Essays in this section explore the politics of race, with specific focus on the African American experience during the 1930s, and how the labor movement and its many radicals fared under the programs of the New Deal. The final section reviews the legacies and outcomes of the New Deal. These essays chart President Roosevelt's response to the rise of overseas fascism during the late 1930s and the importance of memory in studying the New Deal and the Great Depression.

Over eighty years since Franklin D. Roosevelt took the oath as president, Americans are still debating what happened or what did not happen in the 1930s to help the nation recover from its worst economic depression. Proponents and detractors have cast the New Deal in many lights—veiled socialism, liberalism, state-ism, communism, or other dangerous or welcomed "isms." Decades of scholarship, hindsight, memory, and modern-day discussions reveal the incongruities, complexities, and dichotomies of the period. The essays in this volume explore the nature, effects, and outcomes of the New Deal, by analyzing the historical debates since the 1930s. Most importantly, these essays allow students to have a broad view of the New Deal and the Great Depression before writing chapters of their own.

CHAPTER ONE

Historical Interpretations of the New Deal and the Great Depression

AARON D. PURCELL

Before the ascendancy of Franklin D. Roosevelt to the presidency in 1933, Americans lacked a host of reassurances; for many, employment, food, stability, prosperity, and hope had all become scarce. The Great Depression officially began with the collapse of the stock market in October 1929.[1] President Herbert Hoover's efforts at economic recovery were varied. Hoover largely followed the tradition of limited involvement in the economy by the federal government. He relied on American businesses to stop the downward spiral and trusted that philanthropic and religious groups could reach the struggling masses. Many of Hoover's recovery efforts mirrored New Deal agencies, but the size and scale of his approach paled in comparison. While some of Hoover's programs yielded small signs of recovery, overall his measures proved ineffective in reversing the nation's economic plunge.[2]

The arrival of Roosevelt in the early 1930s changed the political landscape and offered Americans, more than anything, a sense of hope. Compared with Hoover, Roosevelt's charisma, charm, and confidence inspired optimism. Roosevelt and his team of advisors, the "brain trust," promised great change through experimentation. Solutions came in the form of federal assistance, with government programs that were part of what he called, in the closing lines of his 1932 acceptance speech for the Democratic Party's nomination, "a

New Deal for the American people."[3] New Deal programs started in early 1933, with a flurry of activity during Roosevelt's First Hundred Days in office. With Roosevelt's encouragement, Congress created a variety of new federal agencies and programs, designed to reach Americans in need. The first New Deal programs were created to provide employment, regulate the economy, stabilize banking, reclaim or protect the natural environment, and in the process reignite the American spirit.[4]

The scale and scope of Roosevelt's initial recovery efforts were unprecedented. Up to then the only interaction most Americans had with the federal government was receiving their mail. But the New Deal created a relationship between local communities and lawmakers in Washington, D.C. Roosevelt's effective use of the radio to address Americans in his "fireside chats" strengthened the ties between the voters and the executive office.[5] Early New Deal programs brought some immediate results: millions returned to work, the national banking structure regained its footing, the government pumped new money into the economy, public works projects focused on better managing the natural environment, and the nation's infrastructure improved dramatically. Despite such advances, many of the larger shadows of the Great Depression, such as unemployment, abject poverty, environmental ruin, farm foreclosures, and homelessness worsened.

The programs of the First New Deal, 1933-1934, were uneven and drew considerable criticism. Opponents from the political right characterized the New Deal as socialism, or worse. Those on the left charged that the new federal programs had not brought about the recovery Roosevelt promised.[6] Most damaging to Roosevelt, the Supreme Court made several rulings against key New Deal programs, ending agencies such as the Agricultural Adjustment Administration and the National Recovery Administration (NRA). The elimination of these cornerstone First New Deal agencies that addressed the nation's agricultural and industrial woes weighed heavily on Roosevelt's broader agenda and overshadowed his political future.[7]

In 1935, Roosevelt launched the programs of the Second New

Deal. These programs, which most notably included the Social Security Act, were more pragmatic and less experimental than those launched during the First New Deal. Roosevelt's landslide victory in the 1936 presidential election ensured that a majority of the New Deal's programs lasted through the remainder of the decade.[8] However, the New Deal suffered significant setbacks. In 1937, Roosevelt unsuccessfully attempted to expand the Supreme Court in order to appoint new justices who would be sympathetic to the New Deal. Roosevelt's "court-packing" misstep coincided with another dramatic economic downturn, which effectively erased previous gains in per capita income, employment, and the gross national product.[9]

The programs of the New Deal constituted an important part of national recovery in the last few years of the 1930s. However, in time, New Deal programs gave way to other government initiatives to prepare the nation for war. As the nation and the people transitioned from economic recovery to military preparedness, the Roosevelt administration either terminated New Deal programs or folded them into new government initiatives designed to help fight the Axis powers of Germany, Italy, and Japan. These shifts often obscured the exact results of the New Deal, which left scholars to determine whether it was a catalyst for positive change or detrimental to national recovery.

STUDYING AND INTERPRETING

The history and historiography of the New Deal and the Great Depression are inseparable. It is also impossible to understand the 1930s without considering Roosevelt. He casts an enormous shadow across the twentieth century; his approach to recovery during the Great Depression represents one of his most significant contributions. In the past eighty years, scholars have produced hundreds of studies of the New Deal, the Great Depression, Roosevelt, and the 1930s. Scholarship on these topics has remained steady and recent attention to the programs of the New Deal has produced a groundswell of new writing. This chapter reviews the most significant academic writings on the New Deal and Great Depression to provide readers with recurring themes in this period of study. It does not, however, address the growing list of non-academic books on the subject, because of their political, rather than historical, focus.

A majority of scholars studying the 1930s, regardless of when they were writing, have approached the New Deal by examining the origins, the extent, and the results of the reforms. First, scholars questioned who was responsible for the reforms of the New Deal, with one group maintaining that Roosevelt and his advisors were the key and, and another arguing that the people generally, rather than Roosevelt and his advisors, were the chief instigators in identifying areas for reform. Second, scholars have either interpreted the 1930s as a period of American liberalism in which the New Deal was the engine for change, or they have viewed the New Deal as a conservative moment when government officials sought to appease business, labor, and popular demands for change. As a result, one group of historians portrayed Roosevelt as a near socialist, while other scholars argued that Roosevelt took steps to save capitalism. Finally, scholars have searched for New Deal connections to other reform movements, especially focusing on the Populist Movement of the late nineteenth century, the Progressive Era of the early twentieth century, and the Great Society programs of the 1960s.[10] Historians have argued variously that the New Deal went too far, that it did not go far enough, that it created more problems than it solved, or even that its shaky foundations are the reason for the economic and social instability of the Great Recession of the early twenty-first century.

The varied scholarship on the New Deal and the Great Depression presents an example of how historical interpretation changes over time. One constant across all these studies is the importance of historical revisionism, or the re-examination of previous historical interpretations. The corpus of scholarship on the New Deal and the Great Depression fits well within a few major categories, or schools, of historical interpretative thought that developed. It is important to remember that scholars representing these schools of thought wrote across a wide period of time and their interpretations changed over the decades. A categorical and chronological approach is perhaps the easiest way to digest eighty years of scholarship and understand the mainstream threads of historical interpretation for this period.[11]

Interpretations from Contemporaries

The first wave of publications focused on the New Deal and the Great Depression came from participants and contemporaries. While few of these authors were professional historians, they offered later scholars important perspectives on the period. Frederick Lewis Allen, a journalist who wrote the widely popular *Only Yesterday: An Informal History of the 1920s* (1931), capped off the difficult decade with a sequel titled *Since Yesterday: The 1930s in America* (1939).[12] Other writers tackled the period through significant works of fiction and non-fiction based on the harsh social realities of the Great Depression. Books such as John Steinbeck's *The Grapes of Wrath* (1939) and *Let Us Now Praise Famous Men: Three Tenant Families* (1941) by James Agee and Walker Evans became influential works on the period.[13]

The New Deal and Roosevelt stood at the center of many early studies of the 1930s. One of the first significant volleys against the New Deal and Roosevelt's recovery efforts came from Herbert Hoover. Throughout the decade, Hoover wrote and spoke about the inadequacies of the New Deal. He believed that Roosevelt's approach to remedying the Great Depression threatened free-enterprise economics, the essence of American democratic ideals, and most importantly the liberty of the American people because of an ever-expanding federal government at the expense of states, localities, and self-government. Hoover warned that the government excesses of the New Deal would lead to a revolution similar to those that had taken place in European countries.[14]

Other detractors of the New Deal came from the political right and left. Notables such as Louisiana governor and senator Huey P. Long, radio evangelist Charles E. Coughlin, Democratic Party stalwart and former New York governor Alfred E. Smith, and later Republican Party challenger Wendell Willkie each gained a national following for their harsh criticisms of Roosevelt and the New Deal.[15] Their speeches and writings attracted significant attention from Americans unsatisfied with New Deal recovery. These detractors founded anti-New Deal organizations, the most influential of which was the conservative democratic American Liberty League, organized in 1934.[16]

An important set of contemporary voices came from the people who launched or managed the programs of the New Deal. Many members of Roosevelt's cabinet and his advisors wrote books about their experiences during the 1930s, most with uniformly positive recollections. Commentary on the New Deal came from the pens of such notables as James Farley, the postmaster general and chairman of the Democratic National Committee who was largely responsible for Roosevelt's rise to the presidency, the Secretary of the Interior and director of the Public Works Administration, Harold Ickes, Secretary of Labor Francis Perkins, and key Roosevelt aide and executive director of the National Recovery Administration, Donald Richburg.[17]

Several important figures from the Roosevelt administration published books that questioned the New Deal for failing to do enough. Raymond Moley, an early Roosevelt advisor, and Rexford Tugwell, an economist who drafted early New Deal policies, both criticized the effectiveness of Roosevelt's economic and social recovery efforts. They each argued that the New Deal and Roosevelt had not gone far enough to change the national economy to encourage recovery.[18] Tugwell, Moley, and other contemporaries had been early proponents of the New Deal, but their support turned into opposition as the Great Depression worsened.

Other autobiographies, case studies, and memoirs from former New Dealers and Roosevelt associates appeared during the second half of the twentieth century. Their firsthand participation and recollections remain an important component of New Deal historiography, especially for the role of memory in history. By the end of World War II, the first group of professional historians produced scholarly interpretations of the New Deal, Roosevelt, and the Great Depression.

Progressive Historians

The first scholarly works on the New Deal and the Great Depression appeared in the 1940s, largely from a group categorized as the progressive historians. These scholars viewed American history as an ever-evolving progression, with a crescendo of liberal reform completed largely through the political process. The progressives interpreted American history as a struggle between the majority and the privileged, and argued that reformers wanted to return government, society, and economic power back to the people through their reforms.[19] Charles Beard, Vernon Parrington, and Frederick Jackson Turner were the most significant historians to write in the progressive tradition.[20] Although these three historians produced their most significant scholarship before the 1930s and thus offered little on the New Deal, their school of thought influenced a great number of historians writing in the early post–World War II era.

According to the progressive historians, the reforms of the New Deal were in fact a continuation of the nation's liberal tradition—the demands of the people resulted in tangible social, economic, and political reforms. Many of these writers juxtaposed the New Deal with the Populist Movement, the Progressive Era, and other periods of reform in American history when the people demanded and enacted liberal change over the conservative forces of monopoly and privilege.[21] This approach also supported the concept that trends in American history were cyclical, recurring, and perhaps even predictable.[22]

Arthur Schlesinger Jr., a Harvard professor and son of distinguished historian Arthur Schlesinger Sr., best defined the progressive school approach to evaluating the New Deal, the Great Depression, and Roosevelt. In his three-volume *The Age of Roosevelt* (1957-1960), Schlesinger focused on the life and career of Roosevelt from the end of World War I in 1919 to the beginning of his second term as president in 1936.[23] Much like his *The Age of Jackson* (1945), which won the Pulitzer Prize, Schlesinger approached the late 1920s and early 1930s as a period of cyclical change.[24] He argued that New Deal liberalism, similar to Jacksonian democracy, emerged from the people as a liberal reaction to the conservative forces of big business and privileged interests. Schlesinger viewed the New Deal as a pragmatic solution to remedy the economic collapse of the Great Depression, with Roosevelt as the leading figure in putting economic and political power back in the hands of the people. According to Schlesinger, the urgency of the Great Depression mobilized national reform into a larger political movement that resulted in greater federal oversight of the national economy. Despite its sympathetic cheerleading for New Deal reform, *The Age of Roosevelt* became a landmark work on the period. While historians challenged his arguments about the New Deal, Schlesinger's detail of the period remains unmatched.[25]

Frank Freidel's four-volume *Franklin D. Roosevelt* (1952-1973) took a similar view of the 1930s. Freidel found that Roosevelt and other New Dealers were at the center of 1930s relief efforts and were the torchbearers for the tradition of grassroots liberal reform earlier in the century. He argued that Roosevelt and his advisors cut their teeth on the issues of the Progressive Era (i.e., women's suffrage, urban reform, immigration control, Prohibition, and direct election of officials), before seizing the moment in the early 1930s to enact change. Subsequently, these reformers emulated the ideals of Theodore Roosevelt and Woodrow Wilson, rather than introducing a wave of new reforms.[26]

Other historians addressed the theme of New Deal connections to past periods of reform in American history. Louis M. Hacker's *The Shaping of the American Tradition* (1947) asserted that the New Deal emerged from a tradition of popular liberal reform that promoted so-

cial, economic, and political equality. Hacker went further to connect 1930s reform with past periods of liberal change by calling the
New Deal the "third American Revolution." Likewise, Henry Steele
Commager agreed that the New Deal was another occurrence of
American liberal reform. He noted that the legislation and programs
of the 1930s appeared different because of the sharp contrast with
the national policies of the 1920s Republican Party and the speed
with which the New Deal began, but in general they were quite
similar to the reforms from earlier periods in American history.[27]

During the 1930s, Roosevelt's political opponents lodged frequent volleys at the New Deal, calling it state socialism or a version
of communism. However, most of the progressive historians, who
were generally sympathetic to Roosevelt, downplayed the radical
nature of the New Deal. These historians found that the programs
of the New Deal were more evolutionary than revolutionary. In
their minds, the New Deal was not an attempt to undermine or even
overthrow capitalism, rather the programs of the New Deal concentrated more power at the federal level to enact national change, recovery, and reform. Progressive historians believed that the reforms
of the New Deal improved the capitalist system and strengthened
the federal government's ability to help regulate the economy.[28]

Progressive historians also evaluated the extent and results of
the New Deal. Schlesinger, Freidel, and others argued that the
New Deal, like previous reform movements, expanded the ideals
of democracy to a greater range of Americans. These historians
believed that through federal intervention more of the nation's citizenry had access to the American dream. On the whole, progressive historians agreed that the reforms of the New Deal resulted
in some positive changes. This group of historians recognized that
the New Deal was yet another important period of liberal reform
in American history.[29]

CONSENSUS OR NEOCONSERVATIVE HISTORIANS

The consensus or neoconservative school of historical thought emerged in the 1950s and challenged the interpretations of the progressive historians. Louis Hartz, Daniel Boorstin, and Richard Hofstadter were the most recognized members of the consensus school of historical thought. This group of scholars dominated the 1950s and early 1960s. They believed that consensus marked the development of American history. Unlike progressive historians, who believed that the conflict between the "haves" and the "have-nots" defined the national experience, consensus historians saw unity as the central component in American history. Consensus historians believed that homogeneity, stability, and a shared national character shaped America's past. Their writing also reflected skepticism of mass movements due to the events that defined their time, including the atrocities of World War II and the global polarity caused by the Cold War. While they acknowledged that conflict had erupted between classes, races, and groups, these historians rejected the notion that conflict brought about significant change. Instead, the consensus historians focused on how events and ideas unified people and how those occurrences in American history resulted in larger shifts.[30]

Consensus historians approached the New Deal as a strain of reform different from previous periods in American history. They argued that the leaders of the New Deal viewed the Great Depression as indicative of a collapsing society and economy, which could only be salvaged by federal intervention. The methods of reform used by New Dealers—federal responsibility for the economy, wages, the unemployed, the retired and elderly, agricultural production, and public works—departed from the kind of reforms that took place earlier in the century. Thus, the consensus historians did not believe that the New Deal had connections to previous reform movements, and in fact they argued that Roosevelt and other New Dealers made changes that reversed the course of previous reforms, the repeal of Prohibition being the most obvious example.[31]

Richard Hofstadter best represented the consensus school of thought on the New Deal and the Great Depression. In *The Age of*

Reform: From Bryan to FDR (1955), he argued that the New Deal had little in common with the Progressive Era. Hofstadter's book described the Progressive Era as a period of moral-based reform, which aimed to make government more representative and eliminate the undue influence of monopolies and big business. In comparison, he found the New Deal to be more a reaction to an economic emergency than a clear reform initiative. According to Hofstadter, the New Deal was devoid of a true reform philosophy; instead, he argued that 1930s reform represented a pragmatic approach to fix short-term problems with the economy and American society. Even though Hofstadter took great issue with the reform principles behind the New Deal, he pointed out many of the positive results of the programs. He agreed with Schlesinger and other progressive historians that the New Deal brought recovery to an ailing nation, but Hofstadter was less convinced that the programs represented a significant upswing of genuine reform.[32]

Unlike the progressives, consensus historians were less sympathetic to Roosevelt. They argued that Roosevelt and his advisors did little to combat the massive social problems of the 1930s and chose to offer pragmatic economic and political approaches to recovery. In *An Encore for Reform: The Old Progressives and the New Deal* (1967), Otis Graham Jr. argued that legislators who had been around since the Progressive Era found Roosevelt to be untrustworthy and even devious. Graham argued that the New Deal and Roosevelt's reform efforts had little direction or a clear vision for fixing economic, social, and political problems. In the same vein, Hofstadter labeled Roosevelt an opportunist, who surrounded himself with out-of-touch politicians with little understanding of the severity of the Great Depression. In the first volume of his biography of Roosevelt, political scientist James MacGregor Burns agreed with these evaluations. He asserted that Roosevelt was a master politician who held the nation together with his charisma and influence rather than a clear agenda of reform. Other consensus historians went further, arguing that Roosevelt and the New Deal undermined individual freedoms in favor of expanding the power of the federal government and making concessions to corporate interests.[33]

Consensus historians considered their work highly critical of American society, its economic system, and its institutions. These historians upheld the belief that periods of stability, rather than conflict, defined the American experience. Consensus historians focused on the New Deal believed that Roosevelt's programs were necessary to keep the nation's economic system from total collapse, but they were wary of Roosevelt's motives and economic strategies.

A Transitional Figure

In the early 1960s historian William Leuchtenburg presented a more complex view of the New Deal. In *The Perils of Prosperity* (1958), he described the interwar period as a time of great social and cultural upheaval, which pitted an emerging urban middle class with modernist ideas and economic interests against a more traditional and rural populace. Leuchtenburg argued that the reforms of the New Deal represented the culmination of this shift, as Roosevelt and his advisors devised "modern," big government approaches to solving economic and social problems.[34]

Leuchtenburg expanded his analysis of the 1930s with the landmark book *Franklin D. Roosevelt and the New Deal* (1963). This highly regarded text viewed the New Deal as a "half-way revolution," with its share of successes and failures. Leuchtenburg explained that the New Deal provided some assistance to underrepresented groups, such as farmers and industrial workers, but neglected others, such as sharecroppers and African Americans. According to Leuchtenburg, the strengths of the New Deal included new social programs, economic reforms, and greater federal connections to the populace. While the New Deal brought about many positive effects, he argued that the programs alone did not bring the nation out of its decade-long depression.[35]

Like previous scholars, Leuchtenburg examined the origins and motives of New Deal reform. He agreed with consensus historians that New Dealers had little in common with Progressive Era reformers, largely because the Great Depression was an extreme situation that required a dramatic response. In contrast, however, Leuchten-burg argued that economic motives, rather than human sentimen-tality or sympathy, drove the initiatives of the New Deal. Unlike the consensus historians and more like the progressive historians such as Schlesinger, Leuchtenburg placed Roosevelt at the center of New Deal planning. He argued that unlike Theodore Roosevelt and Woodrow Wilson, Franklin D. Roosevelt took a strong role in initiat-ing and directing reform programs at the federal level. Roosevelt not only spearheaded the reforms of the New Deal, but unlike any other president before he greatly expanded the legislative functions of his office. In the process, Leuchtenburg argued, the federal government grew to assume significant control of the national economy and many areas once reserved for state and local government. Additionally, Leuchtenburg noted Roosevelt's ability to reach Americans through the radio, the press, and federal government programs. Unlike the consensus historians who were critical of Roosevelt, Leuchtenburg argued that Roosevelt used his presidential power to craft, share, and adapt a vision for economic recovery through the New Deal.[36] The next wave of scholars built on Leutchtenburg's work, but they were much more critical of Roosevelt and the New Deal.

THE NEW LEFT HISTORIANS

By the 1960s, the mood of the nation and the landscape of histori-cal writing changed. If there ever had been a consensus or a shared national experience it unraveled and evaporated during the decade. Broader events, such as political upheaval, the culmination of the Civil Rights Movement, and escalating American involvement in and opposition to the war in Vietnam, affected historical inquiry. Not only were there more scholars producing work, but they deliv-ered a wider range of viewpoints, including neoprogressive, left of mainstream liberal, far-right conservative, and even strict Marxist interpretations.[37]

A group of scholars writing from the mid-1960s until the mid-1970s fit within a collective group known as the New Left. Often employing interdisciplinary methods and using untapped evidence, these scholars probed previous historical interpretations for gaps of evidence, perspectives, and themes that earlier historians either ignored or misunderstood. Unlike the consensus historians, this group of scholars believed that struggle and inequality lay at the heart of the American experience. In an effort to expose the important theme of social and economic conflict many of their studies focused on the forgotten roles of women, African Americans, Native Americans, and other minority groups in the course of American history. They sharply criticized Arthur Schlesinger Jr.'s view of American history as a crescendo of democracy marked by liberal reform, instead arguing that genuine democracy declined in favor of private, corporate, and government interests. New Left historians such as Gabriel Kolko and James Weinstein argued that the contraction of democracy further distanced voters from the ability to influence their lives, their government, and their society. This bleak and pessimistic view of history promoted their belief that the political power to enact change rested in the hands of politicians, corporations, private business interests, and the federal government. The overall motives of these groups, New Left historians argued, were disingenuous, self-serving, and contrary to democracy.[38]

During the 1960s a new wave of scholars analyzed the New Deal and the Roosevelt presidency. They focused on the extent of social reform during the 1930s and evaluated the effectiveness of those liberal reforms three decades later. Within the context of the upheaval of the 1960s, these scholars concluded that while the programs of the New Deal had great potential to eradicate poverty, end racial discrimination, and create greater economic equilibrium, on the whole those reforms represented modest steps, if not complete missteps, toward the larger goals of liberalism and social equality. Much like the consensus historians, the scholars of the 1960s regarded Roosevelt as devoid of a clear reform agenda and argued that he was a pragmatic politician who favored business interests over the interests of the people. As a result, these scholars believed that the New Deal solidified economic power and control of the nation in the hands of corporate interests.[39]

New Left scholars of the 1960s and 1970s followed in Leuchtenburg's footsteps by focusing on the shortcomings of Roosevelt and
the New Deal. These scholars focused on narrow topics of the
period. The origins and benefactors of New Deal economic policies served as a common thread in their works. In a chapter on
the New Deal, Barton Bernstein challenged the opinions of liberal
consensus historians by arguing instead that the New Deal merely
protected American corporate capitalism, rather than redistribut-
ing power and reaching out to underrepresented groups and minorities. In his lengthy study of the New Deal and monopoly, Ellis
Hawley argued that the only clear economic policy of the period
was support for private business and modern industrial production. Ronald Radosh's chapter-length study, "The Myth of the New
Deal," was even more direct, arguing that New Deal legislation
was carefully constructed to justify, maintain, and further advance
a corporate-led capitalist system.[40]

Paul Conkin's *The New Deal* (1967) was perhaps the most influential of the New Left accounts of the 1930s. In this slender
volume, Conkin argued that programs of the New Deal lacked
long-term goals. Roosevelt, whom he found to be intellectually
incapable of understanding the complexities of the Great Depression, relied too heavily on the advice of intellectuals and bureaucrats, rather than listening to social activists, radicals, and political
critics. Conkin rejected the assertion that the New Deal expanded
democracy. Instead, he argued that during the 1930s Americans
lost their the ability to make policy decisions and influence national change, as a small number of leaders and lawyers in Washington, D.C., took control of the nation's and the people's future.
According to Conkin, Roosevelt's greatest asset was the ability to
inspire people to believe in New Deal recovery. However, Roosevelt failed to connect that sense of hope to tangible programs and
initiatives. Within the context of the late 1960s, Conkin concluded
that the New Deal supported a subsidized and regulated welfare
system that remained the same since taking hold in the 1930s.[41]

By the early 1970s New Left scholars questioned the origins, extent, and effectiveness of the New Deal. Their works approached

these larger questions through studies of social welfare, race, labor, agriculture, radical groups on the right and the left, and the effects of New Deal programs in rural and urban areas. Roosevelt's lack of long-term planning, especially in terms of social and economic reform, emerged as a consistent theme. However, the majority of these scholars came to the same conclusion, espoused by William Leuchtenburg, that the New Deal addressed certain problems, ignored others, and created a host of new long-term problems.[42]

SOCIAL, CULTURAL, AND SPECIALIZED STUDIES

Beginning in the 1970s, the historical profession splintered into numerous fields, subfields, and schools of thought. Building on the New Left's criticism of consensus and its focus on conflict, a new generation of scholars approached history with a bottom-up, rather than a top-down, analysis. They utilized research methods and approaches that focused on social aspects of history. Standard political and economic studies receded as new scholarship on the middle, working, and lower classes emerged. Groups on the margins of historical accounts, such as women, Native Americans, African Americans, immigrants, and the white working class caught the attention of historians. Studies focused on race, class, gender, sexuality, ethnicity, and identity became part of a growing movement known collectively as social history. A large number of scholars used social history methods to both recover ignored chapters of history and revamp traditional interpretations of the past.[43]

Interdisciplinary research also influenced historical scholarship of this period. Historians worked with related disciplines such as sociology, anthropology, American studies, political science, and architecture to create a focus on cultural history. Building on the work of social historians, these scholars examined the importance of popular culture, memory, linguistic meaning, built environments, and the social construction of identity. In addition, a number of historians focused on specific American regions, recurrent trends across the expanse of the nation's history, and how the American experience fit into international developments. These social and cultural shifts in historical study broadened the range of historical scholarship, but the fragmentation and specialization of study also made their writing much less uniform.[44]

Scholarship on the New Deal and the Great Depression expanded significantly during the past three decades, with a heavy focus on cultural and social aspects of the period.[45] But even with the proliferation of new studies, no single work has fully replaced William Leuchtenburg's *Franklin D. Roosevelt and the New Deal* (1963). Leuchtenburg's assessment that the New Deal produced some important, but uneven, reforms has withstood criticism from both the historical right and left.[46] However, several historiographical trends and new approaches have refocused questions that have significantly added to Leuchtenburg's fifty-year-old analysis.

First, recent scholars examined the social and cultural changes brought about by the Great Depression and the New Deal. These narratives combined the traditional details of the period with more individual voices from the period. Robert McElvaine's *The Great Depression: America, 1929–1941* (1983) demonstrated this kind of social synthesis of the period. McElvaine viewed the Great Depression as an unprecedented period in modern American history, not just because it affected millions in innumerable ways, but because it halted and temporarily reversed the pattern of unlimited consumption, unbridled individualism, and social disintegration in American society. Similarly, historian T. H. Watkins argued in two books that the economic collapse of the late 1920s enabled Americans to assess themselves and their culture. By the end of the 1930s, looming fear and uncertainty, he asserted, had been replaced by a sense of hope and confidence in national community, government, and wider political democracy.[47]

Other scholars focused on individual realities of the Great Depression. Books on the Dust Bowl, migrant workers, sharecroppers, the unemployed, laborers, women, African Americans, and children offered perspectives on the millions of Americans affected by the national crisis.[48] While many books acknowledged the extreme suffering of the period, others focused more on the triumphs of the 1930s. Morris Dickstein's *Dancing in the Dark: A Cultural History of the Great Depression* (2009) offered a sweeping synthesis of how art, media, film, literature, and images created during the period resulted in a new sense of American social purpose. Similar to McElvaine and Watkins, he argued that the experiences of the 1930s solidified a faith in American society and community that created a new cultural milieu.[49]

The implementation of New Deal reforms and their lasting effects on society, especially at the local and state levels, attracted a large amount of scholarly attention. Anthony Badger's *The New Deal: The Depression Years, 1933-1940* (1989) described how the New Deal affected industry, labor, agriculture, welfare, and politics. Badger argued that the social programs of the New Deal represented a clear break from past government-sponsored reforms, but local, state, and regional forces tempered those initiatives. For example, the administration of many New Deal programs conformed to pre-existing labor and employment practices, especially in the South, where Jim Crow laws and non-union hiring dominated. In *The New Dealers: Power Politics in the Age of Roosevelt* (1993), Jordan Schwarz also stressed the importance of regional influence over the New Deal. He argued that the political heft and economic needs of the South and the West resulted in massive public works projects for these regions, all of which supported private investment.[50]

Historians took great interest in the economic and political connections between the government and corporations. In *New Deals: Business, Labor, and Politics in America, 1920-1935* (1994), Colin Gordon argued that the New Deal built upon preexisting private business practices and corporate networks to develop national policies for banking, social welfare, and labor. In fact, the federal government needed the help of corporations to design and manage the programs of the New Deal. Gordon believed that the New Deal originated from national business demands, but that corporate leaders became uneasy with the programs' agreements, regulations, and concessions. By the end of the 1930s, he contended, private business practices were politicized and under greater federal control.[51]

Scholars continue to examine the character of Franklin D. Roosevelt in biographical and topical studies. Books by Patrick Maney, Kenneth Davis, and Geoffrey Ward probed Roosevelt's personal life and career.[52] But what has changed in the past few decades is that these studies incorporate the voices of many of his associates, advisors, and counterparts into the narrative. Studies on Eleanor Roosevelt and New Dealers have provided a fuller account of Roosevelt's inner circle and how decisions were made in the White House.[53] Because of the popularity of biography and interest in the period there are numerous books about Roosevelt and the 1930s written by journalists, freelance writers, and other non-academics. While some of these books have merit, the majority of these popular treatments have an obvious present-day, political point-of-view that precludes the methodology and objectivity that define the historian's craft.[54]

Recent works on the New Deal revisited some of the earliest debates of the field. Several books examined the New Deal's connections to other periods, especially the postwar era. David Kennedy's Pulitzer Prize-winning *Freedom From Fear: The American People in Depression and War, 1929-1945* (1999) connected the context of the 1930s to overseas events that ultimately resulted in American involvement in World War II. In this lengthy analysis of the 1930s, he argued that the New Deal created a sense of security for both privileged and underprivileged Americans. By doing so, Kennedy found that the New Deal established a new set of political, cultural, and economic standards, which had a direct influence on postwar society. Kennedy believed that New Deal programs lasted far beyond their initial purposes to provide relief, recovery, and reform. Instead, he argued, the New Deal became the backbone of American society in the second half of the twentieth century.[55]

Today's scholars reexamined the nature and extent of liberal reform in the New Deal. Alan Brinkley, in *The End of Reform: New Deal Liberalism in Recession and War* (1995), argued that the idea of New Deal reform developed into a postwar definition of liberalism. He believed that the concept of New Deal liberalism influenced liberal politics, policies, and action well into the 1960s. Brinkley argued that postwar liberals attempted to cure societal ills and fix the problems with industrial capitalism by using large-scale centralized government programs—an approach reminiscent of the New Deal.[56] Other scholars suggested that the "Roosevelt revolution" of the 1930s created a New Deal order. This group of liberal Democrats and activists, they believed, shepherded the government-sponsored social reforms of the Great Society programs of the 1960s.[57]

A similar argument for connecting the New Deal to postwar liberal reform came from Alonzo Hamby. In *Liberalism and its Challengers: FDR to Reagan* (1985), Hamby argued that the New Deal opened up the democratic process to more Americans, and this brand of democratic liberalism became a regular facet of modern American politics. He found that the adaptation of New Deal ideals created a mixed legacy of reform. Hamby found that the programs of the New Deal improved civil liberties, civil rights, and economic inequity, but that many of those programs fell short because they were administered by an expanding bureaucratic system that proved inefficient, competitive, and unable or unwilling to help those in need.[58]

The scholarship of social and cultural historians pushed studies of the New Deal and the Great Depression into more specialized topics. Apart from the infrequent works of synthesis, the majority of today's historical writing on the 1930s incorporates social history methods to reach broader conclusions about the period. Views of history from the bottom up or from historically neglected groups have added new voices to the scholarship of the period.

CONCLUSION

Historians representing different schools of thought evaluated the New Deal and the Great Depression through a variety of sources, research methods, divergent and convergent perspectives, and the influences of their own time. The 1930s brought the nation a host of long-lasting social programs, an expanded role for the government, a new conceptualization of the presidency, greater economic regulation, and many cultural shifts. Historians continue to debate the successes, failures, partial victories, and remnants of the New Deal. In general, there has been a noted shift from early sympathy for the programs and leaders to a more realistic evaluation that the accomplishments of the New Deal were mixed and tempered by multiple factors.

In the past few decades historians writing from a social and cultural perspective expanded our understanding of the 1930s. The most fertile areas of study included labor relations, politics, minority groups, race, agriculture, the natural environment, radicalism, social programs, the arts, the economy, overseas intervention, memory, and regional or local topics within the context of the New Deal. The purpose of this volume is to review and showcase the growing historical literature within those subfields. These and other contributions allow scholars to unearth new directions of research on the period and continue historical debates about the New Deal and the Great Depression.

NOTES

1. See John Kenneth Galbraith, *The Great Crash, 1929* (New York: Houghton Mifflin, 1954).

2. See Robert Sobel, *Herbert Hoover at the Onset of the Great Depression* (Philadelphia: Lippincott, 1975); Gene Smith, *The Shattered Dream: Herbert Hoover and the Great Depression* (New York: Morrow, 1970); Harris Gaylord Warren, *Herbert Hoover and the Great Depression* (New York: Oxford University Press, 1959).

3. Franklin D. Roosevelt, "'I Pledge to You—I Pledge Myself to a New Deal for the American People,' July 2, 1932," in *The Public Papers and Addresses of Franklin D. Roosevelt,* comp. Samuel I. Rosenman (New York: Random House, 1938), 1:659.

4. See Elliot A. Rosen, *Hoover, Roosevelt, and the Brains Trust: From Depression to New Deal* (New York: Columbia University Press, 1977); Adam Cohen, *Nothing to Fear: FDR's Inner Circle and the Hundred Days that Created Modern America* (New York: Penguin, 2009).

5. See Russell D. Buhite and David W. Levy, eds., *FDR's Fireside Chats* (Norman: University of Oklahoma Press, 1992); and Lawrence W. Levine,

Cornelia R. Levine, and Michael Kazin, eds., *The Fireside Conversations: America Responds to FDR during the Great Depression* (Berkeley: University of California Press, 2010).

6. See Alan Brinkley, *Voices of Protest: Huey Long, Father Coughlin, and the Great Depression* (New York: Vintage Books, 1983).

7. William E. Leuchtenburg, *Franklin D. Roosevelt and the New Deal, 1933-1940* (New York: Harper and Row, 1963), 143-48.

8. Some historians argued that a "Third New Deal," began in 1937. They characterize this third period as attempts during Roosevelt's second term to preserve legislative gains to that point. See John W. Jeffries, "A 'Third New Deal'? Liberal Policy and the American State, 1937-1945," *Journal of Policy History* 8 (December 1996): 387-409.

9. See Burt Solomon, *FDR v. The Constitution: The Court-Packing Fight and the Triumph of Democracy* (New York: Walker, 2009); Barry Cushman, *Rethinking the New Deal Court: The Structure of a Constitutional Revolution* (New York: Oxford University Press, 1998); G. Edward White, *The Constitution and the New Deal Court* (Cambridge: Harvard University Press, 2000); "*AHR* Forum: The Debate Over the Constitutional Revolution of 1937," *American Historical Review* 110 (October 2005): 1046-115; and Lawrence M. Friedman, *American Law in the Twentieth Century* (New Haven: Yale University Press, 2002).

10. Colin Gordon, "Rethinking the New Deal," *Columbia Law Review* 98 (December 1998): 2033-36.

11. The most notable historiographical treatments of the New Deal and the Great Depression include "The New Deal: Revolution or Restoration?" in *Interpretations of American History: Patterns and Perspectives,* eds. Francis G. Couvares, Martha Saxton, Gerald N. Grob, and George Athan Billias, seventh edition (New York: The Free Press, 2000), 2:223-38; Alan Brinkley, "Prosperity, Depression, and War, 1920-1945," in *The New American History,* ed. Eric Foner (Philadelphia: Temple University Press, 1997), 133-58; Alan Brinkley, "The New Deal in American Scholarship," in *The State of U.S. History,* ed. Melvyn Stokes (New York: Berg, 2002), 115-29; Lisa McGirr, "The Interwar Years," in *American History Now,* eds. Eric Foner and Lisa McGirr (Philadelphia: Temple University Press, 2011), 125-50.

12. Frederick Lewis Allen, *Only Yesterday: An Informal History of the 1920s* (New York: Harper and Brothers, 1931); Frederick Lewis Allen, *Since Yesterday: The 1930s in America* (New York: Harper and Brothers, 1939).

13. John Steinbeck, *The Grapes of Wrath* (New York: Viking Press, 1939); James Agee and Walker Evans, *Let Us Now Praise Famous Men: Three Tenant Families* (Boston: Houghton Mifflin, 1941).

14. Herbert Hoover, *The Challenge to Liberty* (New York: Charles Scribner's Sons, 1934); Herbert Hoover, *American Ideals Versus the New Deal* (New York: Charles Scribner's Sons, 1936); Herbert Hoover, *America's Way Forward* (New York: Charles Scribner's Sons, 1939).

15. Albert Fried, *FDR and His Enemies* (New York: Palgrave, 1999); Brinkley, *Voices of Protest;* Huey P. Long, *Every Man a King: The Autobiography of Huey P. Long* (New Orleans: National Book, 1933); Charles E. Coughlin, *A Series of Lectures on Social Justice* (1935; reprint, New York: DeCapo Press, 1971); Wendell Willkie, *This is Wendell Willkie: A Collection of Speeches and Writings on Present-Day Issues* (New York: Dodd, Mead, 1940).

16. George Wolfskill, *The Revolt of the Conservatives: A History of the American Liberty League, 1934-1940* (Boston: Houghton Mifflin, 1962).

17. James Farley, *Behind the Ballots: The Personal History of a Politician* (New York: Harcourt, Brace, 1938); James Farley, *Jim Farley's Story: The Roosevelt Years* (New York: McGraw Hill, 1948); Harold Ickes, *Back to Work: The Story of PWA* (New York: Macmillan, 1935); Harold Ickes, *The Autobiography of a Curmudgeon* (New York: Reynal and Hitchcock, 1943); Francis Perkins, *The Roosevelt I Knew* (New York: Penguin, 1946); Donald Richburg, *My Hero: The Indiscreet Memoirs of an Eventful but Unheroic Life* (New York: Putnam, 1954).

18. Raymond Moley, *After Seven Years* (New York: Harper and Brothers, 1939); Rexford Tugwell, *The Democratic Roosevelt: A Biography of Franklin D. Roosevelt* (New York: Doubleday, 1957).

19. "The Progressive Movement: Elitist or Democratic?" in *Interpretations of American History,* 2:179.

20. Richard Hofstadter, *The Progressive Historians: Turner, Beard, Parrington* (New York: Alfred A. Knopf, 1968); Ernst A. Breisach, *American Progressive History: An Experiment in Modernization* (Chicago: University of Chicago Press, 1993); *Interpretations of American History,* 2:9-10.

21. "New Deal," in *Interpretations of American History,* 2:226.

22. See Arthur M. Schlesinger Jr., *Cycles of American History* (Boston: Houghton Mifflin, 1986).

23. Arthur M. Schlesinger Jr., *The Age of Roosevelt,* 3 vols. (Boston: Houghton Mifflin, 1957-1960).

24. Arthur M. Schlesinger Jr., *The Age of Jackson* (Boston: Little, Brown, 1946).

25. Schlesinger, *Age of Roosevelt;* "New Deal," in *Interpretations of American History,* 2:226.

26. Frank Freidel, *Franklin D. Roosevelt,* 4 vols. (Boston: Little, Brown, 1952-1973); Richard S. Kirkendall, ed., *The New Deal: The Historical Debate* (New York: John Wiley and Sons, 1973), 2.

27. Louis M. Hacker, "The Third American Revolution," in *The New Deal: Revolution or Evolution?* ed. Edwin C. Rozwenc (Lexington, MA: D.C. Heath, 1959), 1-19; Louis M. Hacker, *The Shaping of the American Tradition* (New York: Columbia University Press, 1947), 1125-46; Henry Steele Commager, "Twelve Years of Roosevelt," *American Mercury* 40 (April 1945): 391-401; "New Deal," in *Interpretations of American History,* 2:225.

28. Kirkendall, *The New Deal,* 2.

29. Ibid.

30. Bernard Sternsher, *Consensus, Conflict, and American Historians* (Bloomington: Indiana University Press, 1975), 2-4; Gene Wise, *American Historical Explanations: A Strategy for Grounded Inquiry* (Minneapolis: University of Minnesota Press, 1980), 343-49; *Interpretations of American History*, 2:12-14; Brinkley, "Prosperity, Depression, and War," 136.

31. "New Deal," in *Interpretations of American History*, 2:228.

32. Richard Hofstadter, *The Age of Reform: From Bryan to FDR* (New York: Knopf, 1955), 301-2, 314, 322-25; "New Deal," in *Interpretations of American History*, 2:228; Brinkley, "Prosperity, Depression, and War," 136.

33. Hofstadter, *Age of Reform*, 308-9; Richard Hofstadter, *The American Political Tradition: And the Men Who Made it* (New York: Vintage Books, 1948), 411-13; James MacGregor Burns, *Roosevelt: The Lion and the Fox* (New York: Harcourt, Brace, and World, 1956), ix-x; Otis L. Graham Jr., *An Encore for Reform: The Old Progressives and the New Deal* (New York: Oxford University Press, 1967), 40, 43; "New Deal," in *Interpretations of American History*, 2:228-29.

34. William E. Leuchtenburg, *The Perils of Prosperity, 1914-1932* (Chicago: University of Chicago Press, 1958), 7-11, 271-73; Brinkley, "Prosperity, Depression, and War," 138.

35. Leuchtenburg, *Roosevelt and the New Deal*, 337, 346-47; Brinkley, "Prosperity, Depression, and War," 143; "New Deal," in *Interpretations of American History*, 2:230.

36. Leuchtenburg, *Roosevelt and the New Deal*, 327, 330-31, 334-39, 346; Brinkley, "Prosperity, Depression, and War," 143.

37. Alonzo L. Hamby, "The New Deal: Avenues for Reconsideration" *Polity* 31 (Summer 1999): 666; Alan Matusow, *The Unraveling of America: A History of Liberalism in the 1960s* (New York: Harper and Row, 1984).

38. Hamby, "The New Deal," 666-67; Irwin Unger, "The 'New Left' and American History: Some Recent Trends in United States Historiography," *The American Historical Review* 72 (July 1967): 1238-41; Brinkley, "Prosperity, Depression, and War," 136.

39. "New Deal," in *Interpretations of American History*, 2:229; Jerold S. Auerbach, "New Deal, Old Deal, or Raw Deal: Some Thoughts on New Left Historiography," *The Journal of Southern History* 35 (February 1969): 18-19; Richard S. Kirkendall, "The New Deal as Watershed: The Recent Literature," *The Journal of American History* 54 (March 1968): 839; Brinkley, "Prosperity, Depression, and War," 136; Kirkendall, *The New Deal*, 6.

40. Barton J. Bernstein, ed., *Towards a New Past: Dissenting Essays in American History* (New York: Pantheon Books, 1968), 263-64; Ellis W. Hawley, *The New Deal and the Problem of Monopoly: A Study in Economic Ambivalence* (Princeton: Princeton University Press, 1966), 14-16, 476, 483-87; Ronald Radosh and Murray N. Rothbard, eds., *A New History of Leviathan: Essays on the Rise of the American Corporate State* (New York: E.P. Dutton, 1972), 186-87;

Hamby, "The New Deal," 666; "New Deal," in *Interpretations of American History,* 2:231-32; Brinkley, "New Deal Scholarship," 117.

41. Paul Conkin, *The New Deal* (New York: Thomas Y. Crowell, 1967), 1-2, 103-6; Auerbach, "New Deal," 19-20; "New Deal," in *Interpretations of American History,* 2:230-31.

42. Auerbach, "New Deal," 21-24; Leuchtenburg, *Roosevelt and the New Deal,* 346; Brinkley, "Prosperity, Depression, and War," 144. See John Braeman, "The New Deal and the 'Broker State': A Review of the Recent Scholarly Literature," *Business History Review* 46 (Winter 1972): 409-29; Walter Rundell Jr., "Main Trends in U.S. Historiography Since the New Deal: Research Prospects in Oral History," *The Oral History Review* 4 (1976): 35-47; *The New Deal,* eds. John Braeman, Robert H. Bremner, and David Brody, 2 vols. (Columbus: Ohio State University Press, 1975); Howard Zinn, ed., *New Deal Thought* (New York: Bobbs-Merrill, 1966).

43. Melvyn Stokes, ed., *The State of U.S. History* (New York: Berg, 2002), 1-2; Anthony Molho and Gordon Wood, eds., *Imagined Histories: American Historians Interpret the Past* (Princeton: Princeton University Press, 1998), 11, 91-93; Joyce Appleby, Lynn Hunt, and Margaret Jacob, *Telling the Truth about History* (New York: W.W. Norton, 1994), 146-59.

44. Stokes, *State of U.S. History,* 3-4; Molho and Wood, *Imagined Histories,* 12-14, 95-97; James W. Cook, Lawrence B. Glickman, and Michael O'Malley, *The Cultural Turn in U.S. History: Past, Present, and Future* (Chicago: University of Chicago Press, 2008), 3-7; Appleby, Hunt, and Jacob, *Telling the Truth,* 217-31.

45. See Harvard Sitkoff, ed., *Fifty Years Later: The New Deal Evaluated* (Philadelphia: Temple University Press, 1985).

46. Brinkley, "New Deal Scholarship," 116-17.

47. Robert S. McElvaine, *The Great Depression: America, 1929-1941* (New York: Times Books, 1984; revised edition 1993), xxiii; T. H. Watkins, *The Great Depression: America in the 1930s* (New York: Little, Brown, 1993), 12-18; T. H. Watkins, *The Hungry Years: A Narrative History of the Great Depression in America* (New York: Henry Holt, 1999), xii-xiii.

48. See Timothy Egan, *The Worst Hard Time: The Untold Story of Those Who Survived the Great American Dust Bowl* (Boston: Houghton Mifflin, 2006); Charles Shindo, *Dust Bowl Migrants in the American Imagination* (Lawrence: University of Kansas Press, 1997); Donald H. Grubbs, *Cry From Cotton: The Southern Tenant Farmers' Union and the New Deal* (Fayetteville: University of Arkansas Press, 2000); Lizabeth Cohen, *Making a New Deal: Industrial Workers in Chicago, 1919-1939* (Cambridge: Cambridge University Press, 1990); James J. Lorence, *The Unemployed People's Movement: Leftists, Liberals, and Labor in Georgia, 1929-1941* (Athens: University of Georgia Press, 2009); Lauren Rebecca Sklaroff, *Black Culture and the New Deal: The Quest for Civil Rights in the Roosevelt Era* (Chapel Hill: University of North Carolina Press, 2009);

Lara Campbell, *Respectable Citizens: Gender, Family, and Unemployment in Ontario's Great Depression* (Toronto: University of Toronto Press, 2009).

49. Morris Dickstein, *Dancing in the Dark: A Cultural History of the Great Depression* (New York: W.W. Norton, 2009), xiv-xxii.

50. Anthony J. Badger, *The New Deal: The Depression Years, 1933-1940* (New York: Hill and Wang, 1989; reprint, Chicago: Ivan R. Dee, 2002), 10; Jordan A. Schwarz, *The New Dealers: Power Politics in the Age of Roosevelt* (New York: Alfred A. Knopf, 1993), xi-xii.

51. Colin Gordon, *New Deals: Business, Labor, and Politics in America, 1920-1935* (New York: Cambridge University Press, 1994), 1-5.

52. Patrick J. Maney, *The Roosevelt Presence: A Biography of Franklin D. Roosevelt* (New York: Twayne Publishers, 1992); Kenneth S. Davis, *FDR: The Beckoning of Destiny, 1882-1928* (New York: Putman, 1972); Kenneth S. Davis, *FDR: The New York Years, 1928-1933* (New York: Random House, 1985); Kenneth S. Davis, *FDR: The New Deal Years, 1933-1937* (New York: Random House, 1986); Kenneth S. Davis, *FDR: Into the Storm, 1937-1940* (New York: Random House, 1993); Kenneth S. Davis, *FDR: The War President, 1940-1943* (New York: Random House, 2000); Geoffrey C. Ward, *Before the Trumpet: Young Franklin Roosevelt, 1882-1905* (New York: Harper and Row, 1985); Geoffrey C. Ward, *A First-Class Temperament: The Emergence of Franklin Roosevelt* (New York: Harper and Row, 1989).

53. See Maurine H. Beasley, *Eleanor Roosevelt: Transformative First Lady* (Lawrence: University Press of Kansas, 2010); Joseph P. Lash, *Dealers and Dreamers: A New Look at the New Deal* (New York: Doubleday, 1988).

54. One of the more popular, but politically biased, books on the Great Depression during the past decade is Amity Shlaes, *The Forgotten Man: A New History of the Great Depression* (New York: Harper Perennial, 2007).

55. David M. Kennedy, *Freedom From Fear: The American People in Depression and War, 1929-1945* (New York: Oxford University Press, 1999), xiii-xiv.

56. Alan Brinkley, *The End of Reform: New Deal Liberalism in Recession and War* (New York: Alfred A. Knopf, 1995), 3-5.

57. See Steve Fraser and Gary Gerstle, eds., *The Rise and Fall of the New Deal Order, 1930-1980* (Princeton: Princeton University Press, 1989).

58. Alonzo L. Hamby, *Liberalism and Its Challengers: FDR to Reagan* (New York: Oxford University Press, 1985), 3-5.

PART I

Roosevelt's New Deal

Revolution

CHAPTER TWO

Politics of the 1930s and the New Deal

MICHAEL A. DAVIS

The 1930s marked a watershed in American politics. The Great Depression, which began with the stock market crash of October 1929 and ended with American entry into World War II in 1941, unleashed not only immense economic misery, but also great political upheaval. Republican president Herbert Hoover, elected in a landslide in 1928 as a "champion of the unfortunate," was soon vilified for his "apparent insensitivity" to the economic plight of the American people.[1] By 1932, he was, according to historian William Leuchtenburg, "a pathetic figure, a weary, beaten man, often jeered by crowds as a President had never been jeered before."[2] Associated with economic collapse and the unpopular Hoover, Republicans witnessed their majority status erode at all levels of government throughout the early 1930s.

The election of Democrat Franklin D. Roosevelt to the presidency in 1932 did not improve Republican prospects. Upon entering office in March 1933, Roosevelt launched the New Deal, a series of bold economic reforms to combat the Depression. Meanwhile, Republicans, unfamiliar with minority status and unable to articulate a single response to the New Deal, descended into factionalism, confusion, and further defeat. In the 1936 presidential election, Roosevelt routed his Republican opponent, Kansas governor Alf Landon, receiving a record-breaking 60.8 percent of the popular vote. When the Seventy-Fifth Congress convened in early 1937, at the apogee of Democratic strength, only seventeen Republicans sat in the Senate, and eighty-nine in the House of Representatives. While the party rebounded slightly by the end of the decade, this was more the result of Democratic errors, including Roosevelt's attempt to pack the Supreme Court in 1937, than Republican skill or unity.[3]

Over the course of the decade, party alignments shifted, coalitions formed, and new leaders emerged on the political scene. This landscape was far different from the politics, parties, and personalities that dominated since the late nineteenth century. In fact, the 1930s served as a turning point for twentieth-century American politics. The emergence of a Democratic majority was not the only political change in the 1930s. Voter turnout, which declined in the 1920s, increased significantly during the Depression decade. For the first time in American history, the personal welfare of the population became a national concern, and the federal government assumed responsibility for the nation's economic well-being.[4] Finally, the nation embraced a "new politics" that set in motion greater ideological distinctions (and polarization) between the two leading parties. This "new politics," adopted by Roosevelt early in his first term, stressed "issue-driven coalitions" over traditional, "patron-based" and "service-oriented" party organizations.[5] The result was an interparty realignment in which, over time, the Democratic Party became the distinctly liberal party, and the Republican Party the decisively conservative one.

A voluminous literature exists on American politics in the 1930s. Most monographs and essays concentrate on the ideological, policy, electoral, and personality clashes related to the Great Depression and Roosevelt's New Deal. These writings detail three distinct subject categories: realignment theory, Republican Party challenges, and Democratic Party divisions. The literature reveals several general characteristics of American politics in the New Deal era. First, new voters (i.e., groups outside the core electorate) were mobilized, while many old ones, dissatisfied with Republicans, were converted to the Democratic Party. Second, the Depression was bleak for Re-

publicans, and the party faced multiple challenges, including association with Hoover, blame for the Depression, minority party status,
and lack of a coherent and positive response to the New Deal. And
third, the Democratic Party, while enjoying electoral success and
majority party status, nevertheless confronted serious internal divisions—especially between the conservative and liberal elements of
the "Roosevelt coalition."

The works relating to partisan realignment during the New Deal
are vast and varied in scope. The theory of realignment is intricately
linked to what Harvard political scientist V. O. Key described as a
"critical election."[6] According to Key, critical elections occurred pe-
riodically in American history, generating high levels of voter interest, upsetting the previous balance of power among competing
parties, and producing durable changes in the compositions of the
voter coalitions supporting each party.[7] The term "realignment,"
then, implies a readjusting or reshuffling of the electorate. The main
lines of scholarly debate are over how and when the New Deal realignment occurred. The traditional interpretation among political
scientists, including Key, Walter Burnham, and others, was that Republican voters of the 1920s were converted to Democratic Party
ranks in the 1930s.[8]

In *The American Voter* (1960), Angus Campbell, Philip Converse,
Warren Miller, and Donald Stokes argued that party identification
in the United States was generally stable, and "not readily disturbed
by passing events and personalities." Only in the most extreme of
circumstances—an economic depression, for example—was party
loyalty affected by politics. The authors of *The American Voter* concluded that in the 1930s a partisan realignment occurred when
three groups most affected by the events of that decade switched
their party allegiance. The first group was comprised of young voters who came of age in the 1920s and never developed a strong
sense of party identification. These voters were quick to abandon
the majority Republican Party once severe economic crisis ensued.
A second group, including those who benefited the most from
New Deal policies, moved toward the Democratic Party. The third
group of voters, meanwhile, included minorities, especially Jews

and African Americans. In the case of Jewish voters, the authors speculated that it was the rise of Nazi Germany, and the Roosevelt administration's opposition to it, that contributed to a partisan shift. In the end, the authors emphasized that "the conversion of erstwhile Republicans" was the most significant factor in establishing the Democratic majority of the 1930s.[9]

V. O. Key, in his *The Responsible Electorate* (1966), provided an additional rationale for this conversion—government action and campaign oratory. According to Key, Roosevelt radically transformed American government, and with it, partisan allegiances. Prior to 1933, the federal government "had been a remote authority with a limited range of activity." The New Deal, with its large-scale measures for unemployment relief, public works, and social security, changed those priorities, and made the federal government "an institution that affected the lives and fortunes of most, if not all, citizens." Key argued that "persons of all classes deserted the Republicans to vote for Franklin D. Roosevelt and a change." He suggested that party switching was common in both directions. Governmental actions and political rhetoric, Key concluded, heightened "polarization along class and occupational lines."[10]

In contrast, scholars such as Samuel Lubell and Carl Degler argued that the revival of the Democratic Party in the 1930s was largely "the result of a one-sided mobilization of previous nonvoters."[11] In *The Future of American Politics* (1952), Lubell argued that the Roosevelt revolution of the 1930s originated from previously uninvolved groups, including "women, young people, and the foreign-stock, urban, working class." Overall, Lubell insisted that the Democratic Party began appealing to these groups as early as 1928, and that in the 1930s, Roosevelt awakened them "to a consciousness of the power in their numbers. He extended to them the warming hand of recognition, through patronage and protective legislation."[12]

In an essay titled "American Political Parties and the Rise of the City: An Interpretation" (1964), Carl Degler argued that a shift in voter preference was well underway before 1932, and that this shift was largely the result of voter mobilization. Degler insisted that the GOP had relatively strong ties with urban voters, carrying heav-

ily populated areas in most elections from 1894 to 1928. He demonstrated that the numbers of Democratic voters in these areas
increased tremendously during that period, while the number of
Republican voters changed very little. In other words, there was not
a conversion or "reshuffling" of voters, but a great mobilization of
new voters.[13]

Historian Nancy Weiss took a different position on realignment in *Farewell to the Party of Lincoln: Black Politics in the Age of
FDR* (1983). She attributed the movement of African Americans
away from their traditional loyalty to the GOP and into the Democratic Party to both voter conversion and voter mobilization. Weiss
noted that despite years of neglect from Republicans, especially the
Hoover administration, African American voters remained loyal
to the GOP through the 1932 election. By 1936, however, African
American voters shifted their party allegiance to the Democrats and
became a part of the "Roosevelt coalition." The reason for this shift,
Weiss concluded, was not that the Democratic Party changed its
views on race—it did not—but because African Americans "were
not excluded from the economic benefits of the New Deal."[14]

Scholars of American politics in the 1930s took an interest in
the Republican Party. The GOP declined throughout most of the
1930s because it lacked national leadership and a unified strategy to
combat the new Democratic majority. Specifically, scholars have focused on party behavior and divisions with the Republican Party.[15]
Most scholars argued that Republicans reacted to the New Deal by
increasing their criticism of Roosevelt, rather than aligning their
rhetoric to support some level of federal recovery efforts. The result
was that the party suffered devastating electoral losses in 1934 and
1936, and the loss of their core voting constituency.

Harris Gaylord Warren's *Herbert Hoover and the Great Depression*
(1959) was one of the first monographs to consider Republican politics of the period. According to Warren, Hoover faced three major
problems that made him vulnerable to Democratic attack prior to
the 1932 presidential election. First, he did not enjoy widespread
popularity within his own party, and had never been the choice of
professional politicians. Second, Hoover was unable to live up to

the "Great Engineer" image and high expectations set for him during the 1928 presidential campaign. These unfulfilled expectations undermined Hoover's credibility and leadership. Warren asserted that Hoover "could not provide the confident leadership needed to 'strengthen the moral fiber of the nation' while he summoned the mass intelligence of the country to point the way toward economic recovery and stabilization." And third, Hoover failed to respond to the Democratic national publicity machine that was committed to denying him a second term even before the Depression. Without a publicity structure in place to counter the Democrats' charges, "every mistake, every failure to take action, every over-optimistic statement by any Republican, could be turned to political account." By the end of 1930, Warren concluded, most voters accepted the Democrats' message that "Republicans, and particularly Hoover, were responsible for the depression and favored the rich over the poor."[16]

In an essay included in the multivolume *History of U.S. Political Parties* (1973), historian George Mayer argued that Republicans faced two fundamental problems in the aftermath of their 1932 electoral rout. One was the unpopularity of former president Herbert Hoover, who refused to the follow the examples set by previously defeated incumbents and withdraw from the political arena. Instead, Hoover attempted to retain control over the party, and lead an assault on the highly popular New Deal. Thus, while Roosevelt damaged the party from the outside, Hoover "embarrassed it from within."[17]

The other problem confronting Republicans, Mayer maintained, was the inability of party leaders to articulate an agenda that might "recapture the defectors with Republican predilections." Roosevelt was popular because his relief policies "had put money into the hands of the jobless and impoverished farmers." Many Republican congressmen feared that a direct assault on the New Deal would be disastrous. The Republican National Committee, under the leadership of Henry P. Fletcher, organized a national campaign in 1934 to attack Roosevelt and his policies. Mayer noted that as a response most Republicans "moved uneasily through an ideological twilight zone. They believed that it was imperative to compete with the

New Deal for the support of the masses and yet uphold traditional Republican principles."[18] That November, the GOP, instead of gaining seats in Congress during midterm elections, lost nineteen seats in the House of Representatives and ten in the Senate.

In *Herbert Hoover: The Post-Presidential Years, 1933-1964* (1983), Gary Dean Best analyzed Hoover's weaknesses and his opponents. According to Best, it was clear that Hoover was unpopular with Republican leaders, before, during, and after his presidency. Hoover was, Best insisted, "always something of a loner in the Republican Party," distrusted by both conservatives and western progressives. Conservatives were suspicious of him because of his service during the Wilson administration and because he was a humanitarian and an administrator rather than a professional politician. Western progressives distrusted Hoover in the area of foreign affairs. They suspected that he favored Wilsonian internationalism because of his support for American entry into the League of Nations during the Senate debate of 1919-1920, and because of his years traveling abroad.[19]

The 1936 presidential election was a central event in understanding the changes and crises in the Republican Party. In *Landon of Kansas* (1966), Donald McCoy provided insight into Republican Party divisions during the New Deal era. McCoy detailed Alf Landon's path to the Republican nomination in 1936, his campaign and subsequent defeat that November, and his fight with party conservatives in the late 1930s over "the intellectual and organizational reconstruction" of the Republican Party. Landon was a moderate Kansas governor who won re-election in 1934. He had a record of balancing budgets, fighting oil companies and utility interests, and actively opposing the Ku Klux Klan. As the party's nominee, Landon promised efficiency in government, but insisted that relief would not be withdrawn from those who needed it. Still, he was defeated by Roosevelt in a landslide in 1936, carrying only two states and garnering eight electoral votes.[20]

Throughout his biography, McCoy presented Landon as a champion for moderation within the party. According to McCoy, Landon was undermined in 1936 by conservative elements from both inside and outside of the party. By October, McCoy observed, Landon was "being overshadowed in tone and coverage by those less moderate than he," including Hoover, the American Liberty League, and even his own vice-presidential running mate, Frank Knox. During Roosevelt's second term, Landon once again struggled against Hoover and conservatives for "the intellectual and organizational reconstruction of the Republican party." In the end, McCoy insisted that Landon was a moderate, who "played an important part in shaping the development of his party into what, during the 1950s, would be known as Modern Republicanism."[21]

In a 1971 essay titled "The Election of 1936," William Leuchtenburg presented a slightly different picture of Landon. Although the governor was promoted by many of his supporters as a "'liberal Coolidge,'" Landon distanced himself from both ostentatious wealth and Old Guard Republicanism. In fact, Landon aligned himself with the more conservative, rural populace during the campaign. Still, Leuchtenburg insisted, there were sharp limits to Landon's socalled progressivism. For example, in a speech in Milwaukee in late September, Landon "denounced the Social Security Act as 'unjust, unworkable, stupidly drafted and wastefully financed.'" The most important question of the campaign, he repeatedly told crowds, was "whether our American form of government is to be preserved."[22] Leuchtenburg concluded that Landon was unable to articulate a consistent message, attract a national following, or match Roosevelt's personal magnetism and leadership.

One of the first modern studies to focus comprehensively on Republicans during this critical period was Clyde Weed's *The Nemesis of Reform: The Republican Party during the New Deal* (1994). Weed, a political scientist, examined Republican electoral strategies in the 1930s, noting that they failed to conform to the prevailing theory of party competition, the so-called Downsian model, named after economist Anthony Downs. This model, Weed noted, "sees political parties as rational individuals seeking to advance private ends by influencing the policymaking process." In an effort to maximize electoral gains, parties alter their "appeals in response to changes in policy preferences by the electorate." According to Weed, Republicans in the 1930s did not act in a "Downsian fashion." Republican leaders (i.e., the old guard, eastern business conservatives who controlled the party machinery) were simply unable to comprehend the political realignment that took place. Even in the aftermath of the devastating Republican losses in the 1934 midterm elections, they believed "that normal electoral patterns continued to be skewed by [New Deal] federal expenditures," and that any "disillusionment with the Democratic recovery program would result in the restoration of Republican hegemony under conservative auspices."[23]

In addition, Weed argued that internal divisions within the GOP played an important role in undermining the party's ability to adjust to the new political realities of the New Deal. Like its Democratic counterpart, the Republican Party was a collection of various political interests. Since the late nineteenth century, the combined force of eastern and western Republicans represented the necessary keys to Republican success. When the coalition collapsed—as it did in 1912 when western progressives, with their calls for tariff protection for agricultural goods, cooperative marketing, and farm price increases, bolted the party—Democratic victory followed. While those progressives, disenchanted with Democrat Woodrow Wilson's internationalist foreign policy, returned to the GOP by 1920, the Republican coalition remained very fragile. The Depression, Weed observed, strained the already uneasy GOP coalition, and, in fact, western progressives abandoned Hoover and the party in the elections of 1932 and 1934.[24]

In the end, Weed noted, eastern conservatives mistakenly believed that they could restore the Republican Party to its majority status in 1936 by intensifying the party's anti-New Deal message and nominating a midwesterner, such as Alf Landon, for president. They were wrong, Weed insisted. Despite a few small GOP victories in the northeast in the 1935 off-year elections, the conservative message no longer resonated in the traditional Republican stronghold. Furthermore, Landon's nomination failed to rally western progressives, especially in light of the conservative rhetoric coming out of the party machinery. The effect of all this, Weed concluded, "was to minimize electoral appeal and doom the Republicans to a minority status that even now has not been wholly overcome."[25]

Lewis Gould, in *Grand Old Party: A History of the Republicans* (2003), examined the 1936 election and the party's dramatic shift in ideology during the late 1930s. According to Gould, the Landon-Roosevelt contest advanced "a sharp ideological division between the two parties." For example, Landon stressed in his addresses that Roosevelt was betraying American principles and undermining the Constitution. In turn, Roosevelt connected Republicans with "organized money," and "promised that in his second term 'the forces of selfishness and lust for power' would meet 'their master.'" Despite Landon's defeat, the Republican Party experienced a revival of interest in the late 1930s. Gould pointed to three factors for this upswing. First, Roosevelt's Supreme Court-packing plan, unveiled in early 1937, generated great controversy. Second, labor strife in the automobile and steel industries in 1937 and 1938 "frightened middle-class citizens who were otherwise sympathetic to the administration." And third, the start of a recession in the spring of 1937 undermined public support for Roosevelt and the Democrats. The result was that in the midterm elections of 1938, Republicans won seven seats in the Senate and seventy-five seats in the House of Representatives. The GOP also elected twelve governors, and added many new faces, including Robert A. Taft, Harold Stassen, and Thomas E. Dewey, to the national scene. After eight years in the political wilderness, the Republican Party, Gould concluded, reestablished itself as a reasonable alternative to the Democrats.[26]

In *FDR's Republicans: Domestic Political Realignment and American Foreign Policy* (2010), Robert E. Jenner maintained that "Old Guard" leadership in the party was finally undermined by the results of the 1936 election. Jenner argued that Republicans did not "modify their positions to accommodate the changing viewpoints of the electorate" following Hoover's loss in 1932. Instead, the party "held fast to its philosophy of pioneer individualism and self-help as an answer to the ravages of the Great Depression." In 1936, the Old Guard launched a crusade against the New Deal, by associating the Republican platform with Christian principles, and equating Roosevelt with evil. Appealing to only the most ideologically pure, Old Guard leadership, Jenner noted, "left no room for compromise, consensus building, or coalitions," and ultimately "narrowed the base of voter support." According to Jenner, the 1936 election marked a turning point for the Republican Party. By 1938, Republicans accepted the right of government to exercise economic controls and assume welfare responsibilities, and were generally inclined to support some New Deal reforms.[27]

The Democratic Party has also figured prominently in scholarly works on the politics of the New Deal. Most studies emphasized intraparty disputes between liberals and conservatives. In *After Wilson: The Struggle for the Democratic Party, 1920-1934* (1992), Douglas Craig noted that a "fierce struggle for control of the Democratic party's national organization and philosophical direction took place between 1920 and 1932." This intraparty fight revolved around many things, including "cultural issues such as Catholicism, urbanism, and prohibition," as well as "states' rights, the proper extent of federal activism, the relationship between business and government, and tariff policy."[28]

Similarly, David Burner, in *The Politics of Provincialism: The Democratic Party in Transition, 1918-1932* (1967), maintained that there were a number of potential courses available for Democrats to follow in the early 1930s, including a sharp turn to the political right. For example, the three unsuccessful nominees for president in the 1920s, James Cox, John W. Davis, and Alfred E. Smith, were all conservative voices in the early 1930s, demanding balanced budgets, warning against the persecution of the rich, and condemning Hoover's "road to socialism." Had such views prevailed within the Democratic hierarchy, Burner argued, Democrats might have collapsed under the economic stress, and provided Republicans with an opportunity to rediscover their progressive roots and to occupy the political left. It was Roosevelt, Burner concluded, who united the various factions within the party, and gave the Democrats "a progressive cast."[29]

In his masterful *The Age of Roosevelt: The Politics of Upheaval* (1960), Arthur Schlesinger Jr. articulated another division within the Democratic Party—the old "politics of organization" versus a new "politics of ideology." The traditional Democratic organization was an alliance of northern city bosses and southern barons. They, Schlesinger insisted, "believed in little beyond states' rights and federal patronage; politics was its business, a way of life rather than a way to get things done." The New Deal, however, ushered in a new era in politics, one "bound together, not by habit and by spoils, but by ideas . . . and by a belief in positive government as the instrument of national improvement." They were involved in politics not merely to hold office, but to develop policy. By the end of Roosevelt's first term, this politics of ideology supplanted the politics of organization. The reason, Schlesinger insisted, was that the old party professionals "could not supply the ideas, the imagination, and the administrative drive which Roosevelt needed." Ultimately, Schlesinger argued that the executive branch, an instrument of the politics of ideology under Roosevelt, clashed with the legislative branch, a stronghold of the professional politician.[30]

In *Mr. Democrat: Jim Farley, the New Deal, and the Making of Modern American Politics* (2006), Daniel Scroop contended that Farley was actually a key figure in the transition to this new politics. Scroop did not overstate Farley's case, but insisted that Schlesinger's portrait of the party chairman needed revision. He pointed out that Farley directed the expansion of the Democratic National Committee's special divisions for women, African Americans, and labor. This expansion brought disparate groups and individuals into a coalition. While Farley struggled to adapt to the political environment that the New Deal created, Scroop concluded that he "participated in that creative process, actively contributing to and helping to bring about the transition between the worlds of pre- and post-New Deal politics, even as that politics rendered him impotent."[31]

Much of the scholarly literature examined Roosevelt as a party leader, and his quest to transform the Democratic Party into a party that reflected the welfare-state emphasis of his own liberalism. In *Roosevelt: The Party Leader, 1932–1945* (1991), Sean J. Savage argued that Roosevelt had two distinct and interconnected goals for the party. One was to help make it an "enduring majority party in national politics and public policy." The other goal was to transform it "into a distinctly liberal party in its ideology and policy agenda." As the Democratic Party expanded to include urban-industrial areas in the Northeast and West, southern and conservative influence in the party waned. In 1936, only thirty-five percent of Democrats in Congress came from the South, compared to over seventy-five percent in 1920. Similarly, in the presidential election of 1920 ninety percent of the Democrats electoral votes came from the South, but in 1936 the South provided only twenty-three percent of Roosevelt's Electoral College victory.[32]

Susan Dunn's *Roosevelt's Purge: How FDR Fought to Change the Democratic Party* (2010) examined Roosevelt's desire to transform the Democratic Party into a liberal organization. Dunn chronicled the president's relationship with white southerners and conservatives throughout the late 1920s and early 1930s, culminating with the attempted purge of party conservatives in 1938. She argued that Roosevelt sought "to be all things to all people," and hold all factions of the increasingly eclectic Democratic Party together. According to Dunn, conservative Democrats, mainly in the South, were uncomfortable with many of the early New Deal measures, but yielded to the president because they "believed that they were merely leasing out their party to a short-term progressive agenda." By 1937, these conservatives "saw their party changing before their eyes—and stolen out from under them." These Democrats were also concerned about the move of African Americans into the party and the prospect of advocating racial equality. In response, conservative Democrats sabotaged Roosevelt's second-term agenda in Congress, buried the Fair Labor Standards Act, slashed funds for the Wagner housing program, and defeated the court-packing plan. In 1938, Roosevelt struck back, and campaigned to drive his conservative, anti–New Deal foes out of the party. Insisting that politicians must rise above their sectional biases and local interests, and adopt a national outlook, Roosevelt intervened in Democratic primaries that summer and supported liberal challengers over conservative incumbents.[33]

Dunn insisted that Roosevelt's attempted "purge" of party conservatives was motivated by his sincere belief that America needed

two distinctly ideological parties, one liberal and the other conservative. In the short term, Roosevelt's "purge" failed. Many of
the conservatives he opposed for re-election in 1938 retained their
seats, and by the end of 1939, with the outbreak of World War II
in Europe, Roosevelt reached out to them for foreign policy support. Still, Dunn concluded, Roosevelt's vision ultimately came to
pass. In an ironic twist, beginning in the 1960s, southern Democrats became Republicans. By the late twentieth century, ideology
defined the two parties; the Democratic Party was the liberal party
in America, and the Republican Party the conservative one.[34]

The historiography of American politics in the New Deal is immense and crucial to understanding other components of the decade. In the early 1930s, Democrats replaced Republicans as the
majority party. Repudiated at the polls, Republicans descended into
factionalism and confusion, and faced multiple leadership, message,
and image problems. In the elections of 1934 and 1936, Republicans,
dominated by Old Guard conservatives, pursued a largely anti-New
Deal course, attempting to associate the Roosevelt administration with dictatorship and socialism. However, New Deal reforms
reached many people, including Republican voters who switched
political allegiances. Following Roosevelt's landslide victory in 1936,
a new generation of Republicans emerged, calling for greater efficiency in government, less spending, and a milder version of New
Deal reforms. Meanwhile, the Democratic Party coalesced into a
party of white southerners, northeastern liberals, African Americans, western farmers, and labor interests. This realignment resulted in intraparty challenges, especially with southern and conservative opposition to the New Deal during Roosevelt's second term.
The scholarly literature on American politics in the 1930s highlights
these struggles and the powerful personalities that swirled around
them, and illuminates how the political realignments of that period
affect us today.

Notes

1. Roger Biles, *A New Deal for the American People* (DeKalb: Northern Illinois University Press, 1991), 24.

2. William E. Leuchtenburg, *Franklin D. Roosevelt and the New Deal, 1932–1940* (New York: Harper and Row, 1963), 16.

3. William E. Leuchtenburg, "The Election of 1936," in *History of American Presidential Elections* (New York: Chelsea House, 1971), 3:2842.

4. David F. Prindle, "Voter Turnout, Critical Elections, and the New Deal Realignment," *Social Science History* 3 (Winter 1979): 144.

5. Daniel Scroop, *Mr. Democrat: Jim Farley, the New Deal, and the Making of Modern Politics* (Ann Arbor: University of Michigan Press, 2006), 99.

6. See V. O. Key, "A Theory of Critical Elections," *The Journal of Politics* 17 (February 1955), 3-18.

7. Allan J. Lichtman, *Prejudice and the Old Politics: The Presidential Election of 1928* (Chapel Hill: University of North Carolina Press, 1979), 201.

8. Prindle, "Voter Turnout," 146.

9. Angus Campbell, et al., *The American Voter* (Chicago: University Press of Chicago, 1976), 157, 160.

10. V. O. Key, *The Responsible Electorate: Rationality in Presidential Voting, 1936-1960* (Cambridge: Harvard University Press, 1966), 31, 34.

11. Prindle, "Voter Turnout," 148.

12. Samuel Lubell, *The Future of American Politics* (New York: Harper and Brothers, 1952), 29, quoted in Kristi Anderson, *The Creation of a Democratic Majority, 1928-1936* (Chicago: University of Chicago Press, 1979), 9-10.

13. Carl Degler, "American Political Parties and the Rise of the City: An Interpretation," *Journal of American History* 51 (June 1964): 52.

14. Nancy J. Weiss, *Farewell to the Party of Lincoln: Black Politics in the Age of FDR* (Princeton: Princeton University Press, 1983), 211.

15. Clyde P. Weed, *The Nemesis of Reform: The Republican Party During the New Deal* (New York: Columbia University Press, 1994), 2.

16. Harris Gaylord Warren, *Herbert Hoover and the Great Depression* (New York: W.W. Norton, 1967), 122-23, 250.

17. George H. Mayer, "The Republican Party, 1932-1952," in *History of U.S. Political Parties* (New York: Chelsea House, 1973), 3:2264-67.

18. Ibid., 3:2266, 2270-71.

19. Gary Dean Best, *Herbert Hoover: The Postpresidential Years, 1933-1964* (Stanford: Hoover Institution Press, 1983), 1:xv, 74-75.

20. Donald R. McCoy, *Landon of Kansas* (Lincoln: University of Nebraska Press, 1966), ix.

21. Ibid., 327, 342, 347.

22. William E. Leuchtenburg, *The FDR Years: On Roosevelt and His Legacy* (New York: Columbia University Press, 1995), 109, 113.

23. Weed, *The Nemesis of Reform,* 3-5, 49.

24. Ibid., 13.

25. Ibid., 4.

26. Lewis L. Gould, *Grand Old Party: A History of the Republicans* (New York: Random House, 2003), 273-74, 278.

27. Robert E. Jenner, *FDR's Republicans: Domestic Political Realignment and American Foreign Policy* (New York: Lexington Books, 2010), 75, 81, 183.

28. Douglas B. Craig, *After Wilson: The Struggle for the Democratic Party, 1920-1934* (Chapel Hill: University of North Carolina Press, 1992), 296.

29. David Burner, *The Politics of Provincialism: The Democratic Party in Transition, 1918-1932* (Cambridge: Harvard University Press, 1986), 245-46.

30. Arthur M. Schlesinger Jr., *The Age of Roosevelt* (Boston: Houghton Mifflin, 1960), 3:409, 412, 413.

31. Scroop, *Mr. Democrat,* 100, 102.

32. Sean J. Savage, *Roosevelt: The Party Leader, 1932-1945* (Lexington: University Press of Kentucky, 1991), 1, 13, 45.

33. Susan Dunn, *Roosevelt's Purge: How FDR Fought to Change the Democratic Party* (Cambridge: The Belknap Press of Harvard University Press, 2010), 40, 82, 83, 94.

34. Ibid., 238-39.

CHAPTER THREE

Agriculture and the New Deal

TODD HOLMES

When Franklin D. Roosevelt promised a New Deal for the nation during the 1932 Democratic Convention, few could have realized that within the next year his administration would embark on some of the most revolutionary government programs of the twentieth century. To be sure, the New Deal had numerous facets. But beneath the mantra of "relief, recovery, and reform," the crux of Roosevelt's programs relied on government intervention in the economy. In so doing, the New Deal placed the role of the federal government in the crosshairs of political and historical debate—a debate most fully seen in the realm of agriculture and agricultural policy.

Like other New Deal initiatives, Roosevelt's agricultural policies centered on Keynesian economics—the concept that spending or pumping money into the economy was the key to recovering from a downturn. With a federal price tag of over $8.6 billion, the government established and bankrolled a host of agricultural programs in the 1930s to stave off plummeting crop prices and farm foreclosures. Such programs included the Agricultural Adjustment Administration, the Farm Security Administration (FSA), the Soil Conservation Service, the Farm Credit Administration, and the Commodity Credit Corporation. Many components of these programs, as well as the role of the federal government in the lives of American farmers, have continued into the twenty-first century.

Despite these clear links to the past, agriculture and national agricultural policy as topics within the historical discourse of the New Deal have remained overshadowed by more popular topics like WPA projects, union labor, and Roosevelt himself, and isolated within the regional contexts of the West, South, and Midwest.

To understand the scholarship of New Deal agriculture, it is necessary to bridge such regional demarcations and trace the development of the literature chronologically. Indeed, agriculture offers a much fuller view of the historical debates about the New Deal. As the nation's primary industry, agriculture occupied an important place in the debates on the depression and recovery. Following World War I, sectors of the American economy declined. As early as 1920, farmers were affected by the economic downturn. Yet these discussions did not fit squarely within the historical mold of the New Deal. Traditionally, the historiography of Roosevelt's policies has been characterized by a linear trajectory that, after the 1960s, largely oscillated within a conservative-radical dichotomy. In the realm of agriculture, however, right, left, and center interpretations developed. For the right, the government did too much; for the left, it did not do enough; and for the center, the government, with some blemishes, did the best it could and did it well. In charting the literature from its origins in the South and West to the national debates of the late twentieth century, the discussion captures both the political influence of the times and the peculiar interaction between this tripartite of interpretation.[1]

The literature on the South and West sowed the earliest seeds of critique of New Deal agriculture. While developing alongside the conservative criticism of anti-New Deal organizations like the American Liberty League, the leftist interpretations of the South and West represented the first scholarly work on Roosevelt's agricultural programs. To be sure, both regions were unique as areas where Roosevelt confronted the issues of economy, race, labor, and the cultural idyll of the American farmer. And it was the examination of these unique areas—especially race and labor—in the literature on the South and West that established the leftist critique of New Deal agriculture, and created the paradigms that would profoundly shape the historiographic trends of the respective regions.

During the 1930s southern sociologists took the first scholarly look at New Deal agriculture. *The Collapse of Cotton Tenancy* (1935) by Charles Johnson, Edwin Embree, and W. W. Alexander, offered the earliest critique of Roosevelt's agricultural policies, arguing that the New Deal did not do enough. The Agricultural Adjustment Administration (AAA), established in 1933, sought to correct the problem that plagued American agriculture since the end of the Civil War: surplus and overproduction. Covering eight commodities—corn, wheat, cotton, rice, peanuts, tobacco, milk, and hogs—the AAA subsidized farmers to limit their supply and production in the hopes of achieving higher and more stabilized prices. Yet, as Johnson, Embree, and Alexander argued, the AAA in the cotton South favored planters and undermined the sharecropping and tenancy system, a central part of the region's economy. Because the AAA relied on local power structures dominated by white landlords, black tenants were robbed of their subsidy payments, pushed off the land, and ultimately funneled into the exploited ranks of menial wage laborers. Fellow sociologist Arthur Raper confirmed their conclusions in his work, *Preface to Peasantry* (1936). Using two Georgia counties as case studies, Raper situated Roosevelt's agricultural policies within the historical context of race in the South. He showed that New Deal initiatives, like the AAA and farm credits, largely benefited white landlords, and thus further solidified the region's agricultural aristocracy and its hegemony over the black peasantry.[2]

These early studies of New Deal agriculture in the South produced two important developments. First, they created the foundation of the leftist New Deal critique, as both studies argued that the federal government did not do enough to aid southern sharecroppers and failed to enact much-needed economic reorganization and land reform. Second, the studies contributed significantly in shaping the historiographic trends of race relations and the government in southern agriculture. Building upon these earlier studies in the

1970s, Donald Grubbs's *Cry From the Cotton* (1971) provided one of the most detailed histories of New Deal agricultural policies and southern tenancy. According to Grubbs, the AAA not only displaced up to forty percent of southern sharecroppers but also advanced the racial-economic hierarchy of the South. The AAA did not adjust the racial inequities of its programs, which reinforced subsidies for white landlords and poverty for displaced black workers. Later historical studies on southern agriculture built further upon the works of Grubbs and the leftist New Deal critique to provide a deeper understanding of race relations in Dixie. Historians such as Paul Mertz and Robin D. G. Kelley acknowledged the adverse effects of New Deal agricultural programs and the racial apathy of the Roosevelt administration. Studies by these two scholars examined how rural African American communities addressed impediments to social equality by highlighting the rise of black agency and their grassroots organizational efforts during the 1930s.[3]

Just as sociologists explored the race and labor confluences of New Deal agriculture in the South, journalist and public intellectual Carey McWilliams brought unprecedented attention to western agriculture in his groundbreaking work, *Factories in the Field* (1939). Published only months after John Steinbeck's *The Grapes of Wrath* (1939), McWilliams's study of migrant labor and California agriculture not only put historical flesh on the famous Joad family, but, more importantly, it highlighted the racial stratification of farm labor and the capitalist structure in which it operated—a structure that became known as agribusiness. McWilliams's acute analysis of the exploited labor, land concentration, and corporate control of California's agriculture challenged the idyllic image of the American farmer. "It is no longer agriculture in the formerly understood sense of the term," he proclaimed, "farms have become factories." Indeed, the linking of farms and factories represented a significant assault on the nation's agrarian tradition. McWilliams also argued that farm workers were excluded from every piece of New Deal labor legislation, including the Wagner Act, the Social Security Act, and the Fair Labor Standards Act. He concluded that the New Deal offered little for the "toilers of the land."[4]

McWilliams's view of agriculture in the West as an agribusiness model remained at the center of the historical discourse ever since its publication.[5] In *As You Sow* (1947), Walter Goldschmidt built on McWilliams's model by situating the New Deal as the apex in a long trajectory of federal measures for agribusiness in California and the West. Paul Taylor's *Essays on Land, Water, and the Law in California* (1979), placed McWilliams's agribusiness model within the hydro-engineered landscape of the Golden State, examining New Deal water projects that supplied vital, federally subsidized irrigation systems to farms.[6]

The early literature on New Deal agriculture in the South and West created important and long-lasting historical paradigms. Together, scholarship on agriculture in these two regions constituted the major argument that the New Deal reinforced agricultural policies that were race-based, pro-business, and hurt more than helped the laborers in the field. These regional studies highlighted important failures of the New Deal, and they ultimately argued that the federal government did not do enough.

As the works on the South and West provided the earliest leftist critique, Theodore Schultz's *Redirecting Farm Policy* (1943) established the interpretive lens for the right. An agricultural economist and Nobel Laureate from the University of Chicago, Schultz gave scholarly weight to the economic critiques emanating from conservative groups like the American Liberty League, who throughout Roosevelt's tenure publicly linked New Deal programs, such as the Agricultural Adjustment Administration, with communism. For Schultz, government economic control and the ineffective, "backward looking" operations of the agency, rather than the red nemesis, formed the crux of his critique. Schultz lamented that "agriculture was once the classic example of free enterprise," but New Deal programs like the Soil Conservation Service, Commodity Credit Corporation, and the FSA, as well as smaller operations dealing with crop insurance and farm credit expansion, demonstrated federal control over American agriculture.[7]

Schultz saved his harshest criticisms for the Agricultural Adjustment Administration and its use of price parity, which pegged national price-supply goals for agriculture to those from 1910–1914. He argued that parity represented "the dead hand of the past" whose date range was "obsolete." Schultz described such federal intervention as retarding America's agricultural economy, whereby prices were no longer "employed as economic directives" but as false goals that left agriculture stagnated in the status quo, stemming growth while largely benefiting a prosperous few. Moreover, such parity price formulas necessitated ever-increasing intervention by the federal government in the form of subsidies and storage to offset production. Schultz's economic critique of New Deal agriculture created the foundations for the right, crafting the interpretation that the New Deal went too far.[8]

By the late 1950s and early 1960s, historians such as Arthur Schlesinger Jr. and William Leuchtenburg joined the discourse, putting forth the first histories of Roosevelt and the New Deal.[9] Schlesinger and Leuchtenburg represented the liberal center of the historiography of New Deal agriculture; they highlighted the revolutionary nature of the New Deal—an interpretation that extended to agriculture. In particular, they credited the Agricultural Adjustment Administration with stemming rebellions and farm foreclosures, raising and stabilizing prices, and dealing effectively with the price-surplus crisis to bring prosperity back to rural America. Both scholars, however, pointed out the New Deal's flaws, including the "tragic" conditions of sharecroppers and migrant farm workers. This "halfway revolution" of the New Deal, they argued, was a revolution nonetheless; the government did the best it could, and did it well.[10]

In the 1960s, New Left historians challenged the success of the New Deal, and provided an important bridge between the regional discourses of the South and West and national discussions of New Deal agriculture. The leftist critique transcended race and labor and focused on corporate agribusiness. Political scientist Grant McConnell's *Decline of Agrarian Democracy* (1953) was an early precursor of New Left work, and represented one of the first detailed studies of agribusiness and the New Deal on the national level. Building upon the agribusiness paradigm established by Carey McWilliams and Walter Goldschmidt, McConnell focused on the corporate-dominated American Farm Bureau, tracing its consolidation of agricultural political power and its unparalleled influence on New Deal agricultural policies. According to McConnell, such influence pushed the New Deal to favor large commercial agricultural operations over the nation's small farmer, as seen in the operations of the Agricultural Adjustment Administration and the decline of reform-oriented programs like the FSA. Although focusing on southern sharecroppers and fitting within the southern leftist critique of race relations, David Conrad's *The Forgotten Farmers* (1965) was marked by an acute attention to agribusiness and the conservation of the status quo by Roosevelt and Secretary of Agriculture Henry Wallace. Similarly, Charles Jackson's *The Food and Drug Administration in the New Deal* (1970) provided a unique look at agricultural regulation from the bureaucratic level, documenting the struggle of New Deal liberals like Rexford Tugwell against the agribusiness lobby and the conservative, status-quo perspective of many in the Roosevelt administration.[11]

Carving out new dimensions within the leftist interpretation during the 1960s were works with a more pronounced social science orientation. Economists Leonard Arrington and Don Reading broke important ground in their data analysis of New Deal agricultural and relief payments by sketching a preliminary look at the political economy of the 1930s. Arrington and Reading argued that relief centered on resources and high farm income. They believed that the West received the majority of federal money, which undercut the broader goal of national agricultural reform. Just as the activism of farm labor during the 1960s may have influenced the heightened agribusiness focus of New Left scholarship, the liberal planning of Lyndon Johnson's Great Society may have similarly shaped the respective studies of New Deal planners and agriculture by Ellis Hawley, Richard Kirkendall, and Sidney Baldwin. Works by these scholars detailed the political, bureaucratic, and institutional impediments that hampered the government from doing more.[12]

By the 1960s and 1970s, historians from the liberal center addressed New Deal agriculture largely in response to criticisms from the left. Van Perkins's *Crisis in Agriculture* (1969) provided one of the first national histories of the Agricultural Adjustment Administration. He argued that the agency was revolutionary in nature, calling it a "great success" in stabilizing the prices and production of America's agricultural economy. Yet a striking aspect of Perkins's discussion was his efforts to address arguments from the left. Perkins argued that such criticisms lost sight of the extreme emergency facing both the nation and the Agricultural Adjustment Administration. Christiana McFadyen Campbell's *The Farm Bureau and the New Deal* (1962) also challenged criticisms from the left. She took great issue with Grant McConnell's agribusiness characterization of the American Farm Bureau and its corporate influence on New Deal agriculture. Instead, Campbell argued that the bureau established unity within American agriculture for the first time and was a clear example of a New Deal success.[13]

By the late 1970s, critiques on the right matured. Studies by historians Murray Rothbard and Donald Paarlberg provided a critical analysis of New Deal agricultural agencies, arguing that government intervention did much more damage than good to the national economy and, in particular, American agriculture. The most significant work of the rightist critique, however, focused on the Dust Bowl. Paul Bonnifield's *The Dust Bowl* (1979) blamed the New Deal for the crisis that engulfed America's heartland, arguing that midwestern farmers would have been better off without government involvement. Bonnifield portrayed New Deal agencies, such as the Agricultural Adjustment Administration, the Soil Conservation Service, and the Resettlement Administration (predecessor of the FSA), as dominated by arrogant social engineers whose inappropriate solutions to the Dust Bowl greatly exacerbated the crisis and hardship. Bonnifield's work marked an important growth of the rightist critique, demonstrating what conservatives considered the hubris and unintended consequences of liberal planners during the New Deal.[14]

Donald Worster's subsequent work on the Dust Bowl broadened the leftist critique of the New Deal. For Worster, the Great Depression and Dust Bowl stood together as outcomes of capitalist excess—overindulgence in markets for the former and commercial exploitation of nature in the latter. By attaching capitalism and the environment to the agribusiness paradigm, Worster provided a critical analysis of New Deal agriculture. He used data to demonstrate how programs like the Agricultural Adjustment Administration, the Soil Conservation Service, and the FSA did not go far enough to achieve their stated goals. Like other leftist writers, he detailed the socioeconomic slant of New Deal policies, highlighting the small midwestern farmers who were ignored by the programs. Worster's focus on the environment underscored the contradictions of New Deal agriculture by demonstrating that programs like reclamation and resettlement moved forward while the Agricultural Adjustment Administration restricted agricultural supply and production.[15]

In contrast, R. Douglas Hurt's study of the Dust Bowl gave the New Deal high marks for its role in battling the environmental crisis of the Midwest. He argued that programs like the Agricultural Adjustment Administration and FSA both lessened hardship and stabilized the agricultural economy, while the Soil Conservation Service brought the land under control. Hurt's discussion of Dust Bowl causation also marked an important departure. While Bonnifield blamed the New Deal and Worster criticized American capitalism, Hurt chalked up the Dust Bowl to the ecological mix of drought, wind, and inadequate vegetation. Hurt's study stands as the epitome of the liberal center by consistently arguing that the New Deal did the best it could, and did it well.[16]

The 1980s witnessed a pronounced shift in the scholarship on New Deal agriculture from left to right. The politics of the Reagan era provided the foundation for this change as conservative thought affected the academy as well as American political culture. Part of this shift was a familiar economic interpretation of the New Deal, which centered on the failures of Keynesian economics. Economists such as Robert Higgs and Milton Friedman advanced this critique with works that criticized the level of federal intervention found in New Deal programs. Specifically, they identified the agricultural programs of the New Deal as a prime example of the government doing too much, or, in the words of Higgs, the "free-market regime" giving way to "participatory fascism."[17]

Agricultural economist Donald Paarlberg applied this heightened critique of the right directly to New Deal agriculture in his essay "Tarnished Gold." Characterizing the programs as "obvious failure[s]," Paarlberg built upon his earlier work and posited that American agriculture would have been better off had the government simply given a check to every farmer, rather than intervening in the market. Yet Paarlberg's evidence also supported and borrowed from leftist critiques. For instance, he criticized New Deal farm programs for widening the income gap in agriculture, which benefited agribusiness and skirted reform. Higgs, Friedman, and others on the right intertwined the well-known leftist critiques of agriculture with critiques of state intervention to bolster the argument that the New Deal's agricultural programs represented a dire mistake.[18]

Theodore Saloutos's *The American Farmer and the New Deal* (1982) offered a solid history of New Deal agriculture representative of the liberal center. He shed light on areas outside the more dramatic scope of scholarly attention, such as farm strikes, sharecroppers, and dust storms, while tracing the development of the Roosevelt revolution from the fields to the nation's capital. Saloutos highlighted the 1920s as the spawning ground for the many agricultural proposals encompassed by the New Deal and contextualized the personalities who headed the array of agriculture agencies under Roosevelt. Moreover, in detailing the progress of science and technology, Saloutos identified the root of agricultural overproduction as the overabundance of farmers. Saloutos effectively intertwined this fact with the usual center-oriented caveats of the New Deal's shortcomings, while also implicitly speaking to the farm crisis that struck the Midwest during the 1980s. In the end, Saloutos gave the New Deal high marks for its achievements, an assessment squarely in the liberal center, raving that "with all its limitations and frustrations, the New Deal . . . constituted the greatest innovative epoch in the history of American agriculture."[19]

In recent decades, several centrist scholars continued these debates. David Hamilton's *From New Day to New Deal* (1991) builds on Saloutos's work by tracing the continuity of ideas and proposals regarding agriculture between the administrations of Herbert Hoover and Roosevelt. "The 'revolution of 1933,' at least in the field of farm policy, did not mark the shift from the laissez-faire state to the modern liberal state," Hamilton argued, "but rather the beginning of a new attempt to build the modern associative state." Similarly, Deborah Fitzgerald's *Every Farm A Factory* (2003) situated the New Deal within currents of continuity. By examining the industrial business models taking root in American agriculture during the 1920s, Fitzgerald asserted that agricultural programs accelerated this trajectory, while also offering unprecedented aid and relief.[20]

Other centrist works have focused on the overlooked success of the New Deal in rural America. Brian Cannon's *Remaking the Agrarian Dream* (1996) offered a revisionist account of the FSA—an agency cast as a failure and victim of the American Farm Bureau. Examining the FSA's operations in the mountainous West, Cannon argued that the FSA achieved an impressive track record and represented a New Deal success. Sarah Phillips reframed scholarly thinking on rural America in her book *This Nation, This Land* (2007). Phillips used the Dust Bowl as an example to highlight the New Deal as revolutionary in its coupling of conservation and agricultural programs. She argued that the New Deal linked natural resources and the environmental imbalances of rural farm communities.[21]

Several significant rightist critiques appeared in recent decades as well. Historian Burton Folsom's *New Deal or Raw Deal* (2008) cited the list of failures in New Deal agriculture long championed by critics on the left to advance his argument that Roosevelt's agricultural policies ruined America's agricultural economy. Jim Powell offered a similar critique of the New Deal "assault" on free market capitalism in his book, *FDR's Folly* (2003). Powell employed a methodology akin to Folsom's and argued that the interventionist programs of the New Deal, such as the Agricultural Adjustment Administration, prolonged the Great Depression. The work of historian Gary

Dean Best added to this discourse, with an important combination of rightist and leftist critique. According to Best, New Deal programs, the Agricultural Adjustment Administration in particular, were crafted by "idealists turned amateur economists" steeped in an anti-business sentiment, which ultimately delayed economic recovery. While positing the standard rightist critique that the government did too much, Best also argued that the New Deal "did not do enough" to help business, agriculture, and industry recover.[22]

Recent leftist critiques of the New Deal have been influenced by political economics and food politics. Jim Couch and William Shughart's *The Political Economy of the New Deal* (1998) represented one of the first attempts to trace how political and business interests operated in the period. Using agriculture as a primary lens of examination, Couch and Shughart argued that congressional and presidential politics shaped the funding, disbursement, and focus of the various agricultural programs, which overwhelmingly favored the West. According to Couch and Shughart, these influences stymied the New Deal from doing more to aid small farmers, sharecroppers, and the rural poor.[23]

The popular ascendance of food politics in recent years demonstrated that leftist interpretations have come full circle, while also co-opting themes of the right. Michael Pollan, as well as other scholars and documentary filmmakers, examined American agribusiness and the industrialization of food. Indeed, many of these works built on the agribusiness paradigm crafted long ago by leftist critics like Carey McWilliams, Walter Goldschmidt, and Paul Taylor. While Pollan omitted farm labor from his discussions of agribusiness, he joined leftist writers to argue that New Deal agricultural programs were the springboard for America's state-subsidized model of corporate food production. Yet, similar to rightist scholars co-opting leftist critiques, Pollan borrowed from the right in his argument that the federal government did too much for agribusiness.[24]

In the twenty-first century, New Deal agriculture still represents a fertile field for future scholarship. One such area of exploration is transnational comparisons of agricultural policy between the United States and Europe. Daniel Rogers's book *Atlantic Cross-*

ings (1998) broke new ground in his comparative look at progressivism, and one wonders what new insights could be gained by such an examination of agriculture during the 1930s. Another area ripe for study is agriculture and the environment during the New Deal. Some books addressed this topic, such as David Woolner and Henry Henderson's edited volume *FDR and the Environment* (2005), Neil Maher's *Nature's New Deal* (2008), and Eric Rutkow's *American Canopy* (2012). As these works remind us, trees and forests were as much under the purview of the Department of Agriculture as hogs and soybeans, thus requiring a broader treatment of agriculture and the environment during the New Deal.[25]

American agriculture offers an important perspective on the historical literature and debates of Franklin Roosevelt and the New Deal. Flourishing within an interdisciplinary tripartite of leftist, rightist, and centrist interpretations, the scholarship on Roosevelt's agricultural programs lays bare both the interactions between interpretations and the political influences that underpin them. The New Deal casts an enormous shadow over American politics and the nation's agricultural policies and practices. Now more than ever, it is necessary to understand in full the facets of that shadow.

Notes

1. For early discussions on agriculture in the 1920s, see G. F. Warren, "The Agricultural Depression," *The Quarterly Journal of Economics* 38 (1924): 184-213; Albert Benjamin Genung, *The Agricultural Depression Following World War I and its Political Consequences: An Account of the Deflation Episode, 1921-1934* (Ithaca: Northeast Farm Foundation, 1954). For scholarly discussions on U.S. agriculture during the 1920s and its connection to the Great Depression, see Jakob B. Madsen, "Agricultural Crises and the International Transmission of the Great Depression," *Journal of Economic History* 2 (June 2001): 327-65; Kenneth Finegold, "From Agrarianism to Adjustment: The Political Origins of New Deal Agricultural Policy," *Politics & Society* 11 (March 1982): 1-27; R. Douglas Hurt, *Problems of Plenty: The American Farmer in the Twentieth Century* (Chicago: Ivan R. Dee, 2002), chapters 2-3; Willard Wesley Cochrane, *The Development of American Agriculture: A Historical Analysis* (Minneapolis: University of Minnesota Press, 1993), chapters 7-8.

2. Charles S. Johnson, Edwin Embree, and W. W. Alexander, *The Collapse of Cotton Tenancy: Summary of Field Studies and Statistical Surveys* (Chapel Hill: University of North Carolina Press, 1935); Arthur Raper, *Preface to Peasantry: The Tale of Two Black Belt Counties* (Chapel Hill: University of North Carolina Press, 1936).

3. Donald H. Grubbs, *Cry from Cotton: The Southern Tenant Farmers' Union and the New Deal* (Chapel Hill: University of North Carolina Press, 1971); Paul E. Mertz, *New Deal Policy and Southern Rural Poverty* (Baton Rouge: Louisiana State University Press, 1978); Robin D. G. Kelley, *Hammer and Hoe: Alabama Communists during the Great Depression* (Chapel Hill: University of North Carolina Press, 1990).

4. Carey McWilliams, *Factories in the Field: The Story of Migratory Farm Labor in California* (Boston: Little, Brown, 1939), 48, 266, 277, 303.

5. See Ernesto Galarza, *Farm Workers and Agri-business in California, 1947-1960* (Notre Dame: Notre Dame University Press, 1977); Cletus Daniel, *Bitter Harvest: A History of California Farmworkers, 1870-1941* (Ithaca: Cornell University Press, 1981); Linda Majka and Theo J. Majka, *Farmworkers, Agribusiness, and the State* (Philadelphia: Temple University Press, 1982); Richard Steven Street, *Beasts of the Field: A Narrative History of California Farmworkers, 1769-1913* (Palo Alto: Stanford University Press, 2004); Richard Walker, *Conquest of Bread: 150 Years of Agribusiness in California* (New York: The New Press, 2004).

6. Walter Goldschmidt, *As You Sow* (New York: Harcourt, Brace, 1947); Paul Taylor, *Essays on Land, Water, and the Law in California* (New York: Arno Press, 1979).

7. Theodore Schultz, *Redirecting Farm Policy* (New York: Macmillan, 1943), 1, 7; American Liberty League, *The AAA and Our Form of Government: An Analysis of A Vicious Combination of Fascism, Socialism and Communism* (Washington, D.C.: American Liberty League, 1935). For more on the American Liberty League, see Kim Phillips-Fein, *Invisible Hands: The Making of the Conservative Movement from the New Deal to Reagan* (New York: W.W. Norton, 2009).

8. Schultz, *Redirecting Farm Policy*, 16.

9. Arthur M. Schlesinger Jr., *The Coming of the New Deal* (Boston: Houghton Mifflin, 1959); William E. Leuchtenburg, *Franklin D. Roosevelt and the New Deal, 1932-1940* (New York: Harper and Row, 1963).

10. Leuchtenburg, *New Deal*, 52, 137, 347.

11. Grant McConnell, *The Decline of Agrarian Democracy* (Berkeley: University of California Press, 1953); Samuel Berger, *Dollar Harvest: the Story of the Farm Bureau* (Lexington, MA: Heath Lexington Books, 1971); David Conrad, *The Forgotten Farmers: The Story of Sharecroppers in the New Deal* (Urbana: University of Illinois Press, 1965); Charles Jackson, *Food and Drug Legislation in the New Deal* (Princeton: Princeton University Press, 1970).

12. Leonard Arrington, "Western Agriculture and the New Deal," *Agricultural History* 44 (October 1970): 337-53; Don Reading, "New Deal Activity

and the States, 1933-1939," *Journal of Economic History* 33 (December 1973): 792-810; Ellis W. Hawley, *The New Deal and the Problem of Monopoly: A Study in Economic Ambivalence* (Princeton: Princeton University Press, 1966); Richard S. Kirkendall, *Social Scientists and Farm Politics in the Age of Roosevelt* (Columbia: University of Missouri Press, 1966); Sidney Baldwin, *Poverty and Politics: The Rise and Decline of the Farm Security Administration* (Chapel Hill: University of North Carolina Press, 1968).

13. Van Perkins, *Crisis in Agriculture: The Agricultural Adjustment Administration and the New Deal* (Berkeley: University of California Press, 1969); Christiana McFadyen Campbell, *The Farm Bureau and the New Deal: A Study of Making of National Farm Policy, 1933-1940* (Urbana: University of Illinois Press, 1962).

14. Murray N. Rothbard, *America's Great Depression* (Princeton: Princeton University Press, 1963); Donald Paarlberg, *American Farm Policy: A Case Study of Centralized Decision-Making* (New York: J. Wiley, 1964); Paul Bonnifield, *Dust Bowl* (Albuquerque: University of New Mexico Press, 1979).

15. Donald Worster, *Dust Bowl: The Southern Plains in the 1930s* (New York: Oxford University Press, 1979).

16. R. Douglas Hurt, *Dust Bowl: An Agricultural and Social History* (Chicago: Nelson-Hall, 1981).

17. Robert Higgs, *Crisis and Leviathan: Critical Episodes in the Growth of American Government* (New York: Oxford University Press, 1987), 262; Milton Friedman, *Free to Choose: A Personal Statement* (New York: Harcourt, Brace, Jovanovich, 1980); Milton Friedman, *Tyranny of the Status Quo* (San Diego: Harcourt, Brace, Jovanovich, 1984).

18. Donald Paarlberg, "Tarnished Gold: Fifty Years of New Deal Farm Programs," *The New Deal and Its Legacy: Critique and Reappraisal,* ed. Robert Eden (New York: Greenwood Press, 1989), 42, 47.

19. Theodore Saloutos, *The American Farmer and the New Deal* (Ames: Iowa State University Press, 1982).

20. David E. Hamilton, *From New Day to New Deal: American Farm Policy from Hoover to Roosevelt, 1928-1933* (Chapel Hill: University of North Carolina Press, 1991); Deborah Fitzgerald, *Every Farm A Factory: The Industrial Ideal in American Agriculture* (New Haven: Yale University Press, 2003).

21. Brian Cannon, *Remaking the Agrarian Dream: New Deal Rural Resettlement in the Mountain West* (Albuquerque: University of New Mexico Press, 1996); Sarah T. Phillips, *This Land, This Nation: Conservation, Rural America, and the New Deal* (New York: Cambridge University Press, 2007).

22. Burton Folsom, *New Deal or Raw Deal?: How FDR's Economic Legacy has Damaged America* (New York: Threshold Editions, 2008); Jim Powell, *FDR's Folly: How Roosevelt and His New Deal Prolonged the Great Depression* (New York: Crown Forum, 2003); Gary Dean Best, *Peddling Panaceas: Popular Economists in the New Deal Era* (New Brunswick, NJ: Transaction Publishers, 2005); Gary

Dean Best, *Pride, Prejudice, and Politics: Roosevelt Versus Recovery, 1933-1938* (New York: Praeger, 1991).

23. Jim Couch and William Shughart II, *The Political Economy of the New Deal* (Northampton, MA: Edward Elgar, 1998).

24. Michael Pollan, *Omnivore's Dilemma: A Natural History of Four Meals* (New York: Penguin Press, 2006); Michael Pollan, *In Defense of Food: An Eater's Manifesto* (New York: Penguin Press, 2008); Karl Weber, ed., *Food Inc.: How Industrial Food Is Making Us Sicker, Fatter and Poorer* (New York: Public Affairs, 2009).

25. Daniel Rogers, *Atlantic Crossings: Social Politics in a Progressive Age* (Cambridge: Harvard University Press, 1998); Henry L. Henderson and David B. Woolner, eds., *FDR and the Environment* (New York: Palgrave Macmillan, 2005); Neil M. Maher, *Nature's New Deal: The Civilian Conservation Corps and the Roots of the American Environmental Movement* (New York: Oxford University Press, 2008); Eric Rutkow, *American Canopy: Trees, Forests, and the Making of a Nation* (New York: Scribner, 2012).

CHAPTER FOUR

The Environment and the New Deal

DOUGLAS SHEFLIN

While the New Deal has received tremendous attention from social, political, and economic historians, relatively little consideration has been given to how it and the interwar period more broadly fit into American environmental history. In 2001, historian Paul Sutter pointed out that the narrative accepted by historians to explain twentieth-century conservation emphasized the Progressive Era and the post–World War II period as critically important to our understanding of how ideas about land use and conservation changed over the course of the twentieth century.

That narrative identified the Progressive Era battle over the Hetch Hetchy Dam in California as a starting point. The dispute pitted preservationists like John Muir against conservationists such as Gifford Pinchot and typified the early twentieth-century debate over what to do with America's natural resources. Pinchot's vision of utilitarian conservation won, signaling the primacy of managing resources to ensure efficiency and sustained economic development. This program supposedly held out until after World War II, when Americans began placing more stock in recreation and aesthetics and a broader land ethic, rather than simply attending to economic prospects when thinking about the environment. The controversy surrounding the construction of the Echo Park Dam in Dinosaur National Monument during the late 1940s and early 1950s indicated that Americans made that transition. Unlike the Hetch Hetchy Dam, the Echo Park Dam was never built and symbolized the development of a grassroots environmental movement, a supposedly decisive shift away from Pinchot's conservation toward Muir's preservation.

These two moments received much attention; but, as Sutter observed, there has been little effort to map the course between these events and show how the interwar period, and specifically the New Deal, fits into the picture.[1] Fortunately, the historiography on New Deal environmental thought and politics, arguably the most important and distinctive segment of the interwar conservation story, expanded considerably over the past ten years and rectified the dearth that Sutter noted. Recent works detail the significance of Franklin D. Roosevelt's personal views on land use, the development and growing influence of new sciences like ecology and soil conservation, the translation of environmental concerns into federal policy, and the ways in which those federal policies affected local practices across the country. The basic questions—What was conservation during the 1930s? What role did the federal government play in executing policy? How did Americans respond to these reforms?—continue to drive the historiography as historians wrestle with the New Deal and its legacy. This chapter identifies some of the more recent and notable works on New Deal environmental thought and policy, and shows that it straddled the divide between Progressive Era conservation and postwar environmentalism, constituting an important part of the history of land use in America.

One of the most important recent sources on New Deal environmental history came out in 2002 when Henry Henderson and David Woolner edited a collection of articles based on discussions at the "Recovering the Environmental Legacy of FDR" conference. The bulk of this compilation focused on Roosevelt, particularly his views on conservation and the environment. Roosevelt believed that natural resource use was inseparable from America's prosperity. He upheld that only by protecting their environments could Americans achieve economic well-being. This was of course a timely argument considering the gravity of the Great Depression. By controlling soil erosion, planting forests, mitigating flooding, and other means of trying to manage natural resources efficiently, New Deal programs could rescue America from the Great Depression and return the citizenry to prosperity. This view harkened back to Thomas Jefferson's notion of the agrarian ideal, namely that the direct connection between humans and their environment made Americans better people, better citizens, and more economically secure. That perspective remained an integral part of Roosevelt's vision for bringing America's economy back from the brink of ruin and for protecting its natural resources.[2]

While that sentiment reflected the thoughts of earlier conservationists such as Theodore Roosevelt and Gifford Pinchot, Franklin Roosevelt invoked elements of a more modern approach to resource conservation and environmental management than had his Progressive Era predecessors. According to Brian Black, Franklin Roosevelt's bout with polio and subsequent paralysis limited the ways in which he could physically enjoy the outdoors. Consequently, he took a much more academic, managerial position regarding land use, focusing on regional planning and utilizing new scientific disciplines to forge conservation policy. In essence, Roosevelt looked to organize and systematize the natural world through the use of new ideas and modern technology. He also understood the need to manage the human element within the human-environment relationship. This led to a greater appreciation for not only environmental planning but also social planning—trying to restore the landscape as well as society. Associating the land with those who relied on it required a broader program for resource management. As governor of New York, Roosevelt designed reforestation projects, pushed to buy submarginal land and retire it from production, and brought farmers, foresters, and businessmen together to discuss the state's economic recovery. His experiences in that post gave Roosevelt practice as well as confidence to execute similar programs at the national level.[3]

While Roosevelt certainly deserves credit for his role in bringing his version of environmentalism to the American public, he relied on others to better define his own interpretations of land use and the policies he employed. His administration provided fertile ground for individuals who were, like him, sensitive to environmental degradation and had long been contemplating the relationship between humankind and the environment. These professionals, including ecologists like Paul Sears and Frederic Clements, land planners such as M. L. Wilson and Lewis C. Gray, as well as soil conservationists led by Hugh Hammond Bennett, found a home in the expanding federal government and spent their time and energy encouraging Americans to consider themselves as an important part of the environment.

The first work to examine these experts and the effects of their land use programs was Donald Worster's seminal study *Dust Bowl: The Southern Plains in the 1930s* (1979). Worster's investigation emphasized the role federal agents played in trying to reform how farmers used the land. Some of the agents believed that the Great Depression, a clear crisis of capitalism, presented an opportunity for a dramatic reappraisal of American agriculture. Worster found that agricultural practices had been devoted to maximizing production and expanding into semi-arid lands without accounting for environmental constraints. He argued that many federal employees were sensitive to the historical past of the Great Plains. New Dealers appreciated that the supposed closing of the frontier limited the amount of arable land open to settlement (and much of that not desirable) and necessitated that farmers adapt their practices to sustain their lands. Yet farmers still behaved as though they could simply exhaust one area and move to the next without repercussions, or conversely, try to tend acreage that was fallow and deficient. The combination of distressed topsoil, overuse of the land for agricultural purposes, drought, and heavy winds created a series of deadly dust storms that swept across the country.[4]

Worster posited that New Deal policy did not fully rectify destructive practices in the Great Plains because federal agents failed to break the firm hold that market capitalism had on farmers.

Specialists like ecologists, land planners, and agronomists rarely worked in concert with each other or local farmers. Consequently, government employees were unable to convince farmers to appreciate environmental constraints like aridity and lacked the fortitude to challenge the mantra of production at any cost. When rains returned to the Great Plains, the farmers continued on, business as usual, focused solely on their economic benefit.[5]

Worster's scathing critique of 1930s land use shed light on the New Deal as a distinct period in American environmental history. Worster emphasized how the New Deal was different from earlier eras of conservation in terms of both the scope of federal programs and the ways that federal employees brought conservation to private lands was key to his study. Furthermore, his work set the foundation for later studies by including both federal and local actors. He identified the give-and-take of how federal policy addressed destructive land use and affected Americans on the ground. Worster's environmental history contended that New Deal policies rarely lived up to expectations; that important theme appeared in subsequent environmental histories of the period.

Sarah Phillips's work, *This Land, This Nation: Conservation, Rural America, and the New Deal* (2007), differs from Worster's in that her political and environmental history presents a national perspective on rural problems. Land-use planners like Lewis C. Gray and M. L. Wilson, whom Phillips deemed members of the "New Conservationists," were part of the conservation movement of the 1920s, thought about rural poverty well before 1932, and executed many of their ideas while members of the Roosevelt administration. Phillips argued that the devotees of "New Conservation" faced the central problem of how to bring recovery to all of rural America, instead of just focusing on the environmental degradation that led to the Dust Bowl. Their solution involved a permanent land use policy, based on both environmental and economic sustainability. Only by improving rural living standards across the nation could New Dealers hope to stall the exploitation of natural resources and calm the effects of local and regional environmental problems.[6]

Phillips cited the Tennessee Valley Authority (TVA) as the primary example of federal involvement in planning and land use at the regional level. The planners believed that damming the Tennessee River would reduce the chance of flooding and provide hydroelectricity to locals, while federal employees would also reforest and improve submarginal lands. Farmers who wanted non-agricultural jobs could then find them; those who wanted to work the land could do so under better conditions (on more productive land and with modern conveniences). Providing alternatives to area farmers would present them with options to make money and alleviate stress on fragile lands. The TVA epitomized Roosevelt's perspective that the land had to be considered in relationship to humans. Essentially, healthy land meant healthy people, and by utilizing regional planning, by conserving resources, and by addressing both environmental and social issues, the TVA exemplified that approach. This integration of land and people proved especially prominent throughout the South, as specialists like Hugh Hammond Bennett indicted southern farmers for poor conservation practices, which endangered southern soils as well as the economy. Inattention to soil characteristics, exploitative labor schemes, and a predilection for exhausting resources in one area before moving to another left southern soils degraded. Bennett and others became convinced that the key to economic recovery in the South was to stabilize southern agriculture through controlling soil erosion. The connection between the social and environmental costs of destructive land use thus served as the foundation for reformers to address economic depression, dislocation, and environmental degradation. This perspective, a point of synergy between Roosevelt's views and those of the New Conservationists, gave planners and agronomists access to his administration and therefore the ability to construct federal environmental and agricultural policy.[7]

The resettlement program represents another example of trying to address social as well as environmental concerns. In *Remaking the Agrarian Dream: New Deal Rural Resettlement in the Mountain West* (1996), Brian Cannon argued that New Dealers hoped resettlement could solve both rural poverty and environmental degradation. The resettlement process "involved federal purchase of 'submarginal' farming terrain, restoration and management of that land as timber or grazing reserves, and relocation of the land's impoverished tenant farmers and yeomen upon federally developed resettlement projects with more promising farmland."[8] Unfortunately, it was not that simple in practice. Resettlement thus represented a key example of New Deal environmental thinking, where the desire to keep farmers farming, and doing so successfully, met the rationalization that not all land was fruitful, and that environmental constraints of aridity or soil infertility warranted consideration. Theoretically, resettling farmers would allow them to continue as agriculturalists but under conditions and in locales more amenable to production and less prone to environmental degradation. Furthermore, the vacated lands could then be removed entirely from production, protected as federal lands, and eventually opened to the public for camping, hiking, fishing, and other uses. The Comanche National Grassland in Colorado and the Rita Blanca National Grassland in Texas are two examples of this process.[9] By prioritizing restoration through land retirement, the New Deal effectively created new and distinctive conservation landscapes that demonstrated the conviction to protect endangered lands.

Cannon built on the theme first identified by Worster that one of the ironies of New Deal land use policy was that the perceived need to restore the land and remedy past abuses, had mixed results for land users. Resettlement was one of many programs that never fully delivered on its promises. Relocatees lacked control over their situation, as bureaucrats managed all facets of the transition, and many faced heavy indebtedness since they borrowed money to move. Most importantly, planners found it difficult to provide productive farmland because the "most promising agricultural lands with ready supplies of water in the arid West had been settled." Relocatees were frustrated by bureaucracy, the planners, and discord between federal, state, and local officials. At its core, the resettlement process never fully accounted for the farmers and focused on protecting the land.[10]

This theme of government agents and bureaucrats not being able to contend with environmental and social realities to help people appeared in other recent studies. Marsha Weisiger's *Dreaming of Sheep in Navajo Country* (2009) exposed discord between federal officials and local residents over the sheep reduction program in the Southwest and thus offered a different perspective to support Cannon's argument. According to Weisiger, New Deal officials looked at the Navajo reservation in the American Southwest and were appalled by the level of soil erosion. They designed and implemented a livestock reduction program that could limit the flock and minimize the environmental destruction it created. As in this and other examples, policymakers tried to revitalize the land as a way to revive the economy. Importantly, Weisiger's focus on women and Native Americans extended the literature into important areas of social history.[11]

Conversely, Jess Gilbert asserted that federal workers and locals in fact collaborated on policy and its execution, emphasizing the productive communication between federal experts and farmers. This interpretation has become a minority view of the New Deal's execution but it is a critical counterpoint to Worster, Cannon, Weisiger, and others. Gilbert claimed that many New Dealers, specifically members of the U.S. Department of Agriculture, paid heed to local concerns and traditions. Their goal of changing land use and modernizing rural America required citizen participation, achieved through education, participatory meetings on policy and execution, and local administration of federal programs. These officials, whom Gilbert considered "participatory democrats," realized that state-led, authoritarian reform would not fare as well as changes achieved through the inclusion of local participants. As a result, Gilbert contended, locals played an important role after being included by New Deal officials.[12]

Sarah Gregg's *Managing the Mountains: Land Use Planning, the New Deal, and the Creation of a Federal Landscape in Appalachia* (2010) illustrated how federal land management and restoration disrupted local practices. Rather than trying to save grasslands by limiting livestock as they had in the Southwest, federal planners in Appalachia sought to preserve mountain forests by taking them out of private hands and opening them to recreation-minded urban visitors. Gregg's examination of Vermont and Virginia demonstrated the different local and regional responses to the New Deal. In both states, the Resettlement Administration moved subsistence farmers off submarginal lands to create federally managed and publicly accessible areas. Vermonters resisted federal intrusion because state officials disapproved of top-down control and chose to hold onto as much power as they could to manage their forests and keep farmers on their land. Officials in Virginia were more receptive to federal plans to remove landowners from mountain forests in order to create subsistence homesteads for select residents. The federal government established Shenandoah National Park in 1935 on submarginal lands previously occupied by dispossessed residents. While local and state officials supported the project, affected residents often protested, even going so far as to start fires inside the park after its creation. The different reactions to supporting federal land management revealed that the effectiveness of New Deal policy depended on local implementation. Like the books by Worster, Cannon, and Weisiger, Gregg's portrayal of the dissonance between federal policymakers and local residents is another reminder that the New Deal rarely pleased everyone involved.[13]

In addition, Gregg's work on Shenandoah spoke to other aspects of New Deal environmental thought, namely increased attention to ecology in places like national parks and the rising popularity of outdoor recreation. These two developments represented manifestations of the relatively new ways that Americans thought about the natural world. For example, Alfred Runte explained that the creation of Everglades National Park in 1936 demonstrated New Deal officials' sensitivity to ecology. Runte argued that New Dealers aimed to protect the Everglades because they valued the ecosystem for its distinctive character and integrity. Previously, and especially during the Progressive Era, the celebration of scenic wonders dictated the creation of national parks. In that sense, the Everglades reflected a decided shift.[14] Moreover, as Thomas Dunlap contended, the approach to wildlife management inside national and state parks also changed during the 1930s, reflecting new ways federal employees addressed the natural world by utilizing modern science. National Park Service scientists relied on ecology to argue that each species (even unpleasant vermin) was part of the whole ecosystem, and that each park ecosystem was a unique part of our national past, worthy of protection.[15] The parks thus became more ecologically sound and more appealing to tourists and outdoor enthusiasts who hoped to explore the natural world. New Dealers' use of ecology as justification for preserving parks and protecting wildlife represents one of the more notable aspects of New Deal conservation and was a clear departure from conservation efforts of the Progressive Era.

As Neil Maher's work on the Civilian Conservation Corps (CCC) demonstrated, federal attention to outdoor recreation also represented an important difference between New Deal and Progressive Era views on land use. The CCC employed thousands of young men to combat soil erosion, plant trees, build hiking trails and campgrounds, and construct roads to increase public access to the outdoors. In *Nature's New Deal: The Civilian Conservation Corps and the Roots of the American Environmental Movement* (2008), Maher argued that the thirst for national parks, forests, scenic drives, and fresh air far from the city helped foment the grassroots environmental movement. In essence, the CCC brought conservation into public view with camps and projects across the country, democratizing what had been, during the Progressive Era, a movement of elite experts.[16]

According to Maher, popular support for the CCC and its initiation of a national discussion about preservation and environmental policy made both conservationists and preservationists realize that they shared a few priorities, most notably that unmitigated development in natural areas was problematic. These activists then took it upon themselves to protect the environment through grassroots action instead of relying exclusively on the federal government. That sense of responsibility, a product of the debate sparked by the CCC, led to enough popular support against the construction of

Colorado's Echo Park Dam that the nascent environmental movement succeeded in blocking its creation. With this example, Maher argued that New Deal policy reverberated nationally in democratic as well as indirect and unforeseeable ways.[17] This approach differed from that of Weisiger, Gregg, and others, who argued that top-down, bureaucratic reforms often lost sight of the people most affected.

Maher's analysis of the CCC raised two additional points about New Deal policy. First, the push to beautify America and allow for popular enjoyment was an important component of the New Deal but one not exclusive to the CCC, as Phoebe Cutler demonstrated. Cutler cited a "respect for unadulterated natural settings" as the principle justification for building urban parks, city buildings, and public gardens in cities across the country. To Cutler, such construction, much of it a product of the Works Progress Administration (WPA), was a means to make rural migrants more comfortable with life in the city while also providing beauty in a time of desperation.[18] The WPA employed millions of Americans in various capacities, to build roads and bridges, swimming pools and stadiums, airports and post offices, and even sewage treatment plants. While camp sites or hiking trails may seem more aligned with the history of New Deal environmental thought and politics, Cutler argued that the New Deal "inscribed itself upon the landscape" in multiple ways.[19] In that sense, the New Deal affected Americans in cities, towns, and on farms through changes to the nation's physical landscape.

Second, the national debate about conservation revealed that the CCC had many detractors. For example, according to some wilderness advocates, the rise in outdoor recreation, which helped engender the creation of the CCC, actually threatened the natural world by opening it to the general public. Works by Maher and Paul Sutter acknowledged the vocal criticism of the CCC by groups like the Audubon Society and the Wilderness Society who worried that recreational modernization would have adverse effects on wildlife and the wilderness. Members of these groups argued that human recreation threatened American wilderness and they wanted forests to remain undeveloped and inaccessible to automobiles. In that sense, accessing nature became a growing issue because the sheer number of enthusiasts and their heavy reliance on the automobile posed a risk to wilderness, compelling wilderness advocates to argue that "certain wildlands ought to be protected from road building, motorized recreation, and a state increasingly eager to sponsor outdoor recreational development."[20] The New Deal threatened preservation even while it protected resources from commercial extraction or removed submarginal land from cultivation. Wilderness advocates generally applauded the New Deal's efforts at reforming Americans' relationship with their environment yet indicted the commercialization of nature through recreation.[21] In essence, these books showed that the New Deal could never please everyone and invariably policies left some groups feeling either underappreciated or outright ignored.

Another important theme evident in these works is the ways New Deal land use policy blended conservation and preservation, combining both Progressive Era and postwar views of the natural world. Some elements of New Deal policy resembled the Progressive Era's push for the conservation of natural resources. As Samuel P. Hays explained, Progressive conservationists relied heavily on a faith in applied science and the use of "rational planning to promote efficient development and use of all natural resources."[22] This is perhaps most apparent in how New Dealers approached reclamation and water control projects, whether through the TVA, or on the Columbia and Colorado rivers. Reclamation revolved around the notion of using water to help humankind and had little consideration for preserving ecosystems or protecting wildlife. The central goal remained regional economic development, achieved through impressive, multipurpose dams devoted to hydroelectricity, flood control, and irrigation. By proposing technical solutions for environmental problems like floods or aridity, reclamation advocates hoped to make life easier for local residents.[23] In theory, regional development allowed farmers in arid areas to have more stability and all rural residents to have electric power and enjoy modern conveniences. In practice, it also opened the door for big businesses to take advantage of cheap electricity or access irrigation, largely facilitating economic growth for a select few rather than the community. For example, government officials and private enterprise worked together in California to maximize profits through irrigation, but in so doing they rewarded large land owners and speculators instead of the common farmers.[24]

New Deal programs accounted for the health of the land, even if many of those programs had negative effects on people living on the land. Furthermore, as Maher posited, the national debate about the proposed Echo Park Dam began during the New Deal, as outdoor enthusiasts, conservationists, preservationists, politicians, and federal officials all weighed in on the relationship between Americans and the natural environment.[25] This public recognition of the natural world and a consideration of humans' place in it is part of the New Deal's legacy, according to Richard Andrews. He explained that the New Deal developed an agenda through which "the natural environment could be developed and managed in an integrated fashion for human benefit, that this could be done in ways that restored and conserved nature itself while also building a healthy economy and society, and that government leadership and planning, rather than just the invisible hand of the market, were necessary and effective instruments to accomplish this."[26]

While the New Deal provoked a national sense of environmental awareness, scholars concluded that these programs often proved less than beneficial for those under the thumb of the federal government or even for the environment. The notion of environmental restoration, a departure from Progressive Era approaches to conservation, contributed to the New Deal's programs of soil conservation, resettlement, and preservation of lands. These policies had consequences for Americans. Many found themselves at the mercy of an expanding state. In some cases, the people most responsible for devising policy lacked a cohesive vision and failed to agree on how to best execute policy. This often produced confusion, resistance, frustration, and discord on the part of both administrators and citizens. Factionalism, distaste for bureaucracy, and unfulfilled promises of recovery left many Americans critical of the New Deal.[27]

Histories of New Deal environmental policies have been more objective than incendiary. To date, the New Deal's influence on twentieth-century environmental and conservation history has gained historical attention, and local studies with an emphasis on how federal programs affected Americans have become prominent. However, the field has much room for growth. A more concerted effort to look at popular conceptions of the environment and the operations of programs sponsored by the Agricultural Adjustment Administration and the Soil Conservation Service would supplement our understanding of the 1930s. Also, there must be closer examinations of how the dramatic switch from depression to war influenced New Deal environmental policies and their effectiveness. Finally, the international effects of the New Deal on environmental thought and policies is understudied. Sarah Phillips's work on how soil conservation in the United States helped launch similar efforts in South Africa demonstrated that the New Deal was not confined by America's borders.[28] Such emphasis on transnational history, a relatively recent and certainly notable development within the discipline, may present new interpretations of the New Deal as well as environmental history more broadly. On the whole, however, the subfield of environmental history within the context of the New Deal and the Great Depression has grown tremendously and there are clear indications that the literature will continue to flourish.

NOTES

1. Paul Sutter, "Terra Incognita: The Neglected History of Interwar Environmental Thought and Politics," *Reviews in American History* 29 (June 2001): 289-97.

2. John F. Sears, "Grassroots Democracy: FDR and the Land," in *FDR and the Environment,* eds. Henry L. Henderson and David B. Woolner (New York: Palgrave Macmillan, 2005), 7-16. See also A. L. Reisch Owen, *Conservation under F.D.R.* (New York: Praeger, 1983).

3. Brian Black, "The Complex Environmentalist: Franklin D. Roosevelt and the Ethos of New Deal Conservation," in *FDR and the Environment,* 33-41.

4. Donald Worster, *Dust Bowl: The Southern Plains in the 1930s* (New York:

Oxford University Press, 1979), 182-230. See also R. Douglas Hurt, *The Dust Bowl: An Agricultural and Social History* (Chicago: Nelson-Hall, 1981).

5. Worster, *Dust Bowl,* 229-30. The view that the Dust Bowl was in fact a crisis in American agriculture has been disputed by Geoff Cunfer in his *On the Great Plains: Agriculture and Environment* (College Station: Texas A&M Press, 2005). Cunfer argued that dust storms were basically a brief interruption in a time of relative stability.

6. Sarah T. Phillips, *This Land, This Nation: Conservation, Rural America, and the New Deal* (New York: Cambridge University Press, 2007), 16-24.

7. Phillips, *This Land, This Nation,* 9-12, 21-45; Sarah T. Phillips, "FDR, Hoover, and the New Rural Conservation, 1920-1932," in *FDR and the Environment,* 107-52. Hugh Hammond Bennett's role and the appreciation of soil erosion as a southern issue, and thus not exclusively a western problem, is from Paul Sutter, "What Gullies Mean: Georgia's 'Little Grand Canyon' and Southern Environmental History," *The Journal of Southern History* 76 (August 2010): 579-616.

8. Brian Cannon, *Remaking the Agrarian Dream: New Deal Rural Resettlement in the Mountain West* (Albuquerque: University of New Mexico Press, 1996), 1.

9. Michael E. Lewis, "National Grasslands in the Dust Bowl," *Geographical Review* 79 (April 1989): 161-71.

10. Cannon, *Remaking the Agrarian Dream,* 150-52.

11. Marsha Weisiger, *Dreaming of Sheep in Navajo Country* (Seattle: University of Washington Press, 2009), 1-11, 31-49.

12. Jess Gilbert, "Low Modernism and the Agrarian New Deal: A Different Kind of State," in *Fighting for the Farm: Rural America Transformed,* ed. Jane Adams (Philadelphia: University of Pennsylvania Press, 2003); Jess Gilbert, "Agrarian Intellectuals in a Democratizing State: A Collective Biography of USDA Leaders in the Intended New Deal," in *The Countryside in the Age of the Modern State: Political Histories of Rural America,* ed. Catherine McNicol Stock and Robert D. Johnston (Ithaca: Cornell University Press, 2001).

13. Sara M. Gregg, *Managing the Mountains: Land Use Planning, the New Deal, and the Creation of a Federal Landscape in Appalachia* (New Haven: Yale University Press, 2010), 136-39, 171-213.

14. Alfred Runte, *National Parks: The American Experience* (Lincoln: University of Nebraska Press, 1979). See especially 160-64 and Chapter 6.

15. Thomas R. Dunlap, "Wildlife, Science, and the National Parks, 1920-1940," *Pacific Historical Review* 59 (May 1990): 187-202.

16. Neil M. Maher, *Nature's New Deal: The Civilian Conservation Corps and the Roots of the American Environmental Movement* (New York: Oxford University Press, 2008), 10.

17. Ibid., 220-25.

18. Phoebe Cutler, *The Public Landscape of the New Deal* (New Haven: Yale University Press, 1985), 63.

19. Ibid., 4

20. Paul Sutter, "New Deal Conservation: A View from the Wilderness," in *FDR and the Environment,* 94. See also Paul Sutter, *Driven Wild: How the Fight against Automobiles Launched the Modern Wilderness Movement* (Seattle: University of Washington Press, 2002).

21. Sutter, "New Deal Conservation," 94-98.

22. Samuel P. Hays, *Conservation and the Gospel of Efficiency: The Progressive Conservation Movement, 1890-1920* (Cambridge: Harvard University Press, 1959), 2. See also Donald Worster, *Rivers of Empire: Water, Aridity, and the Growth of the American West* (New York: Pantheon Books, 1985).

23. Richard Lowitt, *The New Deal and the West* (Norman: University of Oklahoma Press, 1993), 81.

24. Worster, *Rivers of Empire,* 17-48.

25. Maher, *Nature's New Deal,* 220-24.

26. Richard N. L. Andrews, "Recovering FDR's Environmental Legacy," in *FDR and the Environment,* 221.

27. Jason Scott Smith, *Building New Deal Liberalism: The Political Economy of Public Works, 1933-1956* (New York: Cambridge University Press, 2006). See especially chapters 3-6 for his explanation of how public works projects became part of a contentious and fiery debate about the nature of the New Deal.

28. Sarah T. Phillips, "Lessons From the Dust Bowl: Dryland Agriculture and Soil Erosion in the United States and South Africa, 1900-1950," *Environmental History* 4 (April 1999): 245-66.

CHAPTER FIVE

The Economy and the New Deal

JENNIFER EGOLF

On June 27, 1936, President Franklin D. Roosevelt took the podium at the Democratic Convention in Philadelphia to accept his party's renomination for president. In this important address, he reviewed the causes for and his solutions to the Great Depression. He explained:

> For too many of us the political equality we once had won was meaningless in the face of economic inequality. A small group had concentrated into their own hands an almost complete control over other people's property, other people's money, other people's labor—other people's lives. For too many of us life was no longer free; liberty no longer real; men could no longer follow the pursuit of happiness. Against economic tyranny such as this, the American citizen could appeal only to the organized power of Government. The collapse of 1929 showed up the despotism for what it was. The election of 1932 was the people's mandate to end it. Under that mandate it is being ended. . . . These economic royalists complain that we seek to overthrow the institutions of America. What they really complain of is that we seek to take away their power. Our allegiance to American institutions requires the overthrow of this kind of power.[1]

Economists and historians explored in great depth the origins of the worst economic crisis in United States history and Roosevelt's attempts to end it. This chapter focuses on historical interpretations of both such causes and Roosevelt's economic policies, as well as on some of the programs and long-term economic effects of the New Deal.

Nearly every historical work analyzing the economics of the 1930s addressed the question of what caused the Great Depression. Preeminent economic scholar John Kenneth Galbraith outlined the major events leading to the Great Depression in his landmark work *The Great Crash, 1929* (1954). He argued that the 1920s, an age of optimism, laid the foundation for economic decline. Succinctly stated, stock market speculation, excessive borrowing at high interest rates, income inequality, corrupt and irresponsible corporate and banking practices, foreign trade imbalances, and ignorant national economic policies contributed to severe economic decline in the early 1930s. Galbraith's study attributed the combination of these factors to the economic decline without placing emphasis on a single factor.[2]

Other scholars weighed the role of unsound banking practices more heavily than other contributing factors. Historians Milton Friedman and Anna Jacobson Schwartz argued that the "crop of bank failures" created a "contagion of fear . . . among depositors." This fear then led to the bank "runs" that prompted the downward economic spiral.[3] However, other scholars argued quite the opposite. Rather than the banking crisis leading to the depression, in *Did Monetary Forces Cause the Great Depression?* (1976), Peter Temin asserted that the banking crisis stemmed from an already declining economy. Similarly, Eugene Nelson White posited that the banking crisis was not a turning point in the Great Depression, but rather a stage of the larger economic downturn.[4]

The divergence of historical opinions on the main causes of the Great Depression indicated the complexity of the economic system of the period. Historian David Hamilton argued that agricultural conditions, such as declining farm income and drought, as well as "bad banking practices and a woefully weak financial structure" contributed significantly to the banking crisis.[5] Recent scholarship, from the perspective of right-leaning scholars, placed the majority of the blame for the Great Depression on the Federal Reserve Board. Historian Jim Powell argued that the Federal Reserve's policy of monetary contraction "became so severe, it brought on a depression in output, employment, and income," and applied more pressure on banks, especially when more people wanted to withdraw their funds. Small town banks, in particular, were unable to handle these "runs" because they failed to diversify their loan portfolios and sources of funds.[6]

In addition to examining the banking crisis, contemporary writers of the period focused attention on unraveling the mystery of the stock market crash in 1929, and the ways it contributed to the weak economy of the 1930s. Writing at the time of the Great Depression, H. Parker Willis attributed the crash to the Federal Reserve Board's inadequate regulation of banks, which loaned money for the primary purpose of stock market speculation.[7] Although many contemporary analysts blamed banks and speculation for the crash, other financial experts, including Irving Fisher, proposed a much more complex set of causes. They pointed to other factors, including the liquidation of foreign holdings with declining values, the overvaluation of common stock, an autumn business recession, a federal capital gains tax, broker loans, as well as overwhelming enthusiasm, which arose from the 1920s "boom" and led to a false belief that stocks would retain high values.[8] Alexander Dana Noyes, a financial editor for the *New York Times,* focused his attention particularly on the latter of Fisher's causes. In *The Market Place: Reminiscences of a Financial Editor* (1938), Noyes explained that the illusion of "boom" on the stock market led to an "orgy" of speculation that preceded the crash.[9]

The works of Frederick Lewis Allen and John Kenneth Galbraith concluded that such over-optimism, which led to speculation, obscured any knowledge of a sudden stock market decline. In fact, both argued that the pervading enthusiasm led financiers, industrialists, and average Americans to engage in risky ventures. None of these groups sensed the impending collapse. Galbraith even proposed that speculation became "central to the culture."[10] In *The Great Boom and Panic: 1921-1929* (1965), Robert T. Patterson agreed that optimism bred rampant speculation. He argued that along with the illusion of boom, inflation (especially of credit) caused the stock market crash, or, in his words, the "corrective panic and depression that followed."[11]

More recently, historian Eugene Nelson White dismissed contemporary claims that the "boom" on the stock market was due to an increased number of broker loans. In *Crashes and Panics: The Lessons From History* (1990), White claimed that, "[i]n early 1928, prices rose and then soared above dividends." The stock prices, which climbed as a result of "real" rather than illusory prosperity and growth, did not fall because of over-speculation and artificially high stock values. Instead, he argued that when prices declined in September 1929, no good news about their return to high levels surfaced to maintain the enthusiasm that generated investment. The lack of "good news," accompanied by the Federal Reserve Board's tightening of credit and raising of interest rates, as well as rumors of declining production, led to the crash in October 1929.[12]

Most scholars and financial analysts agreed that the 1929 stock market crash did not directly cause the Great Depression. However, writers studying the period believed that the stock market collapse severely curbed enthusiasm and optimism. In *The Stock Market Crash—And After* (1930), Irving Fisher wrote, "[t]he chief danger . . . was the danger of fear, panicky fear, which might be communicated from the stock market to business." Taking a similar tack, Noyes noted, "we had entered a different New Era in which nothing could stop the fall of prices or the trade depression." That attitude of economic freefall characterized Wall Street during this period. In his groundbreaking study, *Only Yesterday: An Informal History of the 1920s* (1931), Frederick Lewis Allen commented on how declining optimism led to greater economic decline. He wrote, "[w]ith the Big Bull Market gone and prosperity now going, Americans were soon to find themselves living in an altered world which called for new adjustments, new ideas, new habits of thought, and a new order of values."[13] Thus, as Christina Romer argued, the link between the stock market crash and the Great Depression was the uncertainty that the panic generated in people regarding their futures, and in particular, their incomes and ability to spend.[14] Business confidence also eroded, because of declining consumption and stock values.[15]

Historians have long debated how Roosevelt combated the economic downturn of the 1930s through his New Deal programs. In his 1932 inaugural address, Franklin Roosevelt stated that "[t]he money changers have fled from their high seats in the temple of our civilization. We may now restore that temple to the ancient truths. The measure of the restoration lies in the extent to which we apply social values more noble than mere monetary profit."[16] These words ushered in a new era of economic policies—government management of the economy to encourage higher farm incomes and industrial cooperation, relief programs to encourage spending, and taxation to "redistribute" wealth.

The majority of New Deal contemporaries and scholars agreed that there were two separate and distinct New Deals during the 1930s.[17] Generally, the First New Deal occurred from 1933-1934 and focused on immediate relief, recovery, and reform, although some of the programs were experimental and controversial. Then the programs of the Second New Deal, which were more pragmatic and less experimental than those of their predecessor, began in 1935 and lasted for the remainder of the decade. Economic reforms and new regulatory policies were a central part of New Deal programs of the 1930s.

In 1932, Roosevelt assembled a group of advisors to help chart the course for the New Deal. This original "brain trust," which included Columbia University law professor Raymond Moley, helped shape Roosevelt's legislation of the First Hundred Days. The National Recovery Administration (NRA) and the Agricultural Adjustment Administration (AAA) were two of the most dramatic and controversial programs. Some historians analyzed these two programs, which attempted to manage the economy, by looking for international comparisons.

A few scholars searched for direct connections between the economic reforms of the New Deal and fascist-led programs in Europe during the 1930s. In *Three New Deals* (2006), Wolfgang Schivelbusch drew parallels between Roosevelt's New Deal programs and economic reforms sponsored by Mussolini and Hitler.[18] Similarly, in his article in *The American Historical Review*, "The New Deal, National Socialism, and the Great Depression" (1973), John A. Garraty compared German and American leadership of the period. He noted that the two governments dealt with poverty and high levels of unemployment by establishing direct relief and public works programs. Further, he argued that the NRA and the AAA, like the Nazi's economic planning, attempted to balance the interests of "manufacturers and merchants, inflationists and deflationists, between planners, free enterprisers, and advocates of regulated competition." However, Garraty acknowledged that the severity of the economic crisis led both governments to experiment.[19]

As Garraty and others argued, there were important differences between the New Deal and fascist reforms of the 1930s. For example, the NRA was a voluntary program, while fascist-sponsored economic reforms were mandatory. Industrialists who participated in the NRA often did so at the urging of American citizens, and because government compelled them. Also, although conservatives viewed the AAA as government's managing of the economy, the restrictions on production included only a few overproduced products, such as hogs, cotton, and wheat.[20]

Two decades later, legal scholar James Q. Whitman continued the analysis of the First New Deal's most controversial programs. He stated that "[a] startling number of New Dealers had kind words for Mussolini. . . . And the President himself expressed interest in bringing the programs of 'that admirable Italian gentleman' to America." Only after Italy's invasion of Ethiopia in 1935 did Roosevelt abandon these types of allegedly socialistic programs and began what Whitman referred to as the "second phase," or what most scholars called the Second New Deal. Although many political scientists, especially those writing in the 1980s, placed a neo-corporatist label on some of Roosevelt's early programs, Whitman distinguished between the corporatism arising from fascism and what the First New Deal represented. He argued that the leaders of the NRA only appeared fascist and that American corporatism drew primarily from American traditions.[21]

Because of the controversial components of early New Deal economic initiatives such as the NRA and the AAA as well as the Supreme Court's decision to rule both unconstitutional, Roosevelt's economic policies shifted direction in 1935. Some of Roosevelt's contemporaries criticized the change toward what Alan Brinkley, in *The End of Reform: New Deal Liberalism in Recession and War* (1996), referred to as "rights-based liberalism."[22] By the summer of 1933, Raymond Moley and other early supporters became increasingly critical of the New Deal, largely because they believed that the new policies stifled business and economic growth.[23] In his memoir, *After Seven Years* (1939), Moley suggested that Roosevelt's policies after the First Hundred Days emphasized welfare legislation and favored a more urban, working class.[24] More neutral in tone, Basil Rauch, in his book, *The History of the New Deal,* concluded that the Second New Deal resembled a more left-leaning, progressive reform agenda than programs of the First New Deal.[25]

Historians, including Arthur Schlesinger Jr., disagreed with Moley's and Rauch's assessments of the Second New Deal. In *The Politics of Upheaval* (1960), the third volume in his monumental set on Roosevelt and the 1930s, Schlesinger agreed that two New Deals emerged in Roosevelt's first term. He did not believe that Felix Frankfurter and Louis Brandeis, who advised President Roosevelt during the Second New Deal, shifted the country in a left-of-center direction, but rather, that they attempted to restore "a competitive society within a framework of strict social ground rules." In fact, Schlesinger argued that the policies of the Second New Deal emerged from a coalition between lawyers in the Brandeis tradition and Keynesian economists. Their collective theory proposed that the regulation of business might salvage capitalism. Thus,

rather than manage the economy and prices, as the NRA outlined, Roosevelt intended for his economic policies, after 1935, to
restore a competitive market with some regulations on business.
Schlesinger refused to characterize Roosevelt as "left-leaning," and
he argued that the Second New Deal appeared more conservative
than the first. [26]

To many New Deal scholars, a key determinant of whether a
shift to the left took place involves analyzing how much Keynesian economics the United States adopted in the 1930s. Keynesian
economic theory was based on the work and writings of British
economist John Maynard Keynes. His most influential work, *The
General Theory of Employment Interest and Money* (1936), stressed
the importance of a mixed economy, with a predominant role for
the private sector and a limited one for the government. Keynes's
ideas exemplified economic liberalism in the 1930s, but historians
have disagreed about the degree to which the New Deal offered
Keynesian approaches to improving the economy. [27]

In his article "Was There a Keynesian Economy in the USA between 1933 and 1945?" (1999), Patrick Renshaw explained that although Roosevelt promised to balance the budget and stop federal
overspending, during his election campaign in 1932, he quickly
realized that rising unemployment necessitated government intervention. As a response, Roosevelt adopted the Keynesian theory of
reflation—the federal government pumping new capital into the
economy to improve confidence and increase business activity, or,
more simply and in contemporary terms "spend your way out of
a depression." The massive public works expenditures approved
by Congress were just one example of this practice. However, as
Renshaw pointed out, Roosevelt's commitment to Keynesian ideals
was shaky at best, since Roosevelt's programs arose more from experimentation than a commitment to economic liberalism. Thus,
Roosevelt could have decided to reduce government spending and
refocus on balancing the budget, which he attempted between 1936
and 1938. [28]

Revisionist and New Left historians questioned Roosevelt's dedi-
cation to Keynesian economics. Budget figures demonstrated that

in the 1930s, the Roosevelt administration spent no more than $8.42 billion in one year. In comparison, during World War II yearly expenditures grew to $95.2 billion and the deficit rose to $45 billion.[29] Leftist scholars refuted the assertion that Roosevelt had "primed the pump" and lifted the country out of the depression through his economic policies. In *New Deal Thought* (1966), historian Howard Zinn agreed that even when Roosevelt spent more than conservatives desired, "it was still only a fraction of what the British economist John Maynard Keynes was urging as a way of bringing recovery."[30]

In addition to questioning Roosevelt's implementation of Keynesian economic policies, several historians argued that Roosevelt accepted limited spending on relief programs primarily because he wanted to save capitalism and eliminate the possibility of a socialist or communist revolution. In *Poor People's Movements: Why They Succeed and How They* Fail (1977), Frances Fox Piven and Richard A. Cloward noted that "the largest movement of the unemployed that this country has known," the Workers' Alliance of America (WAA), was pitted against the relief system. They demonstrated that the WAA was no longer necessary for providing or demanding relief after Roosevelt's administration established bureaucratic agencies to handle assistance. In *A People's History of the United States: 1942-Present* (2003), Howard Zinn agreed that Roosevelt's inadequate measures to improve the economy and reduce unemployment saved capitalism and left the disparate economic structure largely intact. Barton Bernstein added, in his book *Towards a New Past: Dissenting Essays in American History* (1968), that "[t]he New Deal failed to solve the problem of depression, it failed to raise the impoverished, it failed to redistribute income, it failed to extend equality." In essence, these scholars believed that Roosevelt did just enough to preserve the capitalist system and not enough to end the Great Depression.[31]

Conservative historians on the right focused on how Roosevelt's spending and taxing policies may have prolonged the Great Depression. One method that Roosevelt could use to both balance the budget and raise revenue for his economic programs, without increasing deficit spending, was through taxation. Thus, Roosevelt raised capital gains, profits, corporate, excise, estate, gift, and income taxes (especially in the higher income brackets) to fund his initiatives. According to conservative analysts, other taxes, which arguably hurt consumers and businessmen alike, included the agricultural processing tax and Social Security payroll taxes. Not only did these revenue-generating efforts defy Keynes's theory of reflation, which favored lowering taxes, but many scholars believed that the tax measures worsened the economy. In *FDR's Folly: How Roosevelt and His New Deal Prolonged the Great Depression* (2003), Jim Powell explained, "[a]ll these taxes meant there was less capital for businesses to create jobs, and people had less money in their pockets." Ironically, Keynes might have argued similarly. Businessmen, in the 1930s, opposed taxes more than deficit spending, and believed that the reduced economic growth from higher taxation would ultimately lead to diminished intake for the federal government, and, thus, was counterproductive.[32]

Scholars have also debated the New Deal's economic legacy for the Democratic Party and for the American people. Ironically, many of today's liberal Democrats adopted conservative critiques of the New Deal. Historian Iwan Morgan examined the Jimmy Carter and Bill Clinton administrations, and concluded that both presidents, "departed from the liberal tenets of the fiscal revolution of the mid-twentieth century." Essentially, these two Democratic presidents abandoned Keynes's consumer-oriented capitalism and returned to a more producer-oriented one that typified the American economy before the Great Depression. According to Morgan, President Carter emerged from a "southern progressive" tradition, which called for "economy and efficiency in government," as well as "compassion for the poor." Thus, he proclaimed himself to be a fiscal conservative with socially liberal values. President Clinton, as Morgan pointed out, took a similar economic stance, which included supporting balanced budgets and welfare reform. In addition, both Carter and Clinton abandoned Keynesian acceptance of inflation to stimulate the economy, as well as the regulatory impulse of the New Deal era. Deregulation represented a critical platform item for liberal Democrats in the last decades of the twentieth century.[33]

For future generations, the New Deal added several important features to the American economy. In *A New Deal for the American People* (1991), historian Roger Biles argued that while Roosevelt's reform programs did not effectively end the Great Depression, the New Deal "implanted several 'stabilizers' that have been more successful in averting another such depression." Biles and others pointed to the significance of the Securities and Exchange Commission, the Glass-Steagall Banking Act (which Congress partially repealed in 1999), and the Federal Deposit Insurance Corporation (FDIC). Another feature that Biles credited to the New Deal involved developing "cradle to grave" security, or a social safety net. However, like Howard Zinn and Barton Bernstein, Biles noted the failure of the New Deal to offer either sweeping economic changes or challenges to the underlying reasons for income inequality. Therefore, Biles believed that "the New Deal preserved more than it changed."[34]

In the late twentieth century, groups of politicians, economists, and reformers expressed their desire to preserve many of the economic accomplishments of the New Deal. Although Democrats did not abandon all of the New Deal's reform agenda, their economic values shifted to the center, causing a break from the economic liberalism that marked the 1930s. Democratic leaders from the postwar period to President Carter appeared more comfortable than Roosevelt with Keynes's consumer-based capitalism. But the economic severity of the Great Depression required significant adjustments and experiments, rather than strict adherence to largely untested economic theories. Those economic adaptations were present throughout the New Deal's recovery, reform, and relief agenda, and many of those programs and efforts are still part of the nation's economic and social fabric.

Many scholars credit the New Deal's economic stabilizers for the United States' ability to avert a crisis of equal magnitude. The Great Recession, which began officially in 2008, led scholars to draw comparisons with the Great Depression, in an attempt to understand its causes and effects, as well as the government's remedies for it.

Economists concluded that similar causes included a decline in manufacturing, a stock market crash, growing economic disparity, and rampant speculation. Paul Krugman, for example, graphed the comparable falls in manufacturing production before and during both crises. Other economists illustrated analogous stock market reactions to economic decline, using a "Bad Bears" graph. Charts, demonstrating rising income inequality in the 1920s and 2000s, also reveal a resemblance in causes.[35] In *The Great Recession: Profit Cycles, Economic Crisis, a Marxist View,* Michael Roberts analyzed speculative booms in the 1920s and 2000s, concluding that the Great Recession, especially its duration, resulted from the "massive expansion of fictitious capital in the form of credit (bank loans, corporate debt, and above all new forms of credit in derivatives, or options to bet on debt prices)." These irresponsible monetary policies contributed to the end of prosperity, much like the 1929 stock market crash; however, Roberts argued that bad banking practices in the 2000s, particularly regarding mortgages, had more dire consequences for the economy than the stock market crash in 1929.[36]

In addition to comparable causes, economists explored the effects of and solutions to the economic crises. Economists generally agree that the two crises affected the global community, even though they began in the United States. Roberts argued that the United States credit crisis in the 2000s produced larger global ripples than in the 1930s. Miguel Almunia agreed that the Great Recession had a greater effect on global trade than the Great Depression. However, because of lessons learned during the 1930s, the government responded more quickly and strongly in the 2000s. Alan Blinder and Mark Zandi credited a bipartisan response to the economic crisis for the faster turnaround in the 2000s. A combination of monetary and stimulus policies, including the Troubled Asset Relief Program (TARP) and the Recovery Act of 2009, helped to "restore stability to the financial system and to end the freefall in housing and auto markets," raised the GDP, created jobs, and lowered unemployment rates.[37] Thus, one legacy of the Great Depression and Roosevelt's response to it included the precedent that the president has the authority to act boldly and decisively in the face of economic collapse.

NOTES

1. Franklin D. Roosevelt, "Acceptance of the Renomination for the Presidency, Philadelphia, Pa., June 27, 1936," in *The Public Papers and Addresses of Franklin D. Roosevelt,* comp. Samuel I. Rosenman (New York: Random House, 1938), 5:233-34.

2. John Kenneth Galbraith, *The Great Crash, 1929* (New York: Houghton Mifflin, 1954), 169, 177-83.

3. David E. Hamilton, "The Causes of the Banking Panic of 1930: Another View," *The Journal of Southern History* 51 (November 1985): 581; Milton Friedman and Anna Jacobson Schwartz, *A Monetary History of the United States, 1867-1960* (Princeton University Press: Princeton, 1936), 308.

4. Peter Temin, *Did Monetary Forces Cause the Great Depression?* (New York: Norton, 1976), 83-95; Eugene Nelson White, "A Reinterpretation of the Banking Crisis of 1930," *The Journal of Economic History* 44 (March 1984): 120.

5. Hamilton, "Causes of the Banking Panic," 585.

6. Jim Powell, *FDR's Folly: How Roosevelt and His New Deal Prolonged the Great Depression* (New York: Three Rivers Press, 2003), 29-31.

7. H. Parker Willis, "Who Caused the Panic of 1929?" *North American Review* 229 (February 1930): 177.

8. Irving Fisher, *The Stock Market Crash—And After* (New York: Macmillan, 1930), 31-55.

9. Alexander Dana Noyes, *The Market Place: Reminiscences of a Financial Editor* (Boston: Little, Brown, 1938), 325-27.

10. Galbraith, *Great Crash,* 83, 93-95; Frederick Lewis Allen, *The Lords of Creation* (New York: Harper and Brothers, 1935), 347-49, 361-63; Frederick Lewis Allen, *Only Yesterday: An Informal History of the 1920s* (New York: Harper and Row, 1931; reprint, 1964), 73.

11. Robert T. Patterson, *The Great Boom and Panic: 1921-1929* (Chicago: Henry Regnery, 1965), 224-26.

12. Eugene Nelson White, "When the Ticker Ran Late: The Stock Market Boom and Crash of 1929," in *Crashes and Panics: The Lessons From History,* ed. Eugene Nelson White (Homewood, IL: Dow Jones-Irwin, 1990), 144-45.

13. Fisher, *Stock Market Crash,* 63, 192, 269; Noyes, *The Market Place,* 337, 351; Allen, *Only Yesterday,* 281.

14. Christina D. Romer, "The Great Crash and the Onset of the Great Depression," *Quarterly Journal of Economics* 105 (August 1990): 598-623.

15. Maury Klein, "The Stock Market Crash of 1929: A Review Article," *The Business History Review* 75 (Summer 2001): 348.

16. Franklin D. Roosevelt, "Inaugural Address, March 4, 1933," in *Public Papers and Addresses of Roosevelt,* 2:12.

17. Some scholars argued that a Third New Deal began in 1937. See John

W. Jeffries, "A'Third New Deal'? Liberal Policy and the American State, 1937-1945" *Journal of Policy History* 8 (December 1996): 387-409.

18. Wolfgang Schivelbusch, *Three New Deals: Reflections on Roosevelt's America, Mussolini's Italy, and Hitler's Germany, 1933-1939* (New York: Picador, 2006).

19. John A. Garraty, "The New Deal, National Socialism, and the Great Depression," *The American Historical Review* 78 (October 1973): 909-12.

20. Ibid., 907-44.

21. James Q. Whitman, "Of Corporatism, Fascism, and the First New Deal," *The American Journal of Comparative Law* 39 (Autumn 1991), 747-50, 755-56.

22. Alan Brinkley, *The End of Reform: New Deal Liberalism in Recession and War* (New York: Random House, 1996), 10.

23. Powell, *FDR's Folly,* 12.

24. Raymond Moley, *After Seven Years* (New York: DeCapo Press, 1939), Chapter 8.

25. Basil Rauch, *The History of the New Deal, 1933-1938* (New York: Creative Age Press, 1944).

26. Arthur M. Schlesinger Jr., *The Politics of Upheaval: The Age of Roosevelt* (Boston: Houghton Mifflin, 1960; reprint, 2003), 3:385, 387-89, 392-93.

27. John Maynard Keynes, *The General Theory of Employment, Interest and Money* (London: Macmillan, 1936).

28. Patrick Renshaw, "Was There a Keynesian Economy in the USA between 1933 and 1945?" *Journal of Contemporary History* 34 (July 1999): 338-40, 343.

29. Ibid., 342.

30. Howard Zinn, ed., *New Deal Thought* (New York: Bobbs-Merrill, 1966; reprint, Indianapolis: Hackett, 2003), xxxiv.

31. Frances Fox Piven and Richard A. Cloward, *Poor People's Movements: Why They Succeed and How They Fail* (New York: Random House, 1977), 41, 67-68, 73, 86, 90; Howard Zinn, *A People's History of the United States: 1942-Present* (New York: Harper Collins, 2003), 402-3; Barton J. Bernstein, "The New Deal: The Conservative Achievements of Liberal Reform," in *Towards a New Past: Dissenting Essays in American History,* ed. Barton J. Bernstein (New York: Pantheon, 1968), 246.

32. Powell, *FDR's Folly,* ix-x; Renshaw, "Was There a Keynesian Economy?" 353-54.

33. Iwan Morgan, "Jimmy Carter, Bill Clinton, and the New Democratic Economics," *The Historical Journal* 47 (November 2004): 1016-18, 1022-23, 1032.

34. Roger Biles, *A New Deal for the American People* (DeKalb: Northern Illinois University Press, 1991), 227-28, 230-33.

35. Miguel Almunia, Agustin Benetrix, Barry Eichengreen, Kevin H. O'Rourke, and Gisela Rua, "Lessons from the Great Depression," *Economic Policy* 25 (April 2010): 221-22; David Talbot, "Saving Holland," *Technology Re-*

view 110 (July 2007): 50-56; Dura Vermeer, "High and Dry Concept," *Technology Review* 110 (July 2007): 56.

36. Michael Roberts, *The Great Recession: Profit Cycles, Economic Crisis, a Marxist View* (N.P.: Michael Roberts, 2009), 9-14, 299.

37. Roberts, *Great Recession,* 256; Almunia, et al., "Lessons from the Great Depression," 222; Alan S. Blinder and Mark Zandi, "How the Great Recession Was Brought to an End," (July 27, 2010): 1, 6, available at http://www.princeton.edu/~blinder/End-of-Great-Recession.pdf.

CHAPTER SIX

Social Programs and the New Deal

STUART PATTERSON

During the 1930s, the federal government took on an unprecedented responsibility—and the requisite new powers—for guaranteeing a basic level of social and economic well-being for its citizens. The New Deal's social programs changed since the 1930s, but the basic framework of federal welfare provisions remains one of the defining features of American life. In this light, the social programs of the New Deal have modern-day relevance and are not merely a scholarly pursuit.

Recent studies illustrate the divisive and politically charged interpretations of the New Deal's social initiatives. For example, in *A Commonwealth of Hope: The New Deal Response to Crisis* (2006), Alan Lawson lauded New Deal planning for its crucial role in creating a coherent social and moral world for modern Americans. In contrast, Jim Powell's *FDR's Folly: How Roosevelt and His New Deal Prolonged the Great Depression* (2004) argued that the New Deal retarded American economic and social development through the 1930s and left a legacy of dangerous precedents that still mar the American polity.[1] With the economic downturn of the late 2000s as a backdrop, historians, including David Kennedy and Eric Rauchway, wrote about the significance of New Deal welfare programs to understand modern-day challenges.[2]

Beyond its uses in political debates and connections to today, the New Deal represents a watershed moment in American history. Historian Jennifer Klein explained that recent scholarly literature on New Deal social programs "has sought to extend [the New Deal] in time and scope." She asserted that the New Deal represented a crossroads for understanding previous and current federal social programs. Klein argued that ongoing or defunct New Deal programs shaped subsequent political and social history.[3] This chapter reviews the ongoing historical examination of the New Deal's social programs.

In the late nineteenth century a number of European nations established national welfare programs.[4] During the Progressive Era, state and municipal governments in the United States took on greater responsibilities for the well-being of their citizens. Public and private reformers instituted new functions for local governments, from ensuring clean water and safe housing to preventing child labor and establishing worker pension funds. However, it was not until the Great Depression, that the U.S. federal government began building a system of welfare programs for the nation as a whole.[5]

During Roosevelt's First Hundred Days there was a rush to pass a comprehensive program of short-term and long-term social legislation. New Dealers designed many measures to relieve the immediate suffering caused by widespread unemployment. Other legislation established long-term programs for recovery. Historians question how comprehensive and intentional Roosevelt's first social programs were. For example, in *Nothing to Fear: FDR's Inner Circle and the Hundred Days that Created Modern America* (2009), Adam Cohen stressed the atmosphere of crisis under which the early New Deal took shape. Cohen believed that the urgency of the moment enabled a program of ongoing reform that otherwise might have been impossible to enact.[6]

The Roosevelt administration's earliest measures for immediate relief were an expansion of efforts started a year earlier under Herbert Hoover's Emergency Relief Administration. Renamed by New Dealers as the Federal Emergency Relief Administration (FERA), this agency distributed direct aid—much of it surplus food, clothing, and other necessities—to those with the greatest need. However, FERA's direct aid programs were unpopular during the 1930s. Conservative critics argued that direct aid supported idleness and dependency, while beneficiaries themselves complained of the stigma of receiving a "dole," typically by way of a humiliating "means test" used to determine exact levels of need among recipients. Jeff Singleton's *The American Dole* (2000) demonstrated the ongoing stigmatizing of recipients of direct relief from the Hoover administration through the New Deal and later. Jennifer Mittelstadt's *From Welfare to Workfare* (2005) showed how later administrators of direct relief and social security provisions attempted, with little success, to reduce this stigma. More local studies of New Deal direct relief such as Peter Fearon's *Kansas in the Great Depression* (2007) and Jack Irby Hayes Jr.'s *South Carolina and the New Deal* (2001) documented how poor administration and discriminatory practices hampered FERA's direct relief efforts.[7]

In 1935, FERA operations ceased or were redistributed to other agencies, most notably to the Works Progress Administration (WPA). The WPA signaled the increasing importance of paid "work relief," rather than direct aid. The WPA and similar programs employed millions and built thousands of schools, post offices, housing complexes, roads, and other public works projects, many of which are still in use today. Studies such as Nick Taylor's *American-Made: The Enduring Legacy of the WPA* (2008) demonstrated that New Deal public works projects have modern-day relevance. Other scholars looked at the significance of work relief projects within the evolution of New Deal programs. Historians Jason Scott Smith and Robert Leighninger argued that the public works programs of the New Deal shaped policy, stimulated the economy, and left deep social marks on communities. However, Leighninger lamented that today most of these accomplishments are largely forgotten.[8]

During the 1930s, the Public Works Administration (PWA) focused on improving society through public housing projects. Under the guise of "slum clearance" in many major American cities, the PWA pioneered the design and construction of high-density housing complexes for tens of thousands of low-income and middle-income families. Historians remain divided in their views of New Deal public housing. D. Bradford Hunt argued that the Wagner-Steagall Housing Act was the first step in a "blueprint for disaster," especially in Chicago. He argued that the legislation prepared the way for the disastrous segregation and neglect of the poor that followed World War II. In her article "A House Divided: Public Housing Policy in New Orleans," Margaret C. Gonzalez-Perez told a similar story in the Crescent City. Yet others, such as Gail Radford, praised early New Deal public housing designs for their attention to local control of community-oriented institutions even as she lamented the loss of such visions in subsequent federal public housing policy. And S. J. Fuertes similarly viewed New Deal housing as a "paradise" for early residents that nonetheless succumbed to less progressive policies following the late 1930s.[9]

Other New Deal programs focused on building single-family homes were much more successful in improving housing. In 1934, the government began insuring mortgage loans for new homes with the creation of the Federal Savings and Loan Insurance Corporation and the Federal Housing Administration (FHA). Adam Gordon argued that these programs were systematically discriminatory on the basis of race, which propelled middle-class white homeownership while simultaneously depressing ownership among African Americans. Gordon's work, like many recent studies of FHA discrimination, looked back to Kenneth T. Jackson's landmark study of New Deal suburban housing policy, *Crabgrass Frontier: The Suburbanization of the United States* (1985). Jackson showed in detail how FHA policies changed the entire geography of the nation by spurring a huge growth of private housing following World War II while systematically restricting African American homeownership in major metropolitan areas and rapidly growing suburbs. Jennifer Klein argued that New Deal housing policies served at best as a spur to women and people of color to resist New Deal liberal paternalism. At the same time, in *Building the Dream* (1981), Gwendolyn Wright offered the ambivalent judgment that, given the context of the Depression, New Deal housing policy negotiated "a politics of desperation and idealism" in an attempt to create more substantial and lasting private housing for the poor.[10]

New Deal social programs were just as prevalent in rural areas. Small farmers suffered from poor crop yields and low prices since the end of World War I. Measures such as the Agricultural Adjustment Act of 1933 regulated the production of farm goods and agricultural prices, and established farm subsidies. Historians, including Richard Kirkendall in *Social Scientists and Farm Politics in the Age of Roosevelt* (1966) and Jess Gilbert and Monica Richmond Gisolfi, argued that the politics surrounding such programs led to the rise of large commercial farming enterprises, at the expense of smaller family farms.[11]

Other New Deal agencies such as the Farm Security Administration (FSA), originally named the Resettlement Administration, established forthrightly reform-minded rural policies designed to preserve small farms and local control of land use. The FSA's land reclamation and rehabilitation programs operated through loans and grants to small farmers, including tenant farmers and sharecroppers. Recipients used the funds to purchase land and equipment. The FSA resettled thousands of families to new small farms, many of them linked into cooperatively managed agricultural communities, particularly in the rural South.

The first major studies of the Resettlement Administration and the FSA, Sidney Baldwin's *Politics and Poverty: the Rise and Decline of the Farm Security Administration* (1968) and Paul Mertz's *New Deal Policy and Southern Rural Poverty* (1978), charted the idealistic origins of the New Deal's programs for small farmers and their subsequent political challenges. Systemic racial discrimination and accusations of radicalism contributed to the demise of the agencies. Michael Johnson Grant built on Baldwin's work in *Down and Out on the Family Farm* (2002), which presented a more focused study of the FSA's work in the Midwest. He presented a detailed view of the major shift in population over the twentieth century from farms to cities. Emilye Crosby, in *A Little Taste of Freedom: The Black Freedom*

Struggle in Claiborne County, Mississippi (2005), and Erik Gellman and Jarod Roll, in "Owen Whitefield and the Gospel of the Working Class in New Deal America, 1936-1946," focused on the long-term positive effects of the FSA's small grants and loans for African American families in the South. At the same time Stephanie Lewthwaite's writings on Mexican laborers in Los Angeles and Eric V. Meeks in his article "Protecting the 'White Citizen Worker': Race, Labor, and Citizenship in South-Central Arizona, 1929-1945," revealed the discriminatory practices that limited the effectiveness of New Deal rural rehabilitation programs.[12]

Paul Conkin's *Tomorrow a New World: The New Deal Communities Program* (1959), told the familiar story of a New Deal agency that started with idealistic goals and fell victim to political pressure. Departing from this narrative, Diane Ghirardo, in *Building New Communities* (1989), and C. J. Maloney, in *Back to the Land* (2011), offered more trenchant critiques of the experimental communities. Ghirardo criticized these programs for their authoritarian, even fascistic policies, while Maloney argued that New Deal communities lacked fiscal and practical discipline.[13]

The Civilian Conservation Corps (CCC), one of the largest rural rehabilitation programs, attracted significant scholarly attention. The CCC put young men to work in military-style corps and camps on projects such as reforestation, erosion control, soil conservation, and wildlife management. The workers earned modest wages, with a portion of their earnings mailed back to their families. As noted, like many New Deal programs, the CCC became the subject of numerous and increasingly localized case studies that tend to celebrate the program's accomplishments. Like many early histories of New Deal agencies, the first major overview of the CCC by John A. Salmond was a case study of the agency's evolution from a highly popular early relief program to its bureaucratically moribund end in the early years of World War II. A more focused recent study, Neil Maher's *Nature's New Deal: The Civilian Conservation Corps and the Roots of the American Environmental Movement* (2008), charted the longer formative effects of the CCC on the nation's environmental consciousness. Like Diane Ghirardo's work on the communities program, Kiran Klaus Patel's *Soldiers of Labor* (2005) reached beyond the national context to compare the CCC to the contemporary youth conservation program in fascist Germany, the Reichsarbeitsdienst. Patel argued that both agencies fostered overtly militaristic cultures, authoritarian bureaucratic structures, and racially discriminatory policies and practices.[14]

Of the New Deal's early social programs, none was as comprehensive as the Tennessee Valley Authority (TVA). On one hand, the TVA aimed to build the vast Tennessee River watershed into a single economic and political entity responsible for generating and managing electric power under public control. On the other hand, the agency's "social and economic division" was set up to unify the region into a social and cultural whole that could help build and maintain its new infrastructure across parts of seven states. While building dams and reclaiming much of the area's lands for reforestation and cultivation, TVA resettled thousands of displaced families into new homes and farms and experimental communities with organized health care and schooling. TVA agents trained the region's residents in agricultural techniques, attempted to revive regional industries such as pottery and weaving, and made efforts to enlist area residents in the agency's administrative and political management. Many critics decried the federal government's intensive remaking of the region. However, historian C. Herman Pritchett argued that the severity of the Depression called for such measures. As it happened, due largely to shifts in the agency's leadership, the TVA's ambitious social programs waned as the more focused goal of creating a publicly controlled power agency gained momentum.[15]

Studies of TVA's history, particularly following World War II, analyzed such administrative and political struggles over control of the agency, focusing on the early struggle between Arthur Morgan, who helped devise and oversee much of the social programming, and David Lilienthal, who focused efforts on creating a publicly run power agency. Both Lilienthal, in *TVA: Democracy on the March* (1944), and Morgan, in *The Making of the TVA* (1974), offered their own interpretations of the agency's aims and outcomes. Indeed, Morgan and Lilienthal have remained the focal points of much historical work examining the TVA's relatively short-lived social programs of the 1930s. Thomas McCraw's *Morgan Versus Lilienthal: The Feud Within the TVA* (1970) described decisive political machinations in the agency's early years, while Roy Talbert's *FDR's Utopian: Arthur Morgan of the TVA* (1987), offered a sympathetic account of Morgan's unimplemented social visions for the agency and the region. More recent and comprehensive studies of the agency's social programs contrasted its early idealism with the less than ideal results for the region's residents. Michael McDonald and John Muldowny's *TVA and the Dispossessed* (1982) and Nancy Grant's *TVA and the Black Americans* (1990) both recounted how many of the region's residents were underserved by the agency's massive resettlement campaigns. Other studies, including David Whisnant's *Modernizing the Mountaineer* (1994), demonstrated how the TVA reinforced paternalistic attitudes and practices dating back to well before the New Deal agency's founding.[16]

The foregoing discussion concerned programs of what many historians called the First New Deal, a period characterized by government-provided relief and efforts to create a comprehensive program of economic and social planning. While there were some successes, the programs of the First New Deal were not cohesive and many suffered from poor administration. A few years into Roosevelt's first term, his administration shifted the overall emphasis toward setting up provisions of basic needs for some groups, notably the elderly and infirm, and protecting the rights of laborers. In 1935, a new set of Second New Deal agencies began work. These programs focused on creating basic economic security through "social insurance" programs and a comprehensive restructuring of industrial-labor relations.

The single most important piece of New Deal social legislation—what Roosevelt himself considered the cornerstone of his administration's entire social and domestic agenda—was the Social Security Act. This legislation established several important social programs, including Old Age Assistance, or financial aid for low-income elderly; Old Age Insurance, or payments to retired workers (from tax revenues collected on the employed); Unemployment Insurance, or payments to workers who lost jobs; and Aid for Dependent Children, or payments to unmarried women (usually widows) with children. Overall, the programs and provisions established by the Social Security Act provided a minimum of means necessary to maintain oneself or one's family in case of unemployment, injury, old age, or illness.[17]

Historians dissected the Social Security Act in numerous ways. Some examined the prior social and political forces that shaped the legislation and its passage, while other historians looked beyond its passage at subsequent changes made to the Act's basic mandate. Recent studies of the lead-up to passage of the act, such as those by Edwin Amenta and Mary Poole, focused on the complex interactions of government and society in shaping public policy, particularly around questions of race and gender. Theda Skocpol and Kenneth Finegold's landmark study *State and Party in America's New Deal* (1995) made the Social Security Act a major case in the development of the American polity.[18] Studies of the complex effects of and changes to the Social Security Act since its passage became central to ongoing political debates over the role of social insurance in American life. Works by Daniel Béland and Jennifer Klein focused on recent efforts to "privatize" Social Security by reducing or removing altogether its function as a federal tax on wages.[19]

The Affordable Care Act, signed into law in 2010, sparked debate over federally mandated insurance. The legislation purports to fulfill one of Francis Perkins's most desired yet ultimately unfulfilled goals for the original Social Security Act: a federal mandate for universal health insurance. Early supporters of the Social Security Act removed provisions for a universal or even a basic health care insurance plan for some Americans in order to pass the legislation. But in support of the Obama administration's new measures, historians Kristin Downey and Beatrix Hoffman both offered historical arguments for the merits of public versus private funding for social welfare.[20] The Social Security Act excluded provisions for agricultural, domestic, and any self-employed or "contract" workers in the old-age insurance program. These exclusions affected large numbers of women and African Americans, groups frequently omitted from social programs of the New Deal. The programs created by the Social Security Act remain an active point of political and social discourse.

Another abiding social issue addressed by Second New Deal legislation, unemployment and job security, drew historians into current political debates. In June 1933, the National Industrial Recovery Act (NIRA) established new regulations for the relationship between workers and employers. It included a series of "codes" by which industries would set prices and levels of production for themselves under oversight from new federal agencies, and section 7(a) of the legislation gave workers the right to form unions and bargain collectively. Different interpretations of the provision led to some of the largest and most violent disputes between workers and employers. In 1935, the Supreme Court ruled the NIRA unconstitutional. Skocpol and Finegold examined the failure of the NIRA in their study of American political culture. In *Backlash: The Killing of the New Deal* (2006), Robert Shogan examined more closely how this setback effectively forestalled much of the New Deal's overall social programming.[21]

The failure of NIRA did not impede all New Deal efforts to support basic labor rights. In 1935 the Roosevelt administration supported the passage of the National Labor Relations Act, sponsored by Senator Robert Wagner of New York, a key ally of the New Deal. Dubbed the "Wagner Act," the bill created a National Labor Relations Board (NLRB) to negotiate disputes between workers and owners, with powers to counteract "unfair labor practices" by employers. By 1937 the Wagner Act survived its own challenge in the Supreme Court, and partly on the strength of that success, Congress passed the Fair Labor Standards Act (FLSA) the following year. This landmark legislation set a federally mandated minimum wage, established maximum work hours per day and week, made provisions for overtime pay, and banned child labor. The basic tenets of the FLSA and the Wagner Act remain the bedrock of present-day labor practices, though historians continue to debate their significance in subsequent developments in labor relations. Karl Klare argued that the Wagner Act had the potential to remake "the premises and institutions of capitalist society," but that the judiciary consistently mitigated the law's possible radical interpretations. Similarly, while the FLSA immediately improved wages for hundreds of thousands of workers, contemporary critics, including George Paulsen, argued that a standardized wage structure provided too little for too few. Charles Morris, a noted scholar of American labor history, recently argued in *The Blue Eagle at Work* (2004) that the full potential of the NLRB as a means of securing labor rights has not been tested, a proposition that has stirred much debate among labor historians.[22]

Taken together, the most recent overall assessments of the New Deal's social programs presented a tempered view of what Roosevelt's long presidency accomplished. Anthony Badger's *The New Deal: The Depression Years, 1933-1940* (1989) set the tone by arguing that the New Deal was relatively restricted politically and administratively from making any really radical reforms, and could not be faulted for merely capitulating to moneyed interests. Eric Rauchway's *The Great Depression and the New Deal* (2008) offered a similar assessment of its limited achievements while placing the New Deal in a comparative international context of economic distress and social reform during the 1930s.[23] While specific aspects of New Deal policy continue to figure centrally in current political debates over health care or labor provisions, the general historical picture of what the New Dealers themselves accomplished has gravitated more and more toward a sober accounting of highly idealistic planning meeting difficult and sometimes harsh political, social, and economic realities.

NOTES

1. Alan Lawson, *A Commonwealth of Hope: The New Deal Response to Crisis* (Baltimore: Johns Hopkins University Press, 2006); Jim Powell, *FDR's Folly: How Roosevelt and His New Deal Prolonged the Great Depression* (New York: Three Rivers Press, 2004).

2. See David M. Kennedy, "What the New Deal Did," *Political Science Quarterly* 124 (Summer 2009): 251-68; Eric Rauchway, "New Deal Denialism," *Dissent* 57 (Winter 2010): 68-72.

3. Jennifer Klein, "New Deal Restoration: Individuals, Communities, and the Long Struggle for the Collective Good," *International Labor and Working Class History* 74 (Fall 2008): quote 42, 42-48.

4. Peter Flora and Arnold Heidenheimer, eds., *The Development of Welfare States in Europe and America* (New Brunswick, NJ: Transaction Books, 1981); Walter Trattner, *From Poor Law to Welfare State: A History of Social Welfare in America* (New York: Free Press, 1999).

5. Carolyn M. Moehling, "The American Welfare State and Family Structure: An Historical Perspective," *The Journal of Human Resources* 42 (Winter 2007): 117-55; Thomas A. Krainz, *Delivering Aid: Implementing Progressive Era Welfare in the American West* (Albuquerque: University of New Mexico Press, 2005); Jacob S. Hacker, *The Divided Welfare State: The Battle over Public and Private Social Benefits in the United States* (Cambridge: Cambridge University Press, 2002).

6. Adam Cohen, *Nothing to Fear: FDR's Inner Circle and the Hundred Days that Created Modern America* (New York: Penguin, 2009).

7. See Jeff Singleton, *The American Dole: Unemployment Relief and the Welfare State in the Great Depression* (Westport, CT: Greenwood, 2000); Jennifer Mittelstadt, *From Welfare to Workfare: The Unintended Consequences of Liberal Reform, 1945-1965* (Chapel Hill: University of North Carolina Press, 2005); Peter Fearon, *Kansas in the Great Depression: Work Relief, the Dole, and Rehabilitation* (Columbia: University of Missouri Press, 2007); Jack Irby Hayes Jr., *South Carolina and the New Deal* (Columbia: University of South Carolina Press, 2001).

8. Jason Scott Smith, *Building New Deal Liberalism: The Political Economy of Public Works* (New York: Cambridge University Press, 2006); Robert Leighninger, *Building Louisiana: The Legacy of the Public Works Administration* (Oxford: University Press of Mississippi, 2007); Robert Leighninger, *Long-Range Public Investment: The Forgotten Legacy of the New Deal* (Columbia: University of South Carolina Press, 2007); Nick Taylor, *American-Made: The Enduring Legacy of the WPA: When FDR Put the Nation to Work* (New York: Bantam, 2008).

9. D. Bradford Hunt, *Blueprint for Disaster: The Unraveling of Chicago Public Housing* (Chicago: University of Chicago Press, 2009); Margaret C. Gonzalez-Perez, "A House Divided: Public Housing Policy in New Orleans," *Louisiana*

History 44 (Autumn 2003): 443-61; Gail Radford, *Modern Housing for America: Policy Struggles in the New Deal Era* (Chicago: University of Chicago Press, 1996); Gail Radford, *From Tenements to the Taylor Homes: The Search for an Urban Housing Policy in Twentieth-Century America* (University Park: Pennsylvania State University Press, 2000); S. J. Fuertes, *When Public Housing was Paradise: Building Community in Chicago* (Westport, CT: Greenwood, 2003).

10. Adam Gordon, "The Creation of Home Ownership: How New Deal Changes in Banking Regulation Simultaneously Made Homeownership Accessible to Whites and out of Reach for Blacks," *The Yale Law Journal* 115 (October 2005): 186-226; Kenneth T. Jackson, *Crabgrass Frontier: The Suburbanization of the United States* (New York: Oxford University Press, 1985); Kevin Fox Gotham, "Racialization and the State: The Housing Act of 1934 and the Creation of the Federal Housing Administration," *Sociological Perspectives* 43 (Summer 2000): 291-317; Klein, "New Deal Restoration"; Gwendolyn Wright, *Building the Dream: A Social History of Housing in America* (Boston: MIT Press, 1981; reprint, New York: Pantheon Books, 1983), 218.

11. Richard S. Kirkendall, *Social Scientists and Farm Politics in the Age of Roosevelt* (Columbia: University of Missouri Press, 1966); Jess Gilbert, "Wisconsin Economists and New Deal Agricultural Policy: The Legacy of Progressive Professors," *The Wisconsin Magazine of History* 80 (Summer 1997): 280-312; Jess Gilbert, "Rural Sociology and Democratic Planning in the Third New Deal," *Agricultural History* 82 (Fall 2008): 421-38; Monica Richmond Gisolfi, "From Crop Lien to Contract Farming: The Roots of Agribusiness in the American South, 1929-1939," *Agricultural History* 80 (Spring 2006): 167-89.

12. See Sidney Baldwin, *Poverty and Politics: The Rise and Decline of the Farm Security Administration* (Chapel Hill: University of North Carolina Press, 1968); Paul E. Mertz, *New Deal Policy and Southern Rural Poverty* (Baton Rouge: Louisiana State University Press, 1978); Michael Johnston Grant, *Down and Out on the Family Farm: Rural Rehabilitation in the Great Plains, 1929-1945* (Lincoln: University of Nebraska Press, 2002); Emilye Crosby, *A Little Taste of Freedom: The Black Freedom Struggle in Claiborne County, Mississippi* (Chapel Hill: University of North Carolina Press, 2005); Erik S. Gellman and Jarod Roll, "Owen Whitfield and the Gospel of the Working Class in New Deal America, 1936-1946," *The Journal of Southern History* 72 (May 2006): 303-48; Stephanie Lewthwaite, "Race, Paternalism, and 'California Pastoral': Rural Rehabilitation and Mexican Labor in Greater Los Angeles," *Agricultural History* 81 (Winter 2007): 1-35; Eric V. Meeks, "Protecting the 'White Citizen Worker': Race, Labor, and Citizenship in South-Central Arizona, 1929-1945, *Journal of the Southwest* 48 (Spring 2006): 91-113.

13. Paul Conkin, *Tomorrow a New World: The New Deal Communities Program* (Ithaca: Cornell University Press, 1959); Diane Ghirardo, *Building New Communities: New Deal America and Fascist Italy* (Princeton: Princeton Uni-

versity Press, 1989); C. J. Maloney, *Back to the Land: Arthurdale, FDR's New Deal, and the Costs of Economic Planning* (Hoboken, NJ: Wiley and Sons, 2011).

14. John A. Salmond, *The Civilian Conservation Corps, 1933-1942: A New Deal Case Study* (Durham: Duke University Press, 1967); Neil M. Maher, *Nature's New Deal: The Civilian Conservation Corps and the Roots of the American Environmental Movement* (New York: Oxford University Press, 2008); Kiran Klaus Patel, *Soldiers of Labor: Labor Service in Nazi Germany and New Deal America, 1933-1945* (New York: Cambridge University Press, 2005).

15. C. Herman Pritchett, *The Tennessee Valley Authority: A Study in Public Administration* (Chapel Hill: University of North Carolina Press, 1943).

16. David E. Lilienthal, *TVA: Democracy On the March* (New York: Harper and Brothers, 1944); Arthur Morgan, *The Making of the TVA* (Buffalo, NY: Prometheus Books, 1974); Thomas K. McCraw, *Morgan Versus Lilienthal: The Feud Within the TVA* (Chicago: Loyola University Press, 1970); Roy Talbert Jr., *FDR's Utopian: Arthur Morgan of the TVA* (Jackson: University of Mississippi Press, 1987); Michael J. McDonald and John Muldowny, *TVA and the Dispossessed: The Resettlement of Population in the Norris Dam Area* (Knoxville: University of Tennessee Press, 1982); Nancy L. Grant, *TVA and Black Americans: Planning for the Status Quo* (Philadelphia: Temple University Press, 1990); David Whisnant, *Modernizing the Mountaineer: People, Power and Planning in Appalachia* (Knoxville: University of Tennessee Press, 1994).

17. Mark H. Leff, "Taxing the 'Forgotten Man': The Politics of Social Security Finance in the New Deal," *The Journal of American History* 70 (September 1983): 359-81.

18. Edwin Amenta, *When Movements Matter: The Townsend Plan and the Rise of Social Security* (Princeton: Princeton University Press, 2006); Mary Poole, *Segregated Origins of Social Security: African Americans and the Welfare State* (Chapel Hill: University of North Carolina Press, 2006); Kenneth Finegold and Theda Skocpol, *State and Party in America's New Deal* (Madison: University of Wisconsin Press, 1995).

19. Daniel Béland, *Social Security: History and Politics from the New Deal to the Privatization Debate* (Lawrence: University Press of Kansas, 2005); Jennifer Klein, *For All These Rights: Business, Labor, and the Shaping of America's Public-Private Welfare State* (Princeton: Princeton University Press, 2003).

20. See Kirstin Downey, *The Woman Behind the New Deal: The Life of Frances Perkins, FDR's Secretary of Labor and His Moral Conscience* (New York: Doubleday, 2009); Beatrix Hoffman, "Health Care Reform and Social Movements in the United States," *American Journal of Public Health* 93 (January 2003): 75-85.

21. Finegold and Skocpol, *State and Party in America's New Deal;* Robert Shogan, *Backlash: The Killing of the New Deal* (Chicago: Ivan R. Dee, 2006).

22. Quote from Karl E. Klare, "Judicial Deradicalization of the Wagner Act and the Origins of Modern Legal Consciousness, 1933-1941," *Minnesota Law*

Review 62 (1978): 265; George E. Paulsen, *A Living Wage for the Forgotten Man: The Quest for Fair Labor Standards, 1933-1941* (London: Associated University Presses, 1995); Marc Dixon, "Union Threat, Countermovement Organization, and Labor Policy in the United States, 1944-1960," *Social Problems* 57 (May 2010): 157-74; Charles Morris, *The Blue Eagle at Work: Reclaiming Democratic Rights in the American Workplace* (Ithaca: Cornell University Press, 2004).

23. Anthony J. Badger, *The New Deal: The Depression Years, 1933-1940* (New York: Hill and Wang, 1989); Eric Rauchway, *The Great Depression and the New Deal: A Very Short Introduction* (New York: Oxford University Press, 2008).

CHAPTER SEVEN

Art and the New Deal

SHARON ANN MUSHER

The severity of the Great Depression is well known to scholars, students, and general audiences. By 1933 more than one-quarter of the population was unemployed or underemployed—a figure that was significantly worse in certain areas. Farm prices were in a long-term downward spiral, industrial production and sales were sharply declining, and capital investments were at a stand-still. Within that context one might have expected the needs of artists paled in comparison to more pressing concerns. But an un-precedented cultural venture emerged out of President Franklin D. Roosevelt's eclectic and experimental New Deal reforms.

From 1933 to 1943, the federal government sponsored a variety of arts programs aimed at rehabilitating unemployed artists and intellectuals, fostering the creation and preservation of explicitly American art, and spreading creative experiences across the nation. In 1936, the New Deal devoted roughly $30 million to hiring more than 40,000 mostly needy writers, dancers, actors, musicians, and visual artists. These artists created hundreds of thousands of works of art—plays, concerts, books, murals, posters, photographs, and sculptures—that were performed, displayed, and made available to millions of Americans.[1]

The cultural projects of the New Deal made a profound difference in people's lives. They provided creative young people, such as painter Arshile Gorky, photographer Dorothea Lange, writer Saul Bellow, and scholar Ralph Ellison, with an artistic community, a job, and a paycheck. The projects had dramatic effects on the people who encountered their work. The various projects exposed many people to art who had never before experienced original paintings, sculptures, plays, and concerts. The programs encouraged relief workers to gather raw materials, such as folk music, designs, and stories, for later imaginative works. They also fostered new artistic techniques and styles, including abstract expressionism, silk screening, and color photography. Collectively, these projects encouraged the use of diverse American objects, songs, and stories to develop an experimental national culture to reach a large audience.

In the vast literature on New Deal arts projects, scholars have recovered the institutional histories of individual art projects, the stories behind the artists employed by them, and the actual works of art they created. Some scholars debated the causes, quality, and consequences of this government sponsored artistic flowering. Other writers examined how the art projects incorporated race, ethnicity, gender, and labor politics. This chapter reviews the historiography of New Deal art projects, while also describing the institutional locus and extent of New Deal projects in the arts.

Several federal organizations administered the New Deal's cultural and arts projects. A series of art projects based in the Department of the Treasury oversaw the construction and decoration of government buildings. Instead of handpicking artists with classical training, the Painting and Sculpture Section chose artists through largely anonymous and open competitions.[2] Project leaders encouraged artists to work collaboratively with local communities to identify stories and iconography connected to what literary critic Van Wyck Brooks called a "usable past," a national tradition that unified contemporaries around common principles and values.[3] The resulting façades, murals, and other decorations celebrated national and local historical traditions. The project's artists drew upon realistic portrayals of local American scenes to forge an indigenous and national aesthetic representation of the nation's greatness. They shifted the iconography in government buildings from ancient Greece and Rome to contemporary American populist themes.[4]

The Works Progress Administration (WPA) was the largest New Deal program focused on the arts. In 1935, Roosevelt expanded his commitment to the arts and created a unit within the WPA called Federal Project Number One (Federal One). The unit administered programs in art, music, theater, dance, and writing. Plays produced by the unit's Federal Theatre Project ranged from homegrown pageants to Shakespearean classics to living newspapers. The productions included socially realistic works written to educate and mobilize audiences around contemporary concerns, such as the rise of fascism and the spread of venereal disease. Other Federal One employees collected folk music, interviewed former slaves, and created water-color renderings of traditional American arts and crafts. Because Federal One offered relief to artists on the basis of need rather than merit, it also provided support for artists whose work did not readily fit into current trends, including ventriloquists and abstract expressionists. Given the diversity of programs incorporated into Federal One, it is difficult to characterize aesthetically the artwork produced under its auspices.[5]

In 1935, Roosevelt created a new department called the Resettlement Administration to aid the rural poor, some of whom lost their land as a result of earlier New Deal legislation. Roy Striker directed the public relations unit of the RA, called the Historical Section. Striker hired established and emerging photographers, such as Walker Evans, Dorothea Lange, and Arthur Rothstein, as well as filmmaker Pare Lorentz, to use the seemingly impartial tool of photography to portray sharecroppers and migrant workers in ways that might persuade administrators and the public to support agricultural reform. In 1937, the Historical Section became part of the Farm Security Administration (FSA). In 1942, the Office of War Information absorbed the unit. These relocations resulted in a changing mission for the organization, and, over time, Historical Section photographers shifted from documenting the plight of displaced sharecroppers and migrant workers to celebrating small-town America, and then promoting the war effort.[6] As a result, the images created by the Historical Section incorporated a range of aesthetic styles, including propaganda, social realism, and daily life.

The first reviews of the New Deal's art projects emerged in the 1930s and both celebrated and criticized government funding of the arts. Contemporary cultural critics, such as educator John Dewey, poet Archibald MacLeish, and writer Lewis Mumford, heaped praise on the government's cultural effort arguing that it was improving the nation's quality of life and democratizing the arts.[7] But by the late 1930s opponents largely drowned out such optimistic evaluations.

On the right, anti–New Dealers, such as Texas senator Martin Dies and Virginia representative Clifton Woodrum, attacked the art projects for wasting government funds, sheltering modernists, leftists, and foreign-born artists, and supporting leftist ideology and racially integrationist politics.[8] For example, in his testimony before Congress in February 1938, North Carolina senator Josiah W. Bailey argued that the government-sponsored play, *One-Third of a Nation,* made the U.S. Congress look like the Soviet parliament by depicting the vice president passing a heavily reduced appropriation for the Wagner-Steagall Housing Bill by banging his gavel on the table rather than calling for a vote.[9]

Opponents also emerged from the left. Anti-Stalinist New York intellectuals, including Clement Greenberg, Dwight McDonald, Harold Rosenberg, and Meyer Schapiro, considered 1930s figurative art kitsch and middlebrow. These critics found resonances between the art programs' nationalistic celebration of the common man and the propaganda of national unity and censorship growing in Germany and Russia. New Left historians, such as Christopher Lasch and Warren Susman, similarly ignored or denigrated New Deal art. Rather than attacking artists and their works, New Left historians focused on the political shortcomings of the New Deal and the Popular Front. Schapiro, for example, described the New Deal as a "reactionary regime" that failed to address contemporary structural and economic problems.[10] Susman suggested that the decade's new media—especially photography, movies, and radio—promoted the ideas of culture and commitment without developing a serious ideological critique. According to Susman, 1930s culture encouraged Americans to conform to a narrowly defined way of life rather than challenging power structures and highlighting national diversity.[11]

While those on the left criticized New Deal art, art historians, curators, and collectors tended to ignore it. In the post-World War II art world, nonfigurative modernism prevailed, and New Deal art, with its emphasis on social realism and propaganda, fell out of favor. Ironically, many abstract expressionist artists, including Stuart Davis, Alice Neel, and Jackson Pollock, relied on the art projects' work relief to survive the Great Depression.[12]

The first significant reinterpretation of New Deal art began in the 1960s, when academics and former participants started to recover some of the works of art and the records of the various projects that had been destroyed, dispersed, stolen, or abandoned in the previous decades. Scholars, including Francis V. O'Connor, Lorraine Brown, George Rawick, and Ann Banks, searched local, state, and national archives programs to recover the forgotten records of the arts projects.[13] Academics and enthusiasts also initiated oral history projects to recapture participants' experiences. The Smithsonian Institution's Archives of American Art interviewed 400 surviving artists and administrators from the Federal Art Project and the Treasury Department's art projects. Similarly, professors at George Mason University conducted roughly 270 interviews, mostly with former members of the Federal Dance and Theatre Projects.[14] A wealth of memoirs, biographies, monographs, edited volumes, travel books, and dissertations emerged from those efforts.[15]

One reason that scholars turned to the art projects during the late 1960s and early 1970s was to guide U.S. arts policy, since the New Deal art projects represented a significant precursor to the then emerging National Endowment for the Arts (NEA) and the National Endowment for the Humanities (NEH). In *Federal Support for the Visual Arts* (1969), art historian Francis V. O'Connor specifically advised against reproducing the Treasury Department's meritorious and commission-based approach to public funding, instead arguing for the implementation of the Federal Art Project's relief-based approach.[16] In contrast, Richard D. McKinzie concluded his careful study of the Federal Art Project and Treasury Department's projects, *The New Deal for Artists* (1973), by advising that the United States not pursue the New Deal model of federal patronage because constant disagreements over what constitutes art and its place in national life would always inhibit public funding of the arts.[17] Few politicians at the time, however, paid heed to the nuances of such scholarly arguments. Wary of being seen as extravagant, they developed merit-based approaches to government patronage that more closely resembled the Treasury Department's program than Federal One's relief-based model. Although the NEA and NEH's jury-based approaches offered government officials more control over public art, they nonetheless failed to ward off the type of political tensions described by McKinzie.[18]

A central argument in reassessing the value of the New Deal's art projects was Jane De Hart Mathews's 1975 interpretation of them as a "quest for cultural democracy." According to Mathews, the arts projects nationalized the Progressive Era's efforts to integrate art into citizens' daily lives.[19] While the cultural effort neither created a national renaissance nor convinced taxpayers and politicians that art was a right and a necessity, it succeeded in making the arts accessible to more diverse audiences and in fostering a "usable past." More recent scholars extended Mathews's argument by focusing on the Federal Art Project. Cultural historian A. Joan Saab argued, in *For the Millions* (2004), that the project's philosophy of participation briefly encouraged citizens to engage in artistic creation and consumption, but a more passive definition of aesthetic experience based on observation returned to prominence during the postwar period.[20] In contrast, Victoria Grieve's *The Federal Art Project and the Creation of Middlebrow Culture* (2009) emphasized the longer historical roots and resonances of the Federal Art Project's cultural democratic philosophy. She argued that it broadly disseminated philosophies originated by progressives and cultural nationalists in the early twentieth century and set the precedent for the postwar expansion of museums, the growth of the domestic art market, and the development of permanent government patronage of the arts.[21]

The cultural projects of the New Deal also encouraged what scholar William Stott, in *Documentary Expression and Thirties America* (1972), described as a "documentary moment." According to Stott, the dearth of information at the beginning of the Depression regarding crucial facts—such as how many people were jobless and how many went hungry—increased public disillusionment with traditional news sources and encouraged eyewitnesses to see the country for themselves. In response, a diverse group of photographers, social workers, and writers gathered images of the working class and publicized them to evoke the empathy of middle-class viewers and encourage them to support reform legislation.[22]

Perhaps the most recognized image of working-class Americans during the Great Depression came from the lens of Historical Section photographer Dorothea Lange. On a rainy afternoon in February or March 1936, Lange drove by a thirty-two-year-old mother, named Florence Owens (later Thompson), who was sitting in a tent on the side of the road in Nipomo, California, with four of her seven children. Something about the scene made Lange turn her car around and return to the site. A late frost destroyed the early pea crop, leaving Owens and her family, as well as some 2,000 men, women, and children without work or wages. Drawing on her background as a portrait photographer, Lange made six exposures over ten minutes moving closer and closer to the mother and using the backs of two of her middle children to frame the Madonna-esque photo of mother and infant that became known as the *Migrant Mother.* Lange asked Owens few questions and did not even record her name. Three of Lange's images, including *Migrant Mother,* appeared in the March 10 and 11 issues of *The San Francisco News* alongside articles about the plight of local migrant workers. The government responded to the publicity by rushing 20,000 pounds of food to the pea-picker's camp.[23]

Migrant Mother, 1936. Dorothea Lange, photographer (Library of Congress).

Beyond calling people to action, New Deal iconography portrayed how Americans lived during the 1930s as well as their hopes and fears. In *And a Time for Hope* (2000), historian James McGovern described *Migrant Mother* as having been "reduced materially to a half-tent," but nevertheless giving "the impression she is resourceful and will somehow survive and does."[24] According to art historian Karal Ann Marling, in *Wall-to-Wall America: A Cultural History of Post Office Murals in the Great Depression* (1982), New Deal iconography helped viewers to cope with everyday life and to maintain faith in their country's ability to restore itself despite hard times.[25] This interpretation of New Deal culture fits with broader representations of 1930s popular or mass culture as suggested by Lawrence Levine and Morris Dickstein. They argued that during the 1930s mass audiences turned to popular culture, such as Superman comics, Walt Disney's "The Three Little Pigs," and screwball comedies, to find "pleasure, escape, illumination and hope when they were most needed."[26]

Although some scholars contend that such conservative imagery helped people to maintain faith in the American dream, others condemned it for misrepresenting those it portrayed. Critics highlighted the way that New Deal art emphasized gendered and racial distinctions, painting men primarily as laborers, women as mothers, and both as white. To return to the example of *Migrant Mother,* historian James Curtis, in *Mind's Eye, Mind's Truth: FSA Photography Reconsidered* (1989), argued that Lange framed her in conformity with national, middle-class, and Caucasian trends. According to Curtis, Lange purposely ignored Owen's four other children, particularly the teenager, because having so many children and having become a mother at such a young age would have made her appear to deviate from white, middle-class norms.[27] In *Dust Bowl Migrants in the American Imagination* (1997), historian Charles Shindo argued that Lange and other leftist artists paternalistically misrepresented migrant workers as white, Christian, and native-born victims to invoke national sympathy and support for reform legislation despite the desires (and experiences) of those they pictured. Indeed, Owens, who was actually a Cherokee descendent born on a reservation in Oklahoma, initially failed to conform to a liberal narrative of gratitude. In the 1950s and again in the 1970s, she objected to the image that left her penniless but made Lange famous. The family's attitude toward the picture shifted when her grown children received $30,000 in contributions in response to their plea for aid for their disabled mother. She died shortly afterward.[28] The controversy surrounding *Migrant Mother*—both the photograph and the person represented in the image—exemplified the problems of documentation and representation.[29]

Scholars in the 1990s reassessed the New Deal's cultural projects on the basis not only of the politics of representation, but also of a broader critique of liberal reform. Such scholars tended to apply philosopher Antonio Gramsci's notion of cultural hegemony to the New Deal art projects. These scholars viewed the cultural effort of creating New Deal art as an example of how capitalists maintained ideological control over the working class by using social relations, institutions, and ideas to naturalize bourgeois values. One of the chief proponents of this position, cultural historian Jonathan Harris, argued in *Federal Art and National Culture: The Politics of Identity in New Deal America* (1995), that the Federal Art Project used community art centers, art in new public buildings, and the Index of American Design—a collection of watercolor sketches of American arts and crafts—to help create a homogenous national culture, history, and tradition.[30] Similarly, in *The WPA Guides: Mapping America* (1999), Christine Bold contended that the Federal Writers' state guides flattened local differences to make them conform to the New Deal's progressive and pluralistic notions of cultural citizenship. Harkening back to arguments made by New Left critics against the New Deal, such critiques of the arts projects condemned them for shutting down leftist discourse and debate in order to conserve and consolidate liberal reform and managerial capitalism.[31] These critics agreed with Warren Susman's assessment of 1930s culture as superficial, and dismissed the political commitments and idealism of leftist artists and intellectuals associated with the arts projects. However, their notion of hegemony ignored conflicting agendas among local and national art administrators, artists, and audiences as well as the more recently documented leftist activism of many arts participants.[32]

Prior to the 1980s, only a few scholars countered this interpretation of the cultural projects as primarily preserving capitalism and its social relations.[33] The publication of Michael Denning's *The Cultural Front: The Laboring of American Culture in the Twentieth Century* (1998), however, caused a paradigmatic shift in the literature.[34] According to Denning, rather than stifling or subverting leftist expression, the art projects, and the federal government more broadly, provided a vehicle for the flowering and dissemination of industrial unionism. In *Making a New Deal: Industrial Workers in Chicago, 1919-1939* (1990), historian Lizabeth Cohen dubbed such an approach, a "culture of unity," arguing that it used mass culture and goods to incorporate white ethnics, African Americans, and women into a working-class culture that promoted the New Deal and the experiences of working people.[35] Denning also reinterpreted New Deal culture's embrace of social realism and documentation, arguing that far from solidifying an unproblematic interpretation of "the people" as white and male, New Deal culture was modernist, experimental, pluralistic, and gender inclusive.[36]

Although Denning did not address visual culture in his wide-ranging work—which analyzed music, theater, writing, film, and cartoons—a number of art historians have further developed his analysis. In *Artists on the Left: American Artists and the Communist Movement, 1926-1956* (2002), Andrew Hemingway argued that many rank-and-file members of the Communist Party of the United States of America and their fellow travelers strongly criticized federal patronage in the first half of the 1930s. By 1935, however, following the simultaneous creation of the relief-based projects and the brief formation of the Popular Front, an anti-fascist political alliance among Democrats, Communist Party members, and their fellow travelers came to embrace the government's cultural efforts. Hemingway acknowledged the preponderance of New Deal images that celebrated heterosexual masculinity. He viewed them as challenging the traditional role assigned to the working class by making visible previously forgotten publics and by creating images and representations that promoted a cooperative ideal and helped working people to realize their own dignity, power, and potential.[37]

Other scholars reinterpreted the art projects as countering homogeneity with heterogeneous pluralism. Helen Langa's *Radical Art* (2004) and Laura Hapke's *Art's Canvas* (2010) examined how female and minority federal artists countered the New Deal's predominant masculine Caucasian narrative.[38] Instead of focusing on the works created by New Deal visual artists, in *Portrait of America: A Cultural History of the Federal Writers' Project* (2003), Jerrold

"Painting Class at the South Side Community Art Center, Chicago," 1942.
Jack Delano, photographer (Library of Congress).

Hirsch drew attention to the efforts of Washington, D.C.-based
art administrators to incorporate racial and ethnic minorities into
the Federal Writers' Project. He argued that despite the programs'
decentralization, state directors' racism, and budget cuts, national
administrators encouraged federal writers to portray a pluralistic nation by interviewing ex-slaves, recording the histories and
folklore of minorities, and incorporating their own experiences
into their state guides.[39] Lauren Sklaroff pushed this argument
even further in *Black Culture and the New Deal* (2009). While ac-
knowledging the racial limits of the projects, she argued that they
represented a federal effort to emancipate and incorporate African Americans culturally even though New Dealers were loath to
respond to African Americans' political demands, refusing to advocate for anti-lynching legislation or laws to defeat the poll tax
because they feared alienating the southern congressional bloc.[40]

Some of the most recent literature on New Deal art returns to
an earlier focus on recovery and celebration. Journalists and writ-

ers retold the stories of the various art projects, targeting general audiences and producing documentary films to accompany their publications.[41] Local historians, community activists, and curators unearthed and published photographs, murals, posters, and easel paintings that draw attention to the accomplishments of art projects, particularly in the West, South, and Midwest.[42]

Three key turning points facilitated this most recent transition: the seventy-fifth anniversary of the New Deal in 2008 during a recession; the Obama administration's initial emergency relief efforts, including a minimal increase in funding for the arts; and growing attacks on the New Deal and Roosevelt from the right. Within this context, highlighting the strengths of New Deal culture serves both as a defense of Roosevelt and his administration and as a call to reevaluate the role that artists and the arts play in our contemporary crisis. It is perhaps not coincidental that Roger Kennedy's title for one of the newest spins on the art projects, *When Art Worked* (2009), was so similar to that given to the six-month cross-country tour that President Barack Obama's appointee to the National Endowment for the Arts, Rocco Landesman, began that November: "Art Works." Both the book and the tour highlighted common themes: the idea that artists do real work and that art plays a critical role in shaping local communities, economies, and American culture as a whole.[43]

Despite such revival efforts, the cultural projects of the New Deal—like those created under the auspices of the NEA and NEH—will continue to draw mixed reviews. To be successful, public art needs to serve both artists' interests and those of a wider public. But artists' aesthetic and social visions often conflict with those espoused by community members and art administrators. The negotiations among such players during the 1930s illuminated the difficulties that publicly funded artists faced in terms of producing new, innovative, and especially controversial artwork while still maintaining the support of congressmen and taxpayers. But they also suggest a range of roles that public art might play in citizens' lives and a variety of ways that the government might shape the nation's cultural development. We need to continue to attend to

the jostling agendas of art administrators, diverse artists, and as-
sorted audiences in both the past and the present to glimpse how
government-funded art worked (and did not) during the 1930s and
how we might make it work again today.

NOTES

1. It is difficult to calculate the total number of participants in the New
Deal art projects and total expenditures because of the wide array of, and
frequent transitions in, government art organizations. This estimate is
based on estimates from Lawrence S. Morris, Executive Assistant of the
Works Progress Administration's Federal One, and estimates for other pro-
grams, including the Treasury Relief Art Project, the Section of Painting and
Sculpture, and the Historical Section of the Resettlement Administration.
See United States, Senate, "A Bill to Provide for a Permanent Bureau of Fine
Arts," March 1, 1938, 75th Congress, 3rd Session (Washington, D.C.: United
States Government Printing Office, 1938), 20:156; Richard D. McKinzie, *The
New Deal for Artists* (Princeton: Princeton University Press, 1973), 42, 75.

2. Marlene Park and Gerald E. Markowitz, *Democratic Vistas: Post Offices
and Public Art in the New Deal* (Philadelphia: Temple University Press, 1984), 6.

3. Van Wyck Brooks, "On Creating A Usable Past," *The Dial* 64 (April 11,
1918): 337–41.

4. See Belisario R. Contreras, *Tradition and Innovation in New Deal Art*
(London: Associated University Presses, 1983).

5. See Susan Quinn, *Furious Improvisation: How the WPA and a Cast of
Thousands Made High Art out of Desperate Times* (New York: Walker, 2008);
Virginia Tuttle Clayton, Elizabeth Stillinger, and Erika Lee Doss, eds., *Draw-
ing on America's Past: Folk Art, Modernism, and the Index of American Design*
(Washington, D.C.: National Gallery of Art, 2002).

6. Jack F. Hurley, *Portrait of a Decade* (Baton Rouge: Louisiana State University Press, 1972).

7. Victoria Marie Grieve, "Art as New Deal Experience: Progressive Aesthetics and the New Deal Federal Art," Ph.D. dissertation, George Washington University, 2004, 155; Jane De Hart Mathews, "Arts and the People: The
New Deal Quest for a Cultural Democracy," *The Journal of American History*
62 (September 1975): 330.

8. Anthony Lee, *Painting on the Left: Diego Rivera, Radical Politics, and San
Francisco's Public Murals* (Berkeley: University of California Press, 1999), 182.

9. U.S. Congress, Congressional Record, 75th Congress, 3rd Sess., 1938
(vol. 83, pt. 2): 2305-6.

10. Lee, *Painting on the Left,* 182; Clement Greenberg, "Avant-Garde and
Kitsch," *Partisan Review* 6 (Fall 1939): 39; Michael Denning, *The Cultural*

Front: The Laboring of American Culture in the Twentieth Century (New York: Verso, 1998), 116-17.

11. Warren I. Susman, *Culture as History: The Transformation of American Society in the Twentieth Century* (New York: Pantheon Books, 1984), 152.

12. Jonathan Harris, *Federal Art and National Culture: The Politics of Identity in New Deal America* (New York: Cambridge University Press, 1995), 5.

13. See Francis V. O'Connor, *The New Deal Art Projects* (Washington, D.C.: Smithsonian Institution, 1972); Francis V. O'Connor, *Art for the Millions; Essays from the 1930s by Artists and Administrators of the WPA Federal Art Project* (Greenwich, CT: New York Graphic Society, 1973); Ann Banks, *First-Person America* (New York: Alfred A. Knopf, 1980); George Rawick, ed., *The American Slave: A Composite Autobiography,* 19 vols. (Westport, CT: Greenwood Press, 1972-1979).

14. See Roy Rosenzweig, ed., *Government and the Arts in Thirties America: A Guide to Oral Histories and Other Materials* (Fairfax, VA: George Mason University Press, 1986); Roy Rosenzweig and Barbara Melosh, "Government and the Arts: Voices from the New Deal Era," *The Journal of American History* 77 (September 1990): 596-608.

15. See Milton Meltzer, *Violins and Shovels: The WPA Arts Projects* (New York: Delacorte Press, 1976); Virginia M. Mecklenburg, *The Public as Patron: A History of the Treasury Department Mural Program* (College Park: University of Maryland, 1979); Joanne Bentley, *Hallie Flanagan: A Life in the American Theater* (New York: Knopf, 1988); Jane De Hart Mathews, *The Federal Theater, 1935-39: Plays, Relief, and Politics* (Princeton: Princeton University Press, 1967); John O'Connor and Lorraine Brown, *Free, Adult, and Uncensored: The Living History of the FTP* (Washington, D.C.: New Republic Books, 1978); Jerre Mangione, *The Dream and the Deal: The Federal Writers' Project, 1935-1943* (New York: Avon Books, 1972); Monty Noam Penkower, *The Federal Writers' Project: A Study in Government Patronage of the Arts* (Urbana: University of Illinois Press, 1976).

16. Francis V. O'Connor, *Federal Support for the Visual Arts: The New Deal and Now* (New York: New York Graphic Society, 1969), 108.

17. McKinzie, *New Deal for Artists,* 187-88.

18. See Joseph Wesley Zeigler, *Arts in Crisis: The National Endowment for the Arts Versus America* (Chicago: Chicago Review Press, 1994).

19. Mathews, "Arts and the People," 316-39.

20. A. Joan Saab, *For the Millions: American Art and Culture between the Wars* (Philadelphia: University of Pennsylvania Press, 2004).

21. Victoria Marie Grieve, *The Federal Art Project and the Creation of Middlebrow Culture* (Chicago: University of Illinois Press, 2009), 180.

22. William Stott, *Documentary Expression and Thirties America* (New York: Oxford University Press, 1973), Chapter 4.

23. Linda Gordon, *Dorothea Lange: A Life Beyond Limits* (New York: W.W. Norton, 2009), 236-37.

24. James R. McGovern, *And a Time for Hope* (Westport, CT: Praeger, 2000), 73.

25. Karal Ann Marling, *Wall-to-Wall America: A Cultural History of Post Office Murals in the Great Depression* (Minneapolis: University of Minnesota Press, 1982); McGovern, *And a Time for Hope*. A similar argument can also be seen in Park and Markovitz, *Democratic Vistas*.

26. Lawrence W. Levine, *The Unpredictable Past: Explorations in American Cultural History* (New York: Oxford University Press, 1993), Chapter 11; Morris Dickstein, *Dancing in the Dark: A Cultural History of the Great Depression* (New York: W.W. Norton, 2009), xv.

27. James Curtis, *Mind's Eye, Mind's Truth: FSA Photography Reconsidered* (Philadelphia: Temple University Press, 1989).

28. Charles Shindo, *Dust Bowl Migrants in the American Imagination* (Lawrence: University Press of Kansas, 1997). See Robert Hariman and John Louis Lucaites, *No Caption Needed: Iconic Photographs, Public Culture, and Liberal Democracy* (Chicago: University of Chicago Press, 2007); Wendy Kozol, "Madonnas of the Fields: Photography, Gender, and 1930s Farm Relief," *Genders* 2 (Summer 1988): 1-23.

29. See Paula Rabinowitz, *They Must Be Presented: The Politics of Documentary* (New York: Verso, 1994).

30. Harris, *Federal Art and National Culture*, 7-8.

31. Christine Bold, *The WPA Guides: Mapping America* (Jackson: University Press of Mississippi, 1999). Other works expressing a similar view include Curtis, *Mind's Eye, Mind's Truth;* Barbara Melosh, *Engendering Culture: Manhood and Womanhood in New Deal Public Art and Theater* (Washington, D.C.: Smithsonian Institution Press, 1991).

32. Andrew Hemingway, *Artists on the Left: American Artists and the Communist Movement, 1926-1956* (New Haven: Yale University Press, 2002); Laura Hapke, *Labor's Canvas: American Working-Class History and the WPA Art of the 1930s* (New York: Cambridge University Press, 2008).

33. See David Shapiro, *Social Realism: Art as a Weapon* (New York: Frederick Ungar, 1973); Gerald M. Monroe, "The Artists' Union of New York," Ed.D. dissertation, New York University, 1971.

34. Michael Denning, *The Cultural Front.*

35. Lizabeth Cohen, *Making a New Deal: Industrial Workers in Chicago, 1919-1939* (New York: Cambridge University Press, 1990), 324.

36. Denning, *The Cultural Front,* 120-23. See Jeff Allred, *American Modernism and Depression Documentary* (New York: Oxford University Press, 2009).

37. Hemingway, *Artists on the Left,* 84.

38. Helen Langa, *Radical Art: Printmaking and the Left in 1930s New York* (Berkeley: University of California Press, 2004), 46; Laura Hapke, *Labor's Canvas,* 6.

39. Jerrold Hirsch, *Portrait of America: A Cultural History of the Federal Writers' Project* (Chapel Hill: University of North Carolina Press, 2003).

40. Lauren Rebecca Sklaroff, *Black Culture and the New Deal: The Quest for Civil Rights in the Roosevelt Era* (Chapel Hill: The University of North Carolina Press, 2009).

41. See Quinn, *Furious Improvisation;* David A. Taylor, *Soul of a People: The WPA Writer's Project Uncovers Depression America* (Hoboken, NJ: Wiley, 2009).

42. See Ennis Carter, *Posters for the People: The Art of the WPA* (Philadelphia: Quirk Books, 2008); Betsy Fahlman, *New Deal Art in Arizona* (Tucson: University of Arizona Press, 2009); Jennifer McLerran, *A New Deal for Native Art: Indian Arts and Federal Policy, 1933-1943* (Tucson: University of Arizona Press, 2009); Anita Price Davis, *New Deal Art in North Carolina* (Jefferson, NC: McFarland, 2009); and Anita Price Davis, *New Deal Art in Virginia* (Jefferson, NC: McFarland, 2009).

43. Roger G. Kennedy, *When Art Worked: The New Deal, Art, and Democracy* (New York: Rizzoli, 2009).

PART II

The Fringes of the

New Deal

CHAPTER EIGHT

African Americans and the Politics of Race during the New Deal

GLORIA-YVONNE WILLIAMS

The New Deal marked a pivotal moment in the African American struggle for equality and justice. Franklin D. Roosevelt's New Deal introduced an expanded notion of democracy that transformed American social policy and provided a medium for African Americans to challenge existing racial boundaries. As a progressive Democrat, Roosevelt presented the New Deal as a way to serve the American people regardless of race, creed, or cultural background. In 1933, Roosevelt described his "new national administration" as one that would "restore the confidence" and "bring about governmental action to mesh more with the rights and the essential needs of the individual man and woman."[1] By the mid-1930s the New Deal created economic and political opportunities for African Americans through its policy of inclusion, which at that time was a fundamental step toward gaining recognition of their civil and political rights.

African American leaders and activists embraced the New Deal's reformist agenda as a vehicle to challenge racial inequities throughout government and society. In the 1940s, African American journalists Roi Ottley and Henry Moon viewed the political agency of African American leaders and activists as critical to the advancement and recognition of their full citizenship. Not since Reconstruction had African Americans been given the opportunity to participate in government reforms. Political scientists Minion K. C. Morrison and Richard Middleton IV acknowledged that "[t]he New Deal offered by Franklin Roosevelt is regarded as the first fundamental shift in African American representation."[2] Although most scholars since the 1940s recognized this shift in African American representation, many remained skeptical about the degree of their political influence on New Deal policy.

The New Deal represented an important opportunity for African Americans and other minorities. Since the 1890s the combined forces of segregation, discrimination, and disenfranchisement relegated African Americans as second-class citizens. Jim Crow laws created segregation for public and educational facilities, and those divisions dictated where African Americans lived, worked, socialized, and were educated. In *A New Deal for Blacks: The Emergence of Civil Rights as a National Issue* (1978), Harvard Sitkoff observed that until the 1930s, "[m]ost whites either considered Jim Crow a boon or knew little of the African American plight." However, he pointed out that the perspectives of African Americans began to change in the 1930s due to a convergence of progressive social beliefs about race, the symbolic presence of African Americans in Roosevelt's administration, and the willingness of white New Dealers to ally with African Americans and fight against discrimination and inequality.[3]

In many respects, the interpretation that social change was a failure overshadowed the rich heritage of the New Deal and its reformers. In the 1960s, in particular, New Left historians highlighted the failures of the New Deal. Harvard Sitkoff challenged those criticisms and characterized "the mid-1960s as a torrent of dissent," with a "new generation of historians" who emphasized "racial discrimination in the recovery program," and doubted "the New Deal as a reform movement to benefit the mass of Americans."[4] Similarly, Anthony Badger in *The New Deal: The Depression Years, 1933-1940* (1989), pointed out that radical historians "conscious of continuing racism and poverty in the 1960s, believed that the New Deal had merely served to sustain the hegemony of corporate capitalism."[5] Also, Morton Keller, in *America's Three Regimes: A New Political History* (2007), noted that before the New Left criticism, in the 1960s, "most historians saw the New Deal as the culmination of a reform tradition rooted in Jacksonian democracy, Populism and Progressivism."[6]

Several questions are critical to understanding the major debates about the politics of race during the New Deal, and the multifaceted roles of African Americans. How did African Americans view Roosevelt and the New Deal? How did race influence New Deal reform and legislative change? How successful were New Deal programs in enacting racial, social, and political changes? This chapter focuses on these and other questions with a review of the major works and arguments on the politics of race and the New Deal.

A 1945 article in the *Baltimore Afro-American* characterized President Roosevelt as an activist leader who "Declared For Equality in First Bid for Presidency, [and] Held Fast to Policy." Appearing two days after his death, the article assessed what his leadership meant to African Americans. His rhetoric, according to the writer, was built upon "equal legal and economic opportunity." As a candidate, Roosevelt told a *Baltimore Afro-American* reporter of his belief in those equal opportunities "for all groups, regardless of race, color or creed." During a December 1933 national radio broadcast, he referred to lynching as a "form of collective murder." The article praised Roosevelt's record of legislation for low-cost housing, the development of agencies that provided jobs and education for African American youth, and his stand against disenfranchisement.[7] This contemporaneous portrait of Roosevelt presented him as a voice for democratic rights and equality, but in areas that historians criticized.

This image of Roosevelt contrasts with most scholarly conclusions about his relationship with African Americans. Essentially, most argue that he failed to recognize the plight of the African American masses by not fighting against discrimination and lynching. In response to such negative interpretations, Sitkoff observed that "[p]erhaps no aspect of the New Deal appears more anomalous or paradoxical than the relationship of Afro-Americans and the

administration of President Franklin Roosevelt." But Sitkoff sur-
mised that scholars overlooked the "impact of the New Deal on
civil rights in the context of the prevailing racial conservatism of the
period."[8] Anthony Badger aptly described negative interpretations
as a "gloomy picture" of the New Deal, which "underestimates the
change in status and perception of African American rights as an issue for New Dealers in the 1930s."[9] More recently, sociologist John
Brueggemann's article, "Racial Considerations and Social Policy in
the 1930s: Economic Change and Political Opportunities" (2002),
found "contrasting portrayals reflect[ing] the ambiguity of the New
Deal legacy of race relations." But he concluded that social change
during this era along with the African American struggle for equality planted the seeds for the modern Civil Rights Movement.[10]

The egalitarian rhetoric of the New Deal provided African American leaders and activists a platform for starting a serious national
dialogue about civil and political rights. In *When Negroes March:
The March on Washington Movement in the Organizational Politics for
FEPC* (1959), Herbert Garfinkel viewed the "history of the Thirties
. . . [as] bringing an increased usage of democratic and equalitar-
ian terminology, for it was during that period that radicalism grew
in the despair of world-wide depression."[11] Henry Moon argued,
in *Balance of Power* (1948), that certain factors persuaded African
Americans to embrace Roosevelt's New Deal. He explained that
first, "[t]heir confidence in him stemmed from the conviction that
he was trying to facilitate their long hard struggle to attain full citizenship." Secondly, Moon recalled the meaning of the New Deal to
African Americans as "broad-based and humanitarian . . . [which]
recognized the disadvantaged Negro minority as an integral part of
the American people."[12]

In *The Story of American Freedom* (1998), Eric Foner stressed that
for the African American working class this "quest for economic
freedom" was apparent with the founding of the Congress of Industrial Organizations (CIO), which, unlike the American Federation
of Labor (AFL), did not exclude membership on the basis of race.[13]
Most recently, Thomas Sugrue's *Land of Liberty: The Forgotten Strug-*

gle for Civil Rights in the North (2008) summed up the period's political significance in advocating rights rhetoric. He explained that the "New Deal unleashed great expectations about government and a rhetoric of rights that became increasingly empowering. By pushing national politics leftward, the New Deal made room for dissenters on moral, religious, and economic issues to organize."[14]

In the 1930s several factors triggered a transformation in African American political behavior. As waves of African Americans migrated from the South to the North, the nation's social and political landscape changed. Increasing numbers of African Americans in urban areas such as Chicago, Detroit, and Philadelphia favored Democratic candidates in their local elections. As this voting bloc expanded, the African American electorate used the franchise to "retain and strengthen the New Deal."[15] The growing allegiance to the Democratic Party resulted in a broader coalition of African American activists and leaders pressing Roosevelt for change.

The broad appeal of the New Deal transcended race, class, and region. Roosevelt created a new more inclusive coalition of Democratic voters that included disadvantaged African Americans, southerners who were Democrats by tradition, and people from regions outside of the South, such as northern Democratic voters and those associated with urban political machines. In his 1985 essay, "The New Deal and American Politics," historian Richard Kirkendall argued that the new Democratic Party was built on the president's "rhetoric and his polices." He emphasized that Roosevelt's inclusiveness "was more closely tied to lower-income groups and their organizations than before, and was less dependent upon the South."[16]

Throughout the New Deal, outside activists challenged race and public policy. In his essay "The New Deal and Race Relations" (1985), Harvard Sitkoff argued that there was "pressure for change" exerted by "counter-forces [that] pushed the New Deal toward a more equitable treatment of African Americans." He explained that African Americans "marched, picketed, rallied, and lobbied against racial discrimination" and "boycotted businesses with unjust racial practices." In *The Dual Agenda* (1997), sociologist Dona

Cooper Hamilton and political scientist Charles V. Hamilton discussed the pressure tactics of African American organizations such as the National Association for the Advancement of Colored People (NAACP) and the National Urban League (NUL). They explained that these and other organizations pushed for inclusion and anti-discrimination policies in New Deal legislation. [17]

Direct action protests were also part of racial activism during the 1930s. In *Along the Color Line: Explorations in the Black Experience* (2002), August Meier and Elliott Rudwick analyzed "Don't-Buy-Where-You-Can't-Work" campaigns, in which African Americans picketed, boycotted, and demonstrated against discriminatory hiring practices at white-owned businesses in African American neighborhoods. They concluded that "direct action of the Depression years has been virtually forgotten, and almost totally ignored by historians."[18]

From the inside there were a small number of African American advisors and appointees who influenced the New Deal's racial policies. One method for monitoring and alleviating racial discrimination in hiring practices involved placing African Americans in key national positions, such as economist Robert Weaver in the Department of the Interior and educator Mary McLeod Bethune, who directed the National Youth Administration's (NYA) Division of Negro Affairs. Placing African Americans in New Deal agencies allowed for closer monitoring of local activities, such as verifying that racial discrimination was not part of the federal hiring process. In their edited work *Mary McLeod Bethune: Building a Better World: Essays and Selected Documents* (1999), Audrey McCluskey and Elaine Smith asserted that hiring African Americans for positions of some power curtailed racially based discrimination practices in several New Deal agencies.[19]

Even with support and input from African Americans and other minority groups, Roosevelt's New Deal programs were shaped by the practices and culture of the period, which included race-based segregation and discrimination. Historian Harvard Sitkoff referred to this view of the New Deal—that African Americans supported

Roosevelt even though the New Deal perpetuated discriminatory practices. Sociologist John Brueggemann referred to the decade as an uneven period for race relations. In *Days of Hope: Race and Democracy in the New Deal Era* (1996), Patricia Sullivan concurred, saying that "the depression created constraints as well as opportunities" for African Americans.[20]

Administering federal relief programs resulted in direct conflict with local practices and leadership. For example, New Dealers touted the Agricultural Adjustment Administration (AAA) as offering relief and recovery to farmers and agricultural laborers, but the program displaced tenant farmers and sharecroppers, who were predominantly African American. Warren C. Whatley pointed out in his article, "Labor for the Picking: The New Deal in the South" (1983), that the AAA's programs were under the control of white property owners, which left social and racial divisions in place.[21] In the essay "The New Deal and the Negro" (1975), Raymond Wolters discussed the machinations of the AAA under the control of Henry Wallace and how African Americans were excluded from the program's benefits solely on the basis of race. The NAACP and the Southern Tenant Farmers Union (STFU) pressured the Roosevelt administration to allow African American farmers access to AAA programs. As one result, the Roosevelt administration created the Farm Security Administration (FSA), which was placed under the control of Will Alexander, a white liberal with interests in the welfare of African Americans.[22]

Other New Deal agencies challenged local practices of racial discrimination in hiring workers. In *A New Deal for Blacks* (1978), Sitkoff looked at the Public Works Administration (PWA) and Harold Ickes's administrative approaches. As Secretary of the Interior and head of the PWA, Ickes brought a form of integration into the New Deal by refusing "positions to subordinates who would not work with Blacks." He also insisted that "PWA construction projects hire Afro-Americans as skilled as well as unskilled laborers" in accordance with the PWA's antidiscrimination policy. The PWA was foremost in promoting the use of quotas as a form of proportional equality to guarantee jobs to a percentage of African American applicants. In this respect, proportional equality linked African Americans to labor and economic reform of the period.[23]

Racial quotas during the New Deal became not only federal employment policy, but were the genesis for later affirmative action programs. In *From Direct Action To Affirmative Action: Fair Employment Law and Policy, 1933-1972* (1997), Paul D. Moreno explored the social and political advantages in applying racial quotas during the New Deal. He described the important role of New Deal agencies in changing federal employment policies. Moreno noted that the 1930s "provide a usually unrecognized experiment with the current concept of affirmative action, which lay dormant for the next generation."[24]

Race influenced the perceptions of African Americans who benefited during the early stages of the New Deal. In urban areas African Americans received more direct relief in 1933 and 1935 than job opportunities. African American leaders warned New Deal officials that African Americans also needed access to education and training, which were part of many New Deal jobs. In *Race, Money, and the Welfare State* (1999), political scientist Michael K. Brown explained that the relief practices for African Americans during the New Deal contributed to the stratification of postwar society based on race and economics. Further, sociologist Stephen Pimpare revealed, in *A People's History of Poverty in America* (2011), that the stigma of a "separate public welfare system for African Americans" first became an issue when Reconstruction programs served mostly African Americans. Most importantly, Pimpare argued that this stigma was rooted in the institution of slavery, one of many "repressive institutions that have disproportionately impacted African Americans."[25]

The New Deal was a period when many white liberal politicians, reformers, and activists pushed heavily for social equality for African Americans. In particular, First Lady Eleanor Roosevelt was a force of liberalism whose openness against discrimination motivated other liberal New Dealers. In the Pulitzer Prize-winning *Freedom From Fear: The American People in Depression and War, 1929-1945* (1999), David Kennedy emphasized the influence of Eleanor

Roosevelt on her husband's racial policies. He also noted the influence of Harry Hopkins—who headed several New Deal agencies, including the Federal Emergency Relief Administration (FERA) and the Works Progress Administration (WPA)—on eliminating racial discrimination in federal hiring practices.[26]

Other historians have questioned the intentions and effectiveness of New Dealers who advised Roosevelt on racial matters. John Kirby in *Black Americans in the Roosevelt Era: Liberalism and Race* (1980), found weaknesses in racial liberalism and characterized the relationships between white and African American liberals as patronizing.[27] Other historians took a more balanced view of how White House advisors viewed race. In *The White House Looks South: Franklin D. Roosevelt, Harry S. Truman, Lyndon B. Johnson* (2005), William Leuchtenburg suggested that some of Roosevelt's liberal appointees were "Whites who were conspicuously unsympathetic to the reign of Jim Crow." But Leuchtenburg asserted that Roosevelt did not discourage his advisors from questioning existing racial policies and practices, such as Ickes's desegregation of the Department of the Interior's restrooms and cafeterias.[28]

Other connections between race and public policy appear in studies of resistance of southern Democratic congressmen to New Deal legislation that pertained to expanding rights to African Americans. In *Freedom From Fear* (1999), David Kennedy explored the reaction of powerful southern congressmen to the NAACP's consistent activism for an anti-lynching bill and Roosevelt's responses to this cause. Similarly, Nick Taylor, in *American-Made: The Enduring Legacy of the WPA: When FDR Put the Nation to Work* (2008), explained that a coalition of southern Democrats "erected a bulwark against" progressive legislation and rights for African Americans. In addition, Karen Ferguson's *Black Politics in New Deal Atlanta* (2002) outlined political maneuvers of local and national politicians that thwarted relief programs and improved wages for African Americans.[29]

On the eve of World War II, African American leaders pressured Roosevelt to cease discrimination in hiring practices in the expanding defense industries. In March 1941, African American labor leader A. Philip Randolph organized a march on Washington to raise awareness of racially based discrimination. In *Along the Color Line,* Meier and Rudwick asserted that Randolph believed that "broad, organized mass action was required to put pressure on the political authorities." The march would have mobilized as many as 100,000 African Americans as a growing symbol of national race consciousness.[30]

To prevent the march, President Roosevelt issued Executive Order 8802 in 1941, which established the Fair Employment Practices Committee. This committee monitored discriminatory practices in the defense industries and government. Scholars point to the Fair Employment Practices Committee as a cornerstone of later civil rights legislation, because it expanded opportunities for federal policy challenges to racial boundaries. In *America's Three Regimes* (2007), Morton Keller described the legislation as "the first tentative federal entry into the hitherto forbidden territory of racial equality in the workforce." Further, Keller pointed out that during the Roosevelt administration some of the first civil rights policies aimed at doing "something about race and racism in American life" originated from executive orders, such as the Fair Employment Practices Committee.[31]

Scholars took a great interest in the New Deal as a period of origin for rights advocacy for African Americans. In *Negroes and the Great Depression: The Problem of Economic Recovery* (1970), Raymond Wolters viewed the economic inequality of African American agricultural and industrial workers as a significant problem threatening their recovery. Wolters argued that this inequality became a catalyst for African American political activism. In *A New Deal For Blacks,* Sitkoff placed the struggle for African American rights during the New Deal within the historiography of civil rights activism. His synthesis covered topics critical to understanding racial politics and the New Deal, therefore setting the stage for subsequent studies. In *The Dual Agenda,* Hamilton and Hamilton described the influence of pressure and lobbying campaigns from African American leaders on New Deal social welfare legislation. They explained how civil rights organizations, consisting of African American professionals, fought for "liberal social welfare policies that would benefit not only African Americans but all poor people."[32]

Recent studies pushed the debate on the origins of civil rights activism back to the 1930s. These scholars stressed the significance of African American political activism across class with an emphasis on coalitions of labor groups, professionals, political organizations, and African American New Dealers on Capitol Hill. Aimin Zhang's *The Origins of the African-American Civil Rights Movement, 1865-1956* (2002) chronicled the growth of African American race consciousness and political power during the New Deal. Most recently, in *Land of Liberty,* Sugrue examined the undervalued activism of northern liberals and their interracial coalitions with southerners. Sugrue focused on activists of a particular region, yet he emphasized that the New Deal's "rhetoric of rights . . . became increasingly empowering." Further, he argued that "by pushing national politics leftward, the New Deal made room for dissenters on moral, religious, and economic issues to organize."[33]

The movement that African Americans initiated in the 1930s for advocacy and social change challenged traditional beliefs about race, and developed into a mass movement for equal representation in public policy. In *Lift Every Voice: The NAACP and the Making of the Civil Rights Movement* (2009), Patricia Sullivan reviewed the importance of the New Deal to African Americans. Sullivan argued that the 1930s were a "critical period of black political activism and a formative stage in the evolving movement for freedom and civil rights" in which African American protest and politics merged.[34]

The New Deal facilitated a shift in racial politics and race relations. The ideals, rhetoric, and legislation of the New Deal fostered an environment of racial inclusiveness and increased African American political representation at the federal level. The involvement of African Americans in New Deal programs, their work on Capitol Hill, and their direct involvement with Roosevelt represented a high-water mark for African American rights and representation—a level of national influence and political involvement not equalled since Reconstruction. Social protest from the independent African American press, civil rights organizations, activist leaders, and New Dealers also contributed to the push for greater rights for African Americans during the 1930s.

NOTES

1. Quotes from Franklin D. Roosevelt, *Looking Forward* (New York: John Day, 1933; reprint, New York: Touchstone, 2009), 270.

2. Roi Ottley, *"New World A-Coming": Inside Black America* (Boston: The Riverside Press, 1943); Henry Moon, *A Balance of Power: The Negro Vote* (New York: Doubleday, 1948; reprint, New York: Kraus Reprint, 1969); Minion K. C. Morrison and Richard Middleton IV, "African Americans in Office," in *African Americans and Political Participation,* ed. Minion K. C. Morrison (Santa Barbara, CA: ABC-CLIO, 2003), 288.

3. Harvard Sitkoff, *A New Deal for Blacks: The Emergence of Civil Rights as a National Issue* (New York: Oxford University Press, 1978), 33.

4. Harvard Sitkoff, "Introduction," in *Fifty Years Later: The New Deal Evaluated,* ed. Harvard Sitkoff (New York: McGraw-Hill, 1985), 7-8.

5. Anthony J. Badger, *The New Deal: The Depression Years, 1933-1940* (New York: Hill and Wang, 1989), 3.

6. Morton Keller, *America's Three Regimes: A New Political History* (New York: Oxford University Press, 2007), 207.

7. Audrey Weaver, "Declared For Equality in First Bid for Presidency, Held Fast to Policy," *Baltimore Afro-American,* April 14, 1945.

8. Harvard Sitkoff, "The New Deal and Race Relations," in *Fifty Years Later,* 93.

9. Badger, *The New Deal,* 253-54.

10. John Brueggemann, "Racial Considerations and Social Policy in the 1930s: Economic Change and Political Opportunities," *Social Science History* 26 (2002): 139-77.

11. Herbert Garfinkel, *When Negroes March: The March on Washington Movement in the Organizational Politics for FEPC* (New York: Atheneum, 1969), 21-22.

12. Moon, *Balance of Power,* 21, 27-28.

13. Eric Foner, *The Story of American Freedom* (New York: W.W. Norton, 1998), 195-99, 215-16.

14. Thomas Sugrue, *Land of Liberty: The Forgotten Struggle for Civil Rights in the North* (New York: Random House, 2008), 20.

15. Moon, *Balance of Power,* 21. See also Gunnar Myrdal, *An American Dilemma: The Negro Problem and American Democracy* (New York: Harper Brothers, 1944); Nancy J. Weiss, *Farewell to the Party of Lincoln: Black Politics in the Age of FDR* (Princeton: Princeton University Press, 1983); Aimin Zhang, *The Origins of the African-American Civil Rights Movement, 1865-1965* (New York: Routledge, 2002).

16. Richard S. Kirkendall, "The New Deal and American Politics," in *Fifty Years Later,* 21.

17. Harvard Sitkoff, "The New Deal and Race Relations," in *Fifty Years Later,* 97-98; Dona Cooper Hamilton and Charles V. Hamilton, *The Dual Agenda: The African-American Struggle for Civil and Economic Equality* (New York: Columbia University Press, 1997), 2.

18. August Meier and Elliott Rudwick, "The Origins of Nonviolent Direct Actions in Afro-American Protest: A Note on Historical Discontinuities," in *Along the Color Line: Explorations in the Black Experience* (Urbana: University of Illinois Press, 1976; reprint, 2002), 344.

19. Hamilton and Hamilton, "Dual Agenda," 20; Audrey McCluskey and Elaine Smith, eds., *Mary McLeod Bethune: Building a Better World: Essays and Selected Documents* (Bloomington: Indiana University Press, 1999), xiii, 201.

20. Sitkoff, "The New Deal and Race Relations," in *Fifty Years Later,* 93; John Brueggemann, "Racial Considerations and Social Policy in the 1930s," *Social Science History* 26 (Spring 2002): 140; Patricia Sullivan, *Days of Hope: Race and Democracy in the New Deal Era* (Chapel Hill: University of North Carolina Press, 1996), 43.

21. Warren C. Whatley, "Labor for the Picking: The New Deal in the South," *The Journal of Economic History* 43 (December 1983): 926.

22. Raymond Wolters, "The New Deal and the Negro," in *The New Deal,* eds. John Braeman, Robert H. Bremner, and David Brody (Columbus: Ohio State University Press, 1975), 1:171-78.

23. Sitkoff, *A New Deal for Blacks,* 66, 69.

24. Paul D. Moreno, *From Direct Action to Affirmative Action: Fair Employment Law and Policy, 1933-1972* (Baton Rouge: Louisiana State University Press, 1997), 31-32.

25. Michael K. Brown, *Race, Money, and the Welfare State* (Ithaca: Cornell University Press, 1999); Stephen Pimpare, *A People's History of Poverty in America* (New York: The New Press, 2011), 168, 178.

26. Sitkoff, "The New Deal and Race Relations," in *Fifty Years Later,* 105; David M. Kennedy, *Freedom From Fear: The American People in Depression and War, 1929-1945* (New York: Oxford University Press, 1999), 164, 254, 378-79.

27. John Kirby, *Black Americans in the Roosevelt Era: Liberalism and Race* (Knoxville: University of Tennessee Press, 1980).

28. William E. Leuchtenburg, *The White House Looks South: Franklin D. Roosevelt, Harry S. Truman, Lyndon B. Johnson* (Baton Rouge: Louisiana State University Press, 2005), 63.

29. David Kennedy, *Freedom From Fear,* 340-41; Nick Taylor, *American-Made: The Enduring Legacy of the WPA: When FDR Put the Nation to Work* (New York: Bantam, 2008), 385-87; Karen Ferguson, *Black Politics in New Deal Atlanta* (Chapel Hill: University of North Carolina Press, 2002).

30. Meier and Rudwick, "Origins of Nonviolent Direct Actions," 345.

31. Keller, *America's Three Regimes,* 212-30.

32. Raymond Wolters, *Negroes and the Great Depression: The Problem of Economic Recovery* (Westport, CT: Greenwood Publishing Co., 1970); Sitkoff, *A New Deal for Blacks;* Hamilton and Hamilton, *The Dual Agenda,* 2.

33. Zhang, *Origins of the Civil Rights Movement;* Sugrue, *Land of Liberty,* 20.

34. Patricia Sullivan, *Lift Every Voice: The NAACP and the Making of the Civil Rights Movement* (New York: The New Press, 2009), 191.

CHAPTER NINE

Organized Labor, Reds, and Radicals of the 1930s

GREGORY S. TAYLOR

The Great Depression proved a tumultuous time for organized labor, radical political organizations, and radical political activists. Already at low ebb when the crisis began, their fortunes receded ever further during Herbert Hoover's administration. Those fortunes rebounded dramatically with the election of Franklin D. Roosevelt, the implementation of the New Deal, and a sudden, albeit brief, alliance between workers and the radical left. Historians have long examined these ever-changing fortunes, and in the process raised several fundamental questions about the relationship between organized labor and radicals of the Depression era.

Even before the Great Depression started, the 1920s were difficult for organized labor in America. Although the gross national product grew an average of five percent annually, industrial output increased sixty percent, per capita income rose nearly twenty-five percent, and unemployment hovered near two percent throughout the decade, the average worker suffered. In fact, "the average annual worker's income lagged three-hundred dollars below the yearly earnings necessary for a minimal standard of living."[1] Despite such suffering, the American Federation of Labor (AFL), the nation's largest labor organization, did little to help. It ignored unskilled workers and minorities, and opposed most strikes. As a result, two million members abandoned the AFL for company unions or welfare capitalism in the form of pension plans or profit-sharing programs. Neither alternative provided much benefit, and by the end of the 1920s the majority of American workers were poorly represented and only minimally protected from the dangers of industrial capitalism.

The American Socialist and Communist parties suffered similarly during the 1920s. The Palmer Raids and Red Scare of 1919-1920 were followed by a decade of Nativist sentiment and a fear of radicalism. Sectarianism and internecine strife further ravaged the radical left. The Socialist Party of America, once numbering more than 100,000 members, collapsed to 14,000 by 1921 and totalled 8,000 just prior to the October 1929 stock market crash. The Communist Party of the United States of America (CPUSA), never a large or well organized group, fell from 60,000 members in 1919 to 7,545 in 1930.[2] Thus, the groups that might have radicalized and invigorated the labor movement were in no position to do so when the Depression started.

The continued quiescence of the AFL, worker wariness with radical calls for revolution, the growing labor pool, and the traditional willingness of industry and government to break strikes forcefully further undermined the labor movement during the first years of the Depression. Apart from several successful strikes by agricultural workers in California, who took advantage of the perishable nature of farm produce to win small wage increases, and scattered unemployment demonstrations that won modest relief benefits, labor activism remained ineffective in the early 1930s. Coal miners in Harlan County, Kentucky; cigar makers in Tampa, Florida; and auto workers in Michigan all struck, but their efforts ended in bloody clashes, deaths, blacklisting, and few increases in wages, accommodations, or benefits.[3]

The election of Franklin D. Roosevelt and his dramatic implementation of New Deal legislation reinvigorated both the labor movement and the radical left with programs that aided and abetted labor organizing. Section 7(a) of the National Industrial Recovery Act (NIRA), dubbed the workers' "Magna Charta" by AFL head William Green, guaranteed workers the right to form unions and forbade owner interference in such organizing. The National Labor Relations Act (often dubbed the Wagner Act after its chief proponent New York senator Robert Wagner) reaffirmed workers' rights to organize and strengthened the National Labor Relations Board (NLRB) by empowering it to investigate charges of unfair labor practices. The Fair Labor Standards Act took worker protection a step further: it guaranteed a minimum wage, established a maximum number of working hours per week, provided time-and-a-half for overtime, and prohibited child labor. Thanks to these new protections, labor activism flourished. In 1932 there were approximately 800 strikes involving fewer than 300,000 workers. Those numbers increased to 1,695 strikes and 1.1 million participants in 1933 and 1,856 strikes and 1.5 million participants in 1934.[4] Equally important, workers began to win the strikes. In 1934, for example, the International Longshoreman's Association won a bloody strike in San Francisco that earned them union recognition. Simultaneously, teamsters in Minneapolis stuck for and won pay raises and a closed shop. Not every effort was a success, as labor lost an agricultural strike in January 1934 and a massive textile strike in September of that year, but workers gained momentum, and union membership tripled from 2.8 million in 1933 to 8.4 million by 1939.[5]

A brief alliance between labor and radical groups, made possible in large part by the CPUSA, added to organized labor's momentum. In 1935 the party ended the Third Period, an era begun in 1928 during which it refused to work with other groups and focused on revolution. In its place arose the Popular Front. During this period the CPUSA dropped calls for revolution, and instead sought alliances with labor organizations and focused on concrete economic gains for workers. Although Communists worked on factory floors with AFL organizers and made political pacts with Democrats, their most noteworthy ally during this era was the newly formed Congress of Industrial Organizations (CIO), a derivative AFL group. In 1937 Communists helped CIO-organized steel workers win a ten-percent wage increase, the eight-hour work day, and a forty-hour work week from U.S. Steel, then the world's largest company. That same year Communists helped CIO-sponsored auto workers gain recognition of their union (the United Auto Workers Union) during a sit-down strike against General Motors. The alliance between organized labor and radical organizations continued throughout the decade, and represented a high-water mark for labor organizing and union membership.

The Communists were not the only radicals who got involved with the labor movement during the Great Depression. Several political activists offered their own economic programs designed to revitalize the economy and benefit the working class. Louisiana governor and U.S. senator Huey P. Long blamed the crisis on the nation's economic elite, and he called for limiting the amount of wealth any one individual could possess and distributing the excess to the masses. Long pushed this agenda while in Louisiana by building roads, offering free schoolbooks, and taking on the entrenched powers that ran the state since the Civil War. Once he became senator and assumed national prominence, his "Share Our Wealth Program" called for the redistribution of wealth through a progressive income tax on the wealthy and a guaranteed minimum income for the working poor.

By contrast, radio evangelist "Father" Charles E. Coughlin believed it was big business and the banks that caused the crisis. He demanded greater government regulation of, and intervention in, the economy. Coughlin's National Union for Social Justice called for nationalizing major industries, supported the creation of a government-controlled central bank, and demanded laws to protect labor's right to organize.

Finally, physician Francis Townsend asserted that the crisis was caused by a lack of jobs and an inadequate level of spending. As a solution he offered the Townsend Plan, which proposed a monthly stipend of $200 for the elderly on the promise that they quit their jobs and spend all the money each month. The result, he believed, would be jobs for younger workers, increased spending, and a reinvigorated economy.

The inadequacy of these programs, combined with labor's no-strike pledge during World War II and the CPUSA's subsequent decision to return to a Third Period mindset, ultimately slowed organizing efforts. Despite that fact, with the help of organized labor, Reds, and radicals, American workers made substantial gains from where they had stood a decade prior.

One of the fundamental questions historians ask about such Depression-era organizing efforts is whether workers sought radical socioeconomic reforms or if they merely wanted bread-and-butter improvements to their standard of living. In other words, was labor radicalized to the point that it wanted to significantly remake the capitalist system or did it simply seek minor reforms within that system?

Irving Bernstein's three-volume survey of Depression-era labor activism is perhaps the most prominent statement of the radicalization theory. In his first volume, *The Lean Years* (1960), Bernstein examined the inherent weaknesses of the 1920s economy and asserted that "American workers were in a vulnerable position as the 1920's drew to a close, more so than in any earlier era in the nation's history."[6] This vulnerability led to "turbulence" and the demand for significant changes to the capitalist system. In *Turbulent Years* (1970), Bernstein examined the "turbulence," the demands, and the resulting changes. Among the most fundamental of reforms, he contended, were Section 7(a) of the NIRA and the Wagner Act, both of which made the factory a more agreeable place to work.[7] In the final volume of his study, *A Caring Society* (1985), Bernstein went one step further to contend that the New Deal ensured that "economic power, formerly concentrated in business and banking, was now shared with the government and with the trade union." The result of this shared governance was the creation of "a caring society, a welfare state that preserved many features of capitalism while assisting those too weak to help themselves."[8] Bernstein argued that labor "turbulence" was at the root of these reforms, and while that "turbulence" did not result in the destruction of the capitalist system, it did foster the creation of a radically new social safety net.

Bruce Nelson, in *Workers on the Waterfront* (1988), built on this argument and contended that the Great Depression was an era of "militancy and ideological ferment" during which labor demanded radical reforms that threatened the capitalist system. Specifically, labor tended toward syndicalism, which sought "to transform the world by fundamentally reshaping the pattern of authority and organization in the realm of work." Among the changes workers wanted were control of the means of production and distribution, and an intra-labor alliance to facilitate greater political influence. Nelson admitted that dock workers were exposed to more radical and cosmopolitan ideas than other workers, but nonetheless he contended that all laborers supported drastic socioeconomic reforms.[9]

Not all historians found activism or radicalism within the labor movement, and many argued that workers were far less politically motivated than Bernstein and Nelson believed. In his 2000 essay "Not So 'Turbulent Years': Another Look at America in the 1930s," Melvyn Dubofsky argued that despite a certain amount of working class radicalism, the average American worker was overcome by an "essential inertia" that resulted from racial and ethnic tensions, the lack of an obvious alternative to the contemporary socioeconomic order, and a cultural milieu that focused on "grab[bing] what few joys they could in an otherwise perilous existence."[10] Sidney Verba and Kay Lehman Schlozman agreed, in part, in their 1977 essay "Unemployment, Class Consciousness, and Radical Politics: What Didn't Happen in the Thirties." They perceived a similar inertia, but one that resulted from a lack of class consciousness as well as "the acceptance of the American dream of rugged individualism and optimism about the future."[11] All three historians acknowledged that had there not been this inertia, the "turbulence" of which Bernstein and Nelson wrote might have become a reality. Such was not the case, however, and they depicted workers as willing to concede control of the factory for better wages and the right to unionize.

In *Class Struggle in the New Deal* (1988), Rhonda Levine joined Dubofsky, Verba, and Schlozman with her assertion that workers focused almost solely on traditional economic demands. She went a step further and contended that because workers accepted the status quo they inadvertently undermined their own agenda. Since workers "never threatened the essential nature of the capitalist accumulative process," and never wanted to seize control of the means of production and distribution, they acceded to "the unchallenged hegemony of monopoly capitalism," the "diffusion of labor militancy," and the subordination of labor within the political process. By demanding only minor reform around the edges, Levine asserted, labor strengthened the capitalist system and weakened its own power within that system.[12]

David Milton, in *The Politics of U.S. Labor* (1982), straddled these competing interpretations with the contention that labor and management made a "great bargain" during the New Deal. The bargain occurred when "socialism and independent political action were traded off by the industrial working class for economic rights." Workers, he contended, may have had more radical demands than Dubofsky, Verba, Schlozman, and Levine asserted, but their radicalism did not prevent them from renouncing control of the factory for better wages. Thus, it was neither inertia nor a lack of radical sentiment that kept workers from destroying the capitalist system. Instead, they made a conscious push for short-term economic gains. Milton credited Roosevelt for overseeing this bargain by convincing management to accept the existence of unions and collective bargaining, and by persuading labor to drop demands for radical socioeconomic reform. Whoever was responsible, Milton ultimately agreed with Levine that in the long run labor lost. Workers gained better wages and union recognition, but "found themselves encased in a complex and formal network of legal rules" that limited future organizing efforts.[13]

The debates about what labor wanted inform another hotly contested question for historians: which group did Roosevelt support? Did the president see the New Deal as a way to assist industry and preserve the capitalist system or did he purposefully help labor with the goal of radically remaking the nation?

Sharon Smith supported the former argument. In *Subterranean Fire* (2006), she depicted the New Deal as an industrial tool designed not only to stabilize the capitalist system, but also to undermine labor. She contended that most New Deal legislation was pro-management, and asserted that when Roosevelt finally began to enact labor-friendly legislation it was only to "placate workers enough so that he could get on with the business of stabilizing the U.S. economy." Smith portrayed the pro-labor elements of the Second New Deal as "a calculated move to capture the loyalty of the ascending labor movement for the Democratic Party."[14] Finally, Smith argued that Section 7(a) of the NIRA and the Wagner Act, the laws to which most historians point as evidence of Roosevelt's pro-labor sympathies, were deliberately vague in order to provide management with room to circumvent union activism. Smith thus believed that Roosevelt passed pro-labor legislation only to pacify workers and win them to the Democratic Party, while the bulk of the New Deal's programs benefitted industry and protected the capitalist system.[15]

In *A New Deal for the American People* (1991), Roger Biles demonstrated that Roosevelt was "indifferent" to labor's needs and aided it unintentionally. He asserted that despite the indelible image of Roosevelt as a friend of labor, the president did not foresee the effects of Section 7(a), considered it innocuous, and did not intend it as a signal to organized labor. Furthermore, Biles asserted that the right to collective bargaining, or what he called Roosevelt's "greatest bequest to labor," was an accidental bequest.[16] He contended that the administration did little to enforce collective bargaining rules, allowed business brazenly to ignore the NLRB, and did nothing when industry negotiated in bad faith. Biles thus believed that Roosevelt had no intention of radically remaking the capitalist system; instead he sought to preserve it.[17]

Foster Rhea Dulles took the opposite perspective. In *Labor in America* (1966), he admitted that when Roosevelt took office he did not have a coherent plan to help labor. He did, however, favor labor. Dulles asserted that "a basic understanding and sympathy for the rights of labor were . . . inherent in the emerging philosophy of the New Deal. For the first time in our history a national administration was to make the welfare of industrial workers a direct concern of government and act on the principle that only organized labor could deal on equal terms with organized capital. Heretofore labor unions had been tolerated, they were now encouraged."

Dulles argued that this encouragement was obvious since Roosevelt replaced Section 7(a) with the Wagner Act and the Fair Labor Standards Act after the Supreme Court ruled the NIRA unconstitutional. If, as Smith and Biles contended, Roosevelt implemented labor policies maliciously or accidently, why was he so adamant to replace Section 7(a)? Dulles answered that question by explaining that the president realized the only way to protect workers was to give them the power to defend themselves. The New Deal thus was "pro-labor, but it was pro-labor in order to redress the balance that had been tipped in favor of industry." In balancing the playing field, he argued, the New Deal "looked primarily toward the well-being of the workers."[18]

These debates about what labor desired and who Roosevelt wanted to help form the basis for a third arena of debate. Historians pondered why workers went out on strike when millions were unemployed, and, more importantly, whether or not that activism had any effects on New Deal legislation.

David Brody, in a 1972 article entitled "Labor and the Great Depression," addressed the first of those questions when he asserted that "the labor upsurge of the 1930s must be seen as an extension of the existing trade union movement."[19] While labor was more active in the 1930s than in the 1920s, the decision to strike during the Great Depression was simply the continuation of traditional activism. Workers had no other means of improving their economic lot, so as they had for generations, and regardless of the Depression, they struck.

Robert Zeigler disagreed and, in *American Workers, American Unions* (1994), contended that the Depression "triggered the beginnings of renewed working-class activism." Due to racial, ethnic, and trade divisions, workers lacked class consciousness in the 1920s and early 1930s. That changed during the New Deal thanks to the revival of the AFL, the emergence of the CIO, and the "determination of working people to resist the victimization and distress that the Depression had brought." Zeigler believed this activism was new, and explained that "the most remarkable development of the early New Deal years was the explosion of organizing . . . in industries and trades with little previous unionism or with long records of defeat and desperation." Labor activism, Zeigler believed, was a consequence of the economic crisis. More importantly, this newfound activism was a positive impetus for reform; workers struck and the government responded with labor-friendly legislation.[20]

Michael Goldfield, in his 1989 essay "Worker Insurgency, Radical Organization, and New Deal Labor Legislation," agreed that working-class activism influenced the legislative process. The effects, however, were not positive. Goldfield asserted "that government regulation was necessary to constrain, limit, and control the increasingly militant labor movement" as well as to "slow [the] spread of communism, and diffuse serious challenges to the capitalist system."[21] The New Deal thus was a negative response, restricting and redirecting labor activism. Politicians were afraid of labor's growing power and restlessness, and passed legislation to restrain it.

Not all historians agreed that labor had such an effect. In *Political Ideologies of Organized Labor* (1978), Ruth Horowitz contended that labor activism had little influence on the New Deal. She explained that for most of its history the AFL adopted volunteerism—the idea that labor could not rely on any other agent for help and had to fight its own battles. Only after the New Deal demonstrated Roosevelt's willingness to work with labor did the AFL look to the federal government for aid. While the CIO sought such aid from its inception, Horowitz reminded readers that it was formed in 1935. As such, she made clear that the New Deal could not have been a response to labor's demands because until the mid-1930s labor was not demanding anything from the government.[22]

In their 1990 essay "Explaining New Deal Labor Policy" Theda Skocpol and Kenneth Finegold agreed with Horowitz that labor's influence on New Deal programs was minimal, but disagreed with her as to why. They asserted that "shifts in electoral politics, not increases in workplace militancy, were . . . what heightened 'labor influence' on legislation." In other words, Democrats passed labor legislation because they could. More congressional seats allowed Democrats to implement programs they had always supported but had never been able to pass. Skocpol and Finegold contended that "initial failures and frustrations under the NIRA led these official actors to believe that more state building had to be done—that is, it led them to formulate the strong substantive legal guarantees for independent unions and the means for federal enforcement against business resistance."[23] The weakness of early New Deal legislation, combined with the unconstitutionality of the NIRA, so outraged New Dealers that they determined to pass more labor-friendly legislation. Skocpol and Finegold thus believed that politics, not labor activism, facilitated the New Deal.

In *New Deals* (1994), Colin Gordon rejected the idea that labor activism influenced legislation, and instead contended that "federal social security and labor law grew directly from the search for competitive order and . . . recovery." From Gordon's perspective, industry used the New Deal to diminish the endemic chaos and uncertainty of the era and to stabilize the capitalist system. Thus, industry got exactly what it wanted, as the New Deal provided industrial peace and increased consumption at the modest cost of union recognition and moderate wage hikes.[24] While industry eventually found those costs too high and rejected many programs it initially championed, its early support was responsible for much of the legislation. According to Gordon, industry, not labor, facilitated the New Deal.

These traditional studies of Depression-era labor activism, and the questions they raised, rarely considered the efforts of radical groups, such as the CPUSA. In the last thirty years, scholars examined how the radical left influenced organized labor and laborers. In so doing, the question historians focused on who benefitted the most from this relationship.

In *Labor and Communism* (1977), Bert Cochran argued that labor emerged victorious. Cochran contended that the CPUSA first attracted labor's notice by spotlighting the hardships of coal miners during the Harlan County, Kentucky, strike in 1931. The publicity surrounding the strike facilitated union efforts nationwide, and Communists became highly sought after labor organizers. Once the organizational campaigns were complete, however, labor dropped its Communist allies out of fear that a continued association would undermine its achievements. Cochran summed up this relationship by noting that when questioned about the advisability of working with Communists, CIO leader John L. Lewis responded: "Who gets the bird, the hunter or the dog?"[25] Cochran argued that while labor enjoyed the fruits of this relationship, the Communists, like the dog, gained little.

Similarly, Fraser Ottanelli, in *The Communist Party of the United States of America* (1991), noted that Communists provided the army of skilled and experienced organizers that the CIO needed for its drive into the steel and auto industries. The CIO accepted these organizers because Popular Front "Communists placed the consideration of strengthening the union movement above their own objective of bringing about fundamental changes in U.S. society." In making this move to the political center, the CPUSA won access to the working class. That access was limited, however, and "Communists never gained full acceptance within the CIO. Recruited when needed and closely watched at all times, the moment they finished organizing or gained a following they were quickly transferred or more often summarily dismissed."[26] Despite moderating its politics, Ottanelli asserted, the CPUSA remained too radical for the CIO and the communists gained little from the alliance.

Harvey Klehr, in *The Heyday of American Communism* (1984), reached a different conclusion. Klehr asserted that "the benefits the Communists got from the CIO . . . were plentiful." He noted that "for the first time in its history the Party could claim that it was not only in touch with the union movement, but helping to lead it." Klehr claimed that the CIO "hired, promoted, and aided . . . Communists" with the result that "no other organization so critical in American society had so strong a Communist influence." Klehr admitted, however, that the CPUSA paid a price for these gains. Specifically, the Communists "denuded their own organizations," "relinquished the rigid control they had traditionally exercised over their trade union cadres," and "gave up some long-cherished principles." The Communists accepted this price, and Klehr believed that both the CPUSA and CIO benefitted from the alliance.[27]

The aforementioned works examined the relationship between the CPUSA and labor unions as part of larger studies of the Communist Party. Other historians took a more focused approach. Robin D. G. Kelley's *Hammer and Hoe* (1990) offered a detailed analysis of the interracial Communist movement in Alabama. Kelley noted that the CPUSA-led unionization efforts in and around Birmingham so scared local and state politicians that as early as 1930 they supported AFL efforts to unionize white textile workers. Kelley thus credited the CPUSA with making other unions appear acceptable to management and politicians. More importantly, he asserted that Communists pushed the AFL, and later the CIO, to ever greater activism, supplementing that activism when it fell short. Kelley explained that "[w]hile it is impossible to accurately measure the Party's influence in the labor movement, it is clear that the Communists' impact was far greater than their numbers indicate."[28]

Kelley addressed the important role Communists played in organizing the state's agricultural workers, especially their support for the Sharecroppers Union. Formed in 1931, the union faced violent opposition from local landowners who rejected the union's demands for increased wages and improved living conditions. Despite violence and limited white membership, by 1936 it numbered 10,000 members and spread into Mississippi and Louisiana. Although the union dissolved soon thereafter, Kelley contended that the Sharecroppers Union, and all of the Communist Party's efforts in Alabama, "influenced liberal, labor, and civil rights organizations" for decades to come, and benefitted everyone involved.[29]

A number of historians joined Kelley to study radical work among farm laborers. In *Red Harvest* (1982), Lowell Dyson examined early Communist Party efforts to convince farm workers that they could be saved only by destroying the capitalist system. When that proved too radical, the CPUSA tried to organize farm workers as they had industrial workers and demanded specific economic reforms for the agricultural sector. Dyson concluded that the scattered nature of farming, the lack of organizers, and the continued fear of communism doomed the effort, and provided neither the farmers nor the party any substantive benefits.[30]

In *Cry from the Cotton* (1971), Donald Grubbs reviewed the activities of the Southern Tenant Farmers Union (STFU) and reached a slightly different conclusion. Formed in 1934 by tenant farmers and Socialists in Tyronza, Arkansas, by 1938 the union was an interracial, multistate organization of 35,000 members. Internal struggles and a problematic alliance with the CIO ultimately doomed the union, but Grubbs contended that the STFU encouraged Roosevelt and Secretary of Agriculture Henry Wallace to create the Farm Security Administration (FSA) in 1937. He also concluded that "more significant than the impact of specific STFU proposals on specific persons . . . was the role the union played in creating the climate of opinion in which the United States' only significant assault on rural poverty could be undertaken."[31] Grubbs asserted that the STFU changed the nation's perception of what was possible in the realm of agricultural organizing.

As important as their work in agricultural and industrial unions was, the CPUSA had more unemployed members than employed for most of the New Deal. The CPUSA spent much of its time fighting for and organizing the jobless, and historians examined those efforts as well. In *The Unemployed People's Movement* (2009), James Lorence asserted that Communists helped out-of-work Georgians band "together to purposefully exploit the new opportunities offered by an increasingly activist federal government."[32] This occurred most prominently through unemployment councils, which functioned like industrial and agricultural unions and sought increased relief benefits, additional work programs, bans on evictions, and moratoriums on mortgage payments for those who lost their jobs. Lorence noted that these councils not only ameliorated the worst aspects of the Depression, but showed the unemployed the power of organization and ensured that once workers returned to work they would carry with them a penchant for union activism. Lorence explained that the CPUSA provided both long-term and short-term benefits for all workers, employed or not.[33]

Radical political activists Huey Long, Father Coughlin, and Francis Townsend also have been the focus of recent historical inquiry. Historians were intrigued by what motivated them, what they hoped to gain from their efforts, and how their aspirations affected the working class. Contemporary historians often accused the men of being fascists who sought to organize, inspire, and lead "irrational, antidemocratic uprisings" for their own political gain.[34] Donald Warren's *Radio Priest* (1996) suggested that Father Coughlin held some fascist sensibilities. He defined Coughlin as a demagogue who used the radio to scare the masses for his own benefit. Warren went further and contended that Coughlin had long-standing connections with European fascist movements. He reported that Coughlin wrote a letter to Mussolini in 1933, that he received funds, albeit indirectly, from Nazi Germany, and that from his earliest days he both associated with and supported known fascist groups. While Warren did not directly accuse Coughlin of seeking a fascist overthrow of the American government, he presented the priest as a man with "significant political power" who became a legitimate threat to the nation by arousing the working poor to foster his own radical political agenda.[35]

Instead of linking these radical politicians to fascism, most historians presented them as simple demagogues who worked within the framework of American government and never truly threatened the nation's democratic underpinnings. Richard White Jr.'s *Kingfish* (2006) offered a prime example of those who viewed Long as a demagogue. He refused to accuse Long of being a fascist, but instead described him as a "power addict" whose goal was "acquiring absolute power." White, therefore, contended that whatever else Long did, it was tangential to his real goal of helping himself. Indeed, White noted that for all the good Long did in building roads, providing textbooks, and helping the working class, he left Louisiana deeply in debt and nearly bankrupt. Similarly, he noted that Long's support for ending the poll tax on poor whites was done for his personal political gain, not because it was morally unjust. White admitted that Long initially sought power to help the working poor, but he believed that eventually gaining power became Long's main focus.[36]

In *Demagogues in the Depression* (1969), David Bennett presented both Father Coughlin and Francis Townsend as messianic demagogues who offered programmatic panaceas that spoke to the social, economic, and political fears faced by the nation's working poor. Bennett explained that the two men seduced their "followers into an emotional attachment . . . that would effectively block any group awareness of either the real sources of unhappiness or the real means of solution." He described both men as disingenuous leaders who were willing to lie and exaggerate to achieve political prominence. Although they functioned within the American model of democracy, and thus were not fascists, Bennett believed they were focused on themselves and did little to aid the working class.[37]

Similarly, in *When Movements Matter* (2006), Edwin Amenta noted that while Francis Townsend truly wanted to help the elderly and the working class, he also dearly wanted "to end the Depression and thus become the Lincolnesque figure he fancied himself." Although his plan won the support of many elderly Americans, neither the AFL nor the CIO supported it, and the working class looked to other economic remedies. In the end, Amenta described Townsend as more of an ideologue than a demagogue; regardless of the term, his influence on the working class was minimal.[38]

Other historians gave the three men more credit and present them as "the vanguards of a great progressive social transformation."[39] These historians cast Long, Coughlin, and Townsend as leaders of the larger effort to cure the nation's ills by remaking America's socioeconomic structure. In *Huey Long* (1969) and in the introduction to the 1996 edition of Huey Long's autobiography *Every Man a King,* T. Harry Williams described Long as a clearheaded and Machiavellian politician who used his tactical skills to help the poor. He contended that Long entered politics with this reformist impulse fully formed and that his efforts to expand his power, both in Louisiana and Washington, D.C., were based on the belief that the more power he had the more people he could help. Williams admitted that Long eventually overreached and confused his means with his ends, but ultimately he concluded that Long's drive for power was wholesome and substantial because it succeeded in regulating the powerful for the benefit of the masses.[40]

Charles Tull, in *Father Coughlin and the New Deal* (1965), offered a similar assessment of the Catholic radio priest. Tull asserted that Coughlin fully accepted the Progressive Era's traditional demand for greater government intervention in the economy. He argued that Coughlin had no political agenda or ulterior motive, that his interest lay solely in the betterment of mankind, and that he acted out of kindness and Christian charity. Indeed, Tull stressed that Coughlin's National Union for Social Justice program supported the Catholic Church's traditional search for social justice as found in papal encyclicals by Pius XI and Leo XIII. He concluded that Coughlin was a clear-headed reformer who won wide national support from the working class, among other groups, because of his call for increased governmental control of banks and big business.[41]

Finally, a group of historians contended that Long, Coughlin, and Townsend simply wanted to preserve a society "in which the individual retained control of his own life and livelihood; in which power resided in visible, accessible institutions; in which wealth was equitably (if not necessarily equally) shared." From this perspective, the three were conservative forces who sought to "defend the autonomy of the individual and the independence of the community against encroachments from the modern industrial state." In *Voices of Protest* (1982), Alan Brinkley offered the preeminent version of this perspective. He explained that both Long and Coughlin believed the nation's economic travails were the result of large, faceless institutions destroying the nation's small farmers, bankers, and merchants. Their agenda for saving the nation, therefore, was to take on those powerful forces in the name of returning power to local institutions. In the process, Brinkley argued, both men affirmed the widespread fear that traditional social values were threatened, offered scapegoats for the masses to blame, and offered platforms of reform to return the nation to a time when the individual was preeminent. As a result, both messages were popular with a wide array of Americans, especially the working poor.[42]

All of these questions, and the varied answers rendered, are relevant to understanding the efforts made by labor groups, radical organizations, and radical political activists during the Depression.

Historians studying such efforts, however, all face one final question: who benefitted most from the New Deal? In other words, "Who won?"

Although the goals of each activist differed, most historians agree that Long, Coughlin, and Townsend enjoyed brief moments of success. Each earned fame and widespread support among the poor and working class, but eventually found themselves subsumed by the power of Roosevelt and the New Deal. Neither their supporters nor the workers gained much from the efforts of these radical activists.

By contrast, most historians agree that the CPUSA took advantage of the renewed activism of the era to gain access to the working class and increase its membership rolls. Kelley and Klehr conceded that the party was unable to sustain those gains beyond the era, but both agreed that it emerged from the 1930s at least marginally stronger. Cochran, Dyson, and Ottanelli, by contrast, believed that labor duped the party, and that any gains the party made were largely the result of a disingenuous and unsustainable move to the political center.

The victories by labor during the 1930s were more obvious and substantive: the right to organize, a federal agency to investigate unfair labor practices, a minimum wage, a maximum work week, overtime pay, and the abolition of child labor. Bernstein, Dulles, and Zeigler argued that these gains allowed labor to emerge from the Depression in a very strong position. Levine, Milton, Smith, Biles, Goldfield, and Gordon, however, contended that while the gains labor made were noteworthy, workers remained trapped in a system that continued to exploit them, even if under less onerous circumstances. Industry, by contrast, emerged from the decade empowered; it gave up little for a stable economy and a subordinate labor force.

Historians wrote on the struggles that organized labor, radical political organizations, and radical political activists faced during the Depression. The result has been a focus on six fundamental questions: what did labor seek, with whom did President Roosevelt side, what legislative effect did labor activism have, what role did radical groups play, what role did radical politicians play, and, ultimately, who won? Far from reaching a consensus, historians remain divided. This division continues to inspire academic inquiry, and new historians regularly join the fray to leave their imprint on the debates. Whatever their answers, what remains clear is that organized labor, Reds, and radicals both affected and were affected by the Depression, and their place in this era remains primed for continued historical interpretation.

NOTES

1. Roger Biles, *A New Deal for the American People* (DeKalb: Northern Illinois University Press, 1991), 5.

2. Fraser Ottanelli, *The Communist Party of the United States of America: From the Depression to World War II* (New Brunswick, NJ: Rutgers University Press, 1991), 15.

3. Biles, *A New Deal,* 14.

4. Sharon Smith, *Subterranean Fire: A History of Working Class Radicalism in the United States* (Chicago: Haymarket Books, 2006), 104.

5. Biles, *A New Deal,* 167.

6. Irving Bernstein, *The Lean Years: A History of the American Worker, 1920-1933* (Boston: Houghton Mifflin, 1960), 505.

7. Irving Bernstein, *Turbulent Years: A History of the American Worker, 1933-1941* (Boston: Houghton Mifflin, 1970), 787-89.

8. Irving Bernstein, *A Caring Society: The New Deal, the Worker, and the Great Depression* (Boston: Houghton Mifflin, 1985), 275.

9. Bruce Nelson, *Workers on the Waterfront: Seamen, Longshoremen, and Unionism in the 1930s* (Urbana: University of Illinois Press, 1988), 1, 6, 268.

10. Melvyn Dubofsky, "Not So 'Turbulent Years': Another Look at America in the 1930s," in *Hard Work: The Making of Labor History,* ed. Melvyn Dubofsky (Urbana: University of Illinois Press, 2000), 142, 147.

11. Sidney Verba and Kay Lehman Schlozman, "Unemployment, Class Consciousness, and Radical Politics: What Didn't Happen in the Thirties," *The Journal of Politics* 39 (May 1977): 322.

12. Rhonda Levine, *Class Struggle in the New Deal: Industrial Labor, Industrial Capital, and the State* (Lawrence: University of Kansas Press, 1988), 4, 173.

13. David Milton, *The Politics of U.S. Labor: From the Great Depression to the New Deal* (New York: Monthly Review Press, 1982), 10, 151, 183.

14. Smith, *Subterranean Fire,* 117, 119.

15. Ibid., 117.

16. Biles, *A New Deal,* 168, 171.

17. Ibid., 230-32.

18. Foster Rhea Dulles, *Labor in America: A History,* third edition (New York: Thomas Y. Crowell, 1966), 264, 267, 287.

19. David Brody, "Labor and the Great Depression: The Interpretative Prospect," *Labor History* 13 (Spring 1972): 237.

20. Robert Zeigler, *American Workers, American Unions* (Baltimore: Johns Hopkins University Press, 1994), 33, 54, 67, 71, 89.

21. Michael Goldfield, "Worker Insurgency, Radical Organization, and New Deal Labor Legislation," *The American Political Science Review* 83 (December 1989): 1258, 1274, 1276.

22. Ruth Horowitz, *Political Ideologies of Organized Labor: The New Deal Era* (New Brunswick, NJ: Transaction Books, 1978), 10-11, 241.

23. Theda Skocpol and Kenneth Finegold, "Explaining New Deal Labor Policy," *The American Political Science Review* 84 (December 1990): 1300-301.

24. Colin Gordon, *New Deals: Business, Labor and Politics in America, 1920-1935* (New York: Cambridge University Press, 1994), 2-3.

25. Bert Cochran, *Labor and Communism: The Conflict that Shaped America* (Princeton: Princeton University Press, 1977), 97.

26. Ottanelli, *The Communist Party,* 151, 157.

27. Harvey Klehr, *The Heyday of American Communism: The Depression Decade* (New York: Basic Books, 1984), 240, 250-51.

28. Robin D. G. Kelley, *Hammer and Hoe: Alabama Communists during the Great Depression* (Chapel Hill: University of North Carolina Press, 1990), 76.

29. Ibid., 219.

30. Lowell Dyson, *Red Harvest: The Communist Party and American Farmers* (Lincoln: University of Nebraska Press, 1982), 202.

31. Donald H. Grubbs, *Cry from the Cotton: The Southern Tenant Farmers' Union and the New Deal* (Fayetteville: University of Arkansas Press, 2000), 143.

32. James J. Lorence, *The Unemployed People's Movement: Leftists, Liberals, and Labor in Georgia, 1929-1941* (Athens: University of Georgia Press, 2009), 224.

33. Ibid., 226-29.

34. Alan Brinkley, *Voices of Protest: Huey Long, Father Coughlin and the Great Depression* (New York: Vintage Press, 1983), xi.

35. Donald Warren, *Radio Priest: Charles Coughlin, the Father of Hate Radio* (New York: The Free Press, 1996), 1.

36. Richard D. White Jr., *Kingfish: The Reign of Huey P. Long* (New York: Random House, 2006), 91, 231.

37. David Bennett, *Demagogues in the Depression: American Radicals and the Union Party, 1932-1936* (New Brunswick, NJ: Rutgers University Press, 1969), 4.

38. Edwin Amenta, *When Movements Matter: The Townsend Plan and the Rise of Social Security* (Princeton: Princeton University Press, 2006), 102.

39. Brinkley, *Voices of Protest,* xi.

40. T. Harry Williams, *Huey Long* (New York: Vintage Books, 1981), 283, 326; Huey Long, *Every Man a King: The Autobiography of Huey P. Long* (New York: Da Capo Press, 1996), xxii.

41. Charles Tull, *Father Coughlin and the New Deal* (Syracuse: Syracuse University Press, 1965), 73.

42. Brinkley, *Voices of Protest,* xi.

PART III

Legacies and Outcomes

Overseas Intervention, the Rise of Fascism Abroad, and the Origins of World War II

PETER LUDDINGTON-FORONJY

Historians have divided Franklin D. Roosevelt's presidency into two distinct periods. The first encompasses the years from 1933 through 1938. Historians of Roosevelt's presidency generally agree that during this period Roosevelt turned his back on foreign involvements and focused his attention on ameliorating the hardships caused by the Great Depression. Within this first period, Roosevelt and Congress enacted many of the landmark pieces of legislation that symbolized both the achievements and limitations of Roosevelt's economic reform agenda, which came to be known as the New Deal.

The second period of Roosevelt's presidency began in approximately 1938 when Roosevelt's attention shifted away from domestic reform to focus on international affairs and concluded with his death in April 1945. Roosevelt's abandonment of his domestic economic reform agenda coincided with a crisis in foreign affairs. That crisis escalated in March of 1938 when Hitler ended Austria's independence and made that country part of Germany. It reached its nadir in the fall of 1938, when the leaders of the British and French governments met Adolf Hitler at Munich, and in an attempt to prevent the start of another war, agreed to Hitler's demand that part of Czechoslovakia be given to Germany. Many historians pointed to these events as the crucial moments when Roosevelt returned to his roots as an internationalist, abandoned any further attempts to reform the domestic economy, and became almost exclusively preoccupied with how the United States should respond to the looming threat of war in Europe and the ongoing conflict in Asia. Consequently, historians defined the final six years of Roosevelt's presidency within the parameters of his administration's struggle to rebuild the nation's armed forces, the effort to secure an alliance with Britain and the Soviet Union, the war against the Axis Powers, and finally, his conceptualization of foreign relations for the United States in the postwar world. Historians have studied these interconnected themes through a variety of paradigms.

Many scholars have examined how the war influenced the nature and direction of liberal reform that started during the New Deal. In *The New Men of Power* (1948), sociologist C. Wright Mills argued that postwar liberalism abandoned its traditional role as an opponent of capitalism. According to Mills, leaders within the liberal community became part of the nation's political power structure and were more concerned with protecting their own interests than they were in reforming the domestic economy.[1] Mills's view that postwar liberalism had gone astray attracted a wide audience beyond the field of sociology. His ideas influenced a generation of historians who came of age during the tumultuous 1960s.

Drawing upon Mills's analysis, historians argued that Roosevelt's approach to fighting the war against the Axis powers was the source of postwar liberalism's acceptance of the economic status quo. Many historians argued that in response to the growing menace of Nazi Germany and particularly after the attack at Pearl Harbor, Roosevelt and his supporters formed an alliance with corporate America to supply the materials the government needed in the fight against the Axis powers. They cited Roosevelt's decision to work with corporate America as proof that liberal supporters in government halted domestic reform efforts, and thus liberalism. In *The Rise and Fall of the People's Century* (1973), Norman Markowitz claimed that beginning in 1941, liberals began to suggest in their writings that the war against the Axis powers presented an opportunity for Roosevelt to create an international New Deal. Such a worldwide effort would spread democratic principles and lay the foundation for the start of a "People's Century" that would emerge at the end of the war. Markowitz contended that the Roosevelt administration failed to embrace a genuine effort to restructure the economy, and instead employed the rhetoric of social liberalism in order to garner popular support for the war. Markowitz argued that the administration's rhetoric during World War II suggested that Roosevelt favored replacing capitalism with a form of socialism. However, in practice, the Roosevelt administration and its liberal supporters rejected socialism and favored reforming corporate America.[2] Similarly, labor historian Nelson Lichtenstein argued, in *Labor's War at Home: The CIO in World War II* (1995), that the Roosevelt administration was unwilling to challenge the prevailing capitalist power structure, and offered only mild reforms.[3]

In *Noble Abstractions: American Liberal Intellectuals and World War II* (1999), Frank Warren studied the role of the liberal left during the war years. He claimed that liberal intellectuals supported the war effort as early as December 1941. Warren explained that liberals viewed the war as an idealistic struggle against the evils of fascism, and they believed that the defeat of the Axis powers would usher in a new democratic order in the postwar era. In their writings, intellectuals like Freda Kirchwey and Archibald MacLeish seemed to suggest that the postwar era would be a time when the United States would replace capitalism with democratic socialism. According to Warren, America's liberal intellectuals were not able to push for the economic reforms that they believed were necessary, simply because during the war they had become cheerleaders for the Roosevelt administration and had thus lost their political independence. This transformation made it almost impossible for liberals to question Roosevelt's reliance upon and cooperation with corporate America.[4]

The idea that Roosevelt ended his efforts at reforming the domestic economy after 1938 has recently been challenged. The election of Ronald Reagan as president in 1980 marked a return of conservative ideology in national politics and the resumption of a debate about the role of the federal government in economic affairs and the daily lives of Americans. This debate sparked a reassessment of the merits of many of the domestic reforms that were enacted during the 1930s. At the same time, the scope of Roosevelt's economic reform agenda, particularly during World War II, garnered new interest among historians.

In *Designing a New America: The Origins of New Deal Planning, 1890-1943* (1999), Patrick Reagan challenged the prevailing consensus that Roosevelt ended his attempt to reform the domestic economy in 1938. Reagan argued that Roosevelt viewed the conflict against the Axis powers, in part, as a competition between competing economic systems. He stated that between 1937 and 1943, Roosevelt, in response to "the totalitarian planning in the Soviet Union, Nazi Germany, fascist Italy, and a militarized Japan," developed a "distinctly American national [economic reform agenda] based upon a healthy mistrust of state power, a desire for business-government cooperation, the use of social science expertise, and inclusion of the ordinary citizens as consumer, not just producer." Reagan claimed that this agenda expanded upon the reforms of the New Deal implemented prior to the war. He suggested that a Third New Deal began in 1937 and reached its zenith in March 1943 when Roosevelt submitted to Congress the National Resources Planning Board's (NRPB) multivolume report, which discussed the domestic economic reforms necessary to ensure economic prosperity in the postwar years. The administration was on record as favoring the expansion of America's Social Security system to include "cradle to grave" protection for all citizens.[5]

The NRPB's report called for the federal government to assume responsibility for maintaining a full-employment economy in which individuals who wanted to work would be able to find a job. To accomplish this goal, the report proposed increasing the purchasing power of working-class Americans. According to Reagan, Roosevelt expected that if Americans earned more they would be able to consume more, and this higher rate of consumption would spur private enterprise to greater levels of productivity. Further, this kind of economy would lead to increased levels of employment as businesses expanded to meet the increase in demand for products and services. Reagan argued that Roosevelt wanted these reforms to become part of the economic reconstruction that would define the postwar era.[6]

Cass Sunstein, a law professor at the University of Chicago, contended that Roosevelt pursued an economic reform agenda throughout the war. Like Reagan, Sunstein argued that Roosevelt viewed the war against the Axis powers not only as a matter of the survival of political democracy but also as a chance to reform the capitalist system in order to provide a better standard of living, in the postwar era, for workers throughout the industrialized world.

In *The Second Bill of Rights: FDR's Unfinished Revolution and Why We Need It More Than Ever* (2004), Sunstein extended Roosevelt's attempt at economic reforms until 1944. During the 1944 State of the Union Address, Roosevelt called for the enactment of an "Economic Bill of Rights," which Sunstein believed was a genuine effort to place before Congress a series of economic reforms that would define the postwar social contract between government and the people. Roosevelt described new government obligations and individual rights, including "the right to a useful and remunerative job; the right to earn enough to provide adequate food, clothing and recreation; the right of farmers to earn a decent living; the right of businessmen to be free from monopolies and unfair trade practices; the right of every family to a decent home; the right to adequate medical care; the right to a good education; and the right to protection from economic fears of old age." Sunstein called this speech "the greatest of the twentieth century" and part of a reform movement that continued throughout the war years.[7]

Robert Dallek's *Franklin D. Roosevelt and American Foreign Policy, 1932-1945* (1979) remains the definitive account of Roosevelt's conduct of foreign policy. According to Dallek, prior to being elected president in 1932, Roosevelt was an outspoken advocate for the principles of internationalism and cooperation between nations. However, the economic calamity of the Great Depression coupled with the growing perception among Americans that the country's participation in World War I had been a mistake caused a shift in public opinion about international involvement. Throughout the 1930s, Americans supported politicians who espoused the principles of isolationism. Dallek argued that in response to the realities of domestic politics, Roosevelt downplayed his internationalist credentials during his first two terms in office.[8]

By 1938, however, Roosevelt returned to his internationalist principles as he confronted the growing menace of Nazi Germany. Dallek explained that although a majority of the public remained convinced that American foreign policy should reflect an adherence to the tenets of isolationism, Roosevelt began to challenge this view. Beginning with his quarantine speech in 1937, Roosevelt started to build an argument that Nazi Germany was a threat to the survival of democratic governments around the world, including the United States.[9]

According to Dallek, from 1938 until 1941, Roosevelt pursued a number of initiatives designed to support democracies in Europe. At the same time, Roosevelt rebuilt America's armed forces, whose budgets had been severely reduced since the end of World War I. When the European war started in September 1939, Dallek argued, the American public was still not convinced that Germany's aggression presented a threat to the United States. As a consequence, Americans still opposed sending direct military aide or providing economic assistance to France or Great Britain for fear that such action might drag the nation into another European conflict.[10]

In May 1940, the German military swept across Western Europe. By June, the British Army retreated from mainland Europe and France surrendered. These events alarmed many Americans, who feared the prospect of Germany's domination of Europe. Although Roosevelt was mindful that Americans did not want to become active participants in another European war, Dallek wrote that Roosevelt seized upon this change in public opinion as an opportunity to remind the nation the war pitted Western democracies against fascist regimes. Roosevelt began to articulate the idea that the defeat of the Axis regimes was an opportunity for Western democracies to create, in the postwar era, a new morality in foreign affairs.

In order to convince Americans that war would be worth the sacrifice, Roosevelt maintained that the country needed to adopt a set of humanitarian war aims that would define what was at stake in the conflict.[11]

On August 9, 1941, Roosevelt met Winston Churchill aboard the USS *Augusta* off the eastern coast of Newfoundland, Canada, where the two leaders signed the Atlantic Charter. This document included Roosevelt's eight-part platform of democratic ideas designed to be implemented after the war ended. His postwar reconstruction plan envisioned a new era in international relations in which countries embraced the principles of free trade and developed institutions that would promote international cooperation. The Atlantic Charter also called upon governments to enact legislation that would improve labor standards and expand their systems of social security—the most lasting initiative of the New Deal.[12] After the attack at Pearl Harbor on December 7, 1941, the United States became an active participant in the war, and all the countries that opposed the Axis nations agreed to the principles that Roosevelt articulated in the Atlantic Charter. This alliance became the basis for the United Nations.[13]

Dallek challenged the idea that Roosevelt abandoned his liberal principles during the war. Roosevelt needed to work with corporate America; nevertheless, this did not preclude the president from pursuing the international reforms he believed were needed to secure both a lasting peace and a better standard of living for ordinary workers after the war. Dallek also refuted the argument that Roosevelt's decision to keep the development of the atomic bomb a secret from Stalin was the catalyst that led to the start of the Cold War. According to Dallek, suspicions between the Western democracies and the Soviet Union predated the war. The Grand Alliance was formed because Britain, the United States, and the Soviet Union recognized that Hitler's regime was a far greater threat. When the war ended, the old antagonisms resurfaced.[14]

In the late 1950s and early 1960s a series of clashes between the United States and the Soviet Union represented potential sparks that might escalate the Cold War into a nuclear conflict. In response to the ever-present fear of a nuclear war, historians investigated the origins of the Cold War. In particular, many historians examined the significance of Roosevelt's decision, during World War II, to keep the development of the atomic bomb a secret from Stalin.

Gar Alperovitz's *Atomic Diplomacy* (1965) was one of the first studies on the importance of atomic technology in the formation of the postwar world. In this work, Alperovitz argued that the development of the atomic bomb fundamentally altered the way the United States conducted the pursuit of its foreign policy objectives.[15] Alperovitz's ideas influenced a generation of historians, who reexamined Roosevelt's role in the development of the bomb. In *A World Destroyed: The Atomic Bomb and the Grand Alliance* (1975), Martin Sherwin argued that during World War II, the Grand Alliance between the Soviet Union, Great Britain, and the United States was genuine and could have been extended into the postwar era. However, according to Sherwin, Roosevelt's decision not to include Stalin in the development of the atomic bomb destroyed the Grand Alliance and sowed the seeds of distrust between the United States and the Soviet Union that led to the start of the Cold War.[16]

As Patrick Reagan, Cass Sunstein, and others demonstrated, the prevailing interpretation dividing Roosevelt's presidency into two distinct periods needs re-evaluation. The struggle to reform the domestic economy and to ensure that the benefits of capitalism were shared by a majority of Americans did not end with the start of World War II. As Conrad Black argued in *Franklin Delano Roosevelt: Champion of Freedom* (2003), Roosevelt fused his economic reform agenda with the war against fascism. According to Black, Roosevelt led the "democracies to victory in the war" and his economic reforms prepared the way for "America and its allies . . . to promote the economics of generally distributed wealth everywhere in the world."[17] In *Freedom From Fear* (1999), historian David Kennedy took a much different view of Roosevelt. He contended that Roosevelt had very little to do with the economic prosperity that followed the end of World War II, suggesting instead that this development had more to do with the establishment of global economic interdependence in the postwar years.[18]

The largest shift in the historiography of this subfield relates to Roosevelt's understanding that foreign affairs and the pursuit of economic reforms were integral realms. Roosevelt espoused this dual concept throughout his political career. In the book *Whither Bound?* (1926), Roosevelt argued that the conflict between foreign affairs and economic reform started during the Great War and continued. He claimed that the leaders at Versailles failed to understand that the trajectory of industrial capitalism was leading inexorably toward the unification of each individual nation's economy into an all encompassing global economic unit. According to Roosevelt, the creation of this new economic order was the great "unfinished task" left to the generation that came of age after World War I, and he called upon all "liberal thinkers" to lend their support.[19]

Six years later, during his presidential campaign, Roosevelt returned to the idea that the world needed to create a new international economic order. This time, however, there was an urgency not found in his earlier work. Roosevelt claimed that "[o]ut of economic disputes arise the irritations which lead to competitive armaments and are fruitful causes of war." Future wars, Roosevelt stated, could be avoided if governments were to abandon the predatory practices of economic nationalism. In order to achieve this goal, he believed that the federal government would have to make the promotion of rational "economic interchange . . . the most important item" in the country's foreign affairs.[20]

To avoid another global conflict, Roosevelt argued that the United States, and by implication all governments, needed to pursue "the development of an economic declaration of rights."[21] According to Roosevelt, this new social contract would include the establishment of old-age, sickness, and unemployment insurance.[22] However, Roosevelt insisted that expanding the social safety net was not enough. While these reforms were necessary in order to protect individuals from the vicissitudes of an industrial economy, he argued that nations needed to embrace a new mode of international trade in order to end the current depression and to prevent it from recurring in the future.[23]

According to Roosevelt, in order to sustain a global system of trade, nations needed to shift from an economic model that favored production to one that promoted consumption. In order to promote domestic consumption, in May 1932 he called for increasing the purchasing power of farmers and laborers even if it meant that "the reward to capital, especially capital which is speculative, will have to be less."[24] Four months later, in September 1932, Roosevelt stated that every man had "a right to make a comfortable living" and government "owes everyone an avenue to possess himself of a portion of that plenty sufficient for his needs, through his own work."[25] Roosevelt argued that this agenda, which he referred to as his "reconstruction" plan, did not represent a break with the American political tradition.[26] Instead, the implementation of this plan would be the fulfillment of "the obligations of the apparent Utopia which Jefferson imagined for us in 1776 and which Jefferson, Theodore Roosevelt and Wilson sought to bring to realization."[27] Thus, Roosevelt's reconstruction plan was his rendezvous with destiny. Roosevelt condensed these ideas into the book *Looking Forward* (1933), which appeared just after his election.[28]

After his victory, Roosevelt and his administration promoted the goal of international economic cooperation. With Roosevelt's approval, Secretary of Agriculture Henry Wallace published *America Must Choose: The Advantages and Disadvantages of Nationalism, of World Trade, and of a Planned Middle Course* (1934) and *New Frontiers* (1934), both of which discussed world economic policy. In these books, Wallace reiterated Roosevelt's contention that as the world's creditor nation the United States had to assume responsibility for creating a new global economy that had as its "social objective" securing a new Economic Bill of Rights, not just for Americans but for people throughout the world in order to avoid what Wallace referred to as "another orgy of human killing."[29]

As the United States prepared for entry into World War II, Roosevelt's domestic social and economic policies spilled into foreign affairs. Historians have started to construct a new argument that recognizes that Roosevelt sought to expand the system of social security legislation throughout the industrialized world as a part of his overall strategy for discrediting the political philosophy of fascism and for building a wartime alliance to oppose the Axis powers. Roosevelt stated, in a nationwide address delivered on November 6, 1941, that "social problems and economic problems were not separate water-tight compartments in the international . . . [or] national sphere." And he declared, "[i]n international as in national affairs, economic policy can no longer be an end in itself. It is merely a means for achieving social objectives."[30]

During the war, Roosevelt demonstrated economic objectives. Roosevelt and Adolph Hitler understood that the victor of the war would have the opportunity to shape and control the world's economy. Each leader possessed a very distinctive ideological view of what the postwar settlement would look like. Gerhard Weinberg argued, in *Visions of Victory: The Hopes of Eight World Leaders of World War II* (2005), that when Hitler invaded Poland in September of 1939 it represented the first step in his plan to assert German hegemony over the global market.[31] Weinberg's interpretation challenged the dominant interpretation that World War II began as a European conflict. For example, in *The Last European War: September 1939 to December 1941* (2001), John Lukacs contended that World War II transformed into a global war only after Hitler's decision to invade the Soviet Union in June 1941.[32]

Historians also focused on the connections between the United States and its allies. The "special relationship" that developed between the United States and Great Britain during World War II obscured the fact that both before and during the war the British government viewed Roosevelt's postwar economic agenda as a threat to its national interests. As William Roger Louis recounted in *Imperialism at Bay 1941-1945: The United States and the Decolonization of the British Empire* (1997), the government in London, particularly the members of the Conservative Party, viewed the United States as an economic rival and understood that Roosevelt's postwar plan for promoting economic international cooperation required the dismantling of the British Empire.[33]

David Day explained, in *Reluctant Nation: Australia and the Allied Defeat of Japan, 1942-1945* (1992), that from 1939 until 1941 the British government feared that the United States would use the crisis in Asia as an excuse to expand its economic reach. He argued that the British government sought to curtail the expansion of American business interests into the Western Pacific. However, by early 1942, after the British suffered a series of crushing defeats in Asia and the Japanese military was within reach of the northern shores of Australia, the government in London encouraged the United States to develop military and economic ties with Australia and New Zealand.[34]

Historians are split on whether Roosevelt held a nuanced understanding of global economics. However, after World War II, Roosevelt's global economic reform agenda became the blueprint for postwar economic reconstruction, and his vision still shapes the trajectory of globalization. Industrialized nations throughout the world continue to advance economic policies that promote economic internationalism as the means for achieving the "social objective" of a decent standard of living for all.

NOTES

1. C. Wright Mills, *The New Men of Power* (New York: Harcourt, Brace, 1948).

2. Norman Markowitz, *The Rise and Fall of the People's Century: Henry A. Wallace and American Liberalism* (New York: The Free Press, 1973).

3. Nelson Lichtenstein, *Labor's War at Home: The CIO in World War II* (New York: Basic Books, 1995).

4. Frank Warren, *Noble Abstractions: American Liberal Intellectuals and World War II* (Columbus: Ohio State University Press, 1999).

5. Patrick Reagan, *Designing a New America: The Origins of New Deal Planning, 1890-1943* (Amherst: University of Massachusetts Press, 1999), 208, 222-23.

6. Ibid.

7. Cass Sunstein, *The Second Bill of Rights: FDR's Unfinished Revolution and Why We Need It More Than Ever* (New York: Basic Books, 2004), 1, 13-16.

8. Robert Dallek, *Franklin D. Roosevelt and American Foreign Policy, 1932-1945* (New York: Oxford University Press, 1979).

9. Ibid.

10. Ibid.

11. Ibid.

12. Ibid.

13. "Joint Declaration by the United States of America, China, Great Britain, The Union of Soviet Socialist Republics, and other Signatory Governments," December 19, 1941, Adolph Berle Papers, Franklin D. Roosevelt Presidential Library, Hyde Park, New York.

14. Dallek, *Roosevelt and Foreign Policy.*

15. Gar Alperovitz, *Atomic Diplomacy* (New York: Vintage Books, 1965).

16. Martin Sherwin, *A World Destroyed: The Atomic Bomb and the Grand Alliance* (New York: Knopf, 1975).

17. Conrad Black, *Franklin Delano Roosevelt: Champion of Freedom* (New York: Public Affairs, 2003), 1134.

18. David M. Kennedy, *Freedom From Fear: The American People in Depression and War, 1929-1945* (New York: Oxford University Press, 1999).

19. Franklin D. Roosevelt, *Whither Bound?* (Boston: Houghton Mifflin, 1926), 3, 14, 27.

20. Franklin D. Roosevelt, "Radio Address to the Business and Professional Men's League Throughout the Nation, October 6, 1932," in *The Public Papers and Addresses of Franklin D. Roosevelt,* comp. Samuel I. Rosenman (New York: Random House, 1938), 1:785.

21. Franklin D. Roosevelt, "'New Conditions Impose New Requirements upon Government and Those Who Conduct Government,' September 23, 1932," in *Public Papers and Addresses of Roosevelt,* 1:752.

22. Roosevelt, "Radio Address, October 6, 1932," in *Public Papers and Addresses of Roosevelt,* 1:784.

23. Franklin D. Roosevelt, "Campaign Address on Reciprocal Tariff Negotiations, September 20, 1932," in *Public Papers and Addresses of Roosevelt,* 1:723-26.

24. Franklin D. Roosevelt, "'The Country Needs, the Country Demands Bold, Persistent Experimentation,' May 22, 1932," in *Public Papers and Addresses of Roosevelt,* 1:645.

25. Roosevelt, "'New Conditions,' September 23, 1932," in *Public Papers and Addresses of Roosevelt,* 1:754.

26. Franklin D. Roosevelt, "'I Pledge to You—I Pledge Myself to a New Deal for the American People,' July 2, 1932," in *Public Papers and Addresses of Roosevelt,* 1:649, 657.

27. Roosevelt, "'New Conditions,' September 23, 1932," in *Public Papers and Addresses of Roosevelt,* 1:756.

28. Franklin D. Roosevelt, *Looking Forward* (New York: John Day, 1933; reprint, New York: Touchstone, 2009).

29. Henry A. Wallace, *New Frontiers* (New York: Reynal and Hitchcock, 1934); Henry A. Wallace, *America Must Choose: The Advantages and Disadvantages of Nationalism, of World Trade, and of a Planned Middle Course* (Boston: World Peace Foundation, 1934), 7, 19.

30. Franklin D. Roosevelt, "'The American People Have Made an Unlimited Commitment That There Shall Be a Free World,' November 6, 1941," in *Public Papers and Addresses of Roosevelt,* 10:479-80.

31. Gerhard L. Weinberg, *Visions of Victory: The Hopes of Eight World Leaders of World War II* (New York: Cambridge University Press, 2005), 15-16.

32. John Lukacs, *The Last European War: September 1939 to December 1941* (New Haven: Yale University Press, 2001).

33. William Roger Louis, *Imperialism at Bay 1941-1945: The United States and the Decolonization of the British Empire* (New York: Oxford University Press, 1977).

34. David Day, *Reluctant Nation: Australia and the Allied Defeat of Japan 1942-1945* (New York: Oxford University Press, 1992).

CHAPTER ELEVEN

Memory and the New Deal

MICHAEL W. BARBERICH

Memory is significant for New Deal historiography in at least three ways. First, the New Deal was not entirely "new" but was presented to the American public as a new solution to the economic hardship of the Great Depression. Roosevelt relied upon usable pasts to guide and explain the New Deal to the American public. While the New Deal refers to the collection of programs Roosevelt's administration used to lift the nation out of the Great Depression, the idea of providing the American public with improved circumstances was not new and many of the programs had general or specific precedents. The New Deal revealed continuities with past practice and Roosevelt's presentation of the New Deal used these continuities to encourage support for and defend New Deal programs. The uses of the past and public memory offered Americans of the 1930s a way to understand the New Deal.

Second, the New Deal created several repositories of memory for the United States, recording and influencing its history in the process. According to Michael Kammen, "during the early to mid-1930s, a period that straddled the Hoover and Roosevelt presidencies, American society increasingly needed and sought a meaningful sense of its heritage in crisis times. By 1935-1936 a great many observers believed that a new and vital cultural nationalism had in fact arrived." Collecting Americana was a popular manifestation of public memory in the United States throughout the early twentieth century. However, before the 1930s only a few institutions were responsible for preserving artifacts of American memory. For Kammen, "the 1930s was, undeniably, a distinctively transitional decade in terms of perpetuating and presenting the meaning of America. Never again would that manifest responsibility remain primarily (indeed, almost entirely) in the hands of private individuals and organizations."[1] The New Deal created repositories for American memory, including the National Archives, a presidential library system, and new national parks.

Third, the New Deal, despite being concluded in large part by 1939, had a strong influence and continuing legacy in American politics. Perhaps no other modern presidential administration has had such a profound effect upon the everyday lives of the American people. The New Deal remains a vibrant influence on political action, and all subsequent presidents have been, as William Leuchtenburg stated, "in the shadow of FDR."[2] The legacy of the New Deal concerns the role of the presidency in the federal government and the role of the federal government in the economic and social life of the nation and its citizens.

At the core of promoting the early New Deal was the argument that governmental inaction helped facilitate economic collapse. Roosevelt's election in 1932 was more a result of being the alternative to Herbert Hoover than the promise of a New Deal for the American people. During the campaign and his first year in office, Roosevelt cultivated the perception that Hoover did nothing to forestall the Great Depression and took every opportunity to highlight the difference his administration was making.[3] As a result, the "newness" of the New Deal became a rhetorical commonplace that shaped the historiography and contextual framework of the New Deal.

The programs of the early New Deal thrust the federal government into the everyday lives and practices of people and businesses. As its New Deal programs were implemented in the factories and on the farms, Roosevelt's administration sought to educate the American public about the New Deal's relief and recovery efforts. Leuchtenburg explained that:

To acquaint the country with new moral imperatives and with his departures in public policy, Roosevelt made conscious use of the media almost from the moment he entered the White House. . . . He was fond of calling the press meeting room in the White House his "schoolroom," and he often resorted to terms such as "seminar" or the budget "textbook."[4]

Roosevelt demonstrated the qualities of leadership Herbert Croly cited as necessary for twentieth-century America. In *The Promise of American Life* (1909), Croly argued that economic opportunity was not available to the average American. For Croly, corporations had become the dominant influence in the United States and had corrupted state and local governments in order to establish policies that favored corporate rather than public interest. The federal government was the only entity that could correct the undue influence of corporations. However, the federal government needed a strong executive branch and public support to minimize the undue influence of corporations.[5] Roosevelt fulfilled these requirements in a way no other president had. He not only persuaded the public of a new role for the federal government and the office of the president, he also convinced the public that these new roles evolved from the past. Just as the government worked to provide resources to the unemployed, the president worked to shape and repair the American public's sense of history. As the most obvious example, Roosevelt's fireside chats disseminated the ideals of the New Deal, promoted national interests, and articulated a new public memory.

Roosevelt used the media, especially radio, in ways no other administration had. Having perfected his use of radio while governor in New York, Roosevelt fulfilled the insight Bruce Barton had shared with Calvin Coolidge. In *Fireside Politics* (2000), Douglas Craig related how Barton, a radio advertising agent in the 1920s, suggested to Coolidge the power of radio as a medium for political influence: "[T]he radio has made possible an entirely new type of campaign. It enables the President to sit by every fireside and talk in terms of that home's interest and prosperity . . . if the President will only talk to the folks (not address them) he will re-elect himself."[6] Coolidge used radio to replay addresses. Hoover broadcast speeches live over the radio. But neither president made use of the medium as Roosevelt would with his fireside chats.

The Roosevelt administration also used the radio to balance and respond to the conservative press. Richard Steele explained that, "[f]rom the administration's perspective what radio did *not* air was as important as what it did." [7] While newspapers conveyed the administration's message, they also provided ample criticism of the New Deal. Broadcasters avoided such criticism and, therefore, generally aired the administration's carefully prepared positions. Roosevelt's administration understood Croly's charge to discipline the popular will, "so that the national consciousness will gradually acquire an edifying state of mind towards its present and its future problems."[8]

While Roosevelt's use of radio during the New Deal was politically significant, radio was still a new medium of communication in the 1930s. In *Listening In* (2004), Susan Douglas described the influence radio exerted on American culture through the practice of listening. For Douglas, radio broadcasting made possible an imagined community "on entirely new geographic, temporal and cognitive levels . . . influencing people's desire to seek out, build on, and make more concrete the notion of the nation."[9] The basic genres of entertainment and journalism in broadcasting emerged during the early days of radio. From quiz shows to sporting events to coverage of international events, radio broadcasting produced the forms of information and entertainment that are now used in television and other media.

Roosevelt established presidential communication as an expectation. In *Manipulating the Ether* (1998), Robert Brown provided a detailed description of Roosevelt's fireside chats. Brown wrote that upon his death in April 1945, "the medium that had been such an integral part of Roosevelt's political life was now present to serve him in death."[10] Only Eleanor Roosevelt, the Roosevelt children, and Harry S. Truman knew the president had died before radio broadcast the news to the world. The memorial broadcast following Roosevelt's death received more airtime than the attack on Pearl Harbor and the Normandy invasion.[11]

New Deal programs actively contributed to the public's consciousness and memory of the Great Depression in America. Initially, Roosevelt's programs were thought to have drawn the country out of its economic despair, and government involvement in the economy was considered a public good for many years following. This initial evaluation was shaped by the immediate contributions the administration made to public memory. In his 1936 acceptance speech Roosevelt said that "this generation has a rendezvous with destiny," articulating a sentiment that found an expression in his and the nation's general effort to record and preserve the historical moment as it was lived.[12]

The programs of the New Deal literally transformed the landscape of the United States. Roads, sidewalks, bridges, irrigation systems, post offices, schools, and other landmarks remain as practical reminders of the programs. Some New Deal programs made cultural and archival contributions to public memory. The Federal Writers' and Federal Theatre projects brought members of the cultural workforce into New Deal programs. One contribution of the Writers' Project was a collection of state travel guides and a collection of guides to national parks.[13] T. H. Watkins described the construction of public memory during the Great Depression, using the sense of journalism as "history shot on the wing." Watkins explained that "Americans . . . were looking at themselves as never before, and to a large degree what they saw then is what we remember now. This would have pleased the New Dealers, for much of the imagery that has become part of the common knowledge of the era was created at their behest."[14]

Roosevelt's efforts to record and preserve his administration's responses to crisis cultivated the idea that the government expressed the people's will. His concern was to preserve the articulation of the will of the people and governmental action for future generations. Although Hoover laid the cornerstone for the National Archives building in Washington, D.C., the legislation that chartered the National Archives was not signed into law until June 19, 1934. Roosevelt was actively involved in conceptualizing and building the National Archives. He reviewed the architectural plans for the interior of the building and suggested to archivists that film and audio recordings should be collected and preserved.[15] If Kammen was correct that collecting Americana in the early twentieth century was in part engendered by the lack of historical record and an ambivalence to the past, then the National Archives filled a void. Kammen wrote that "[a]lthough major pieces of supportive legislation have appeared since the mid-1960s, the flurry of government-managed cultural creativity and stocktaking that occurred between 1935 and 1941 remains unique in Unites States history."[16] When Felix Frankfurter asked Roosevelt to provide some guidance for a future memorial for the president, Roosevelt requested a simple stone block, about the size of a desk, to be placed in front of the National Archives building.[17]

Roosevelt's presidential records and personal collections were preserved at his library in Hyde Park, New York. It was the first presidential library and he took an active role in the design of the building and shaping its holdings. Benjamin Hufbauer noted that "Roosevelt so desired to be remembered, and to be remembered in a particular way, that he altered the essential terms of commemoration for the American presidency. No previous president presumed to memorialize himself; self-aggrandizing monuments were thought to be for monarchs, not the elected leader of the United States."[18] Roosevelt built the library with privately donated funds and then, on June 30, 1941, it became part of the National Archives system—a precedent all subsequent presidents have followed. At the beginning of his assessment of the First Hundred Days, Anthony Badger wrote that "the mere existence of the library shaped the legacy Roosevelt bequeathed to his successors and historians in a substantive way."[19]

National parks and the expansion of the National Park Service (NPS) were also an enduring legacy of Roosevelt's contribution to public memory during the New Deal years. As with the administration's New Deal programs and use of media, the development of the National Park Service connected local, regional, and national experiences in a manner that promoted national interests and contributed to discourses of public memory. Established in 1916, the National Park Service was a small agency. However, during the 1930s, it hired professional historians and focused on educating the public. According to John Bodnar, the belief in public education and inspiration through history that existed among professionals in the park service received a "monumental boost" with the coming of the New Deal.[20] In 1935, Congress passed the Historic Sites Act and encouraged a debate over sites of national significance.

Bodnar wrote that "in the 1930s the federal government intervened in the discussion over public memory in a very substantial way and created a national forum for the expression of interests on the subject." Because discourses of public memory are contested, one effect of the federal government's and the park service's administration in selecting and organizing historic sites was to promote specific discourses of public memory over local, regional, or ethnic ones. The middle-class professionals in the park service tended to promote a history of progress and patriotism rather than of local heritage or vernacular expressions.[21]

Roosevelt's administration was integral to the development of the National Park Service during the New Deal years. Kammen explained that the pivotal moment in Horace Albright's leadership of the National Park Service came in April 1933 during a four-hour train ride with Roosevelt returning to Washington from a Sunday visit to a Civilian Conservation Corps camp in Virginia's Blue Ridge Mountains. Albright persuaded Roosevelt that the park service was the appropriate steward of historic sites and within months the president issued an executive order transferring all national military parks, battlefields, and national monuments to park service management.[22] Kammen noted that "[b]y 1939 Congress had in fact disbanded four of the New Deal relief projects that promoted the arts and American culture. A great many voters and their elected officials did not regard artistic innovations and cultural improvement as a public responsibility . . . whereas the National Park Service proved to be enduring, most of the cultural relief programs did not."[23]

The opportunity to participate in site selection and, therefore, the construction of public memory may explain the duration of the National Park Service. Bodnar wrote that:

It was precisely the public demand for historical commemoration that caused Roosevelt to ask [Harold] Ickes by 1939 to limit
the establishment of historic sites in order to keep costs to an
"absolute minimum." But no matter how hard the service attempted to keep the process orderly, political influence, local
pride, and personal feeling constantly intruded into the delib-
erations of the NPS professionals.[24]

The government's enthusiasm for selecting sites of national significance led to many exaggerated proposals. According to Kammen,
"that such a problem arose and could not be readily resolved serves
to remind us that despite the government's rapidly growing role as
a custodian of tradition during the 1930s and beyond, co-operation
between the private and public sectors remained essential."[25] For
Bodnar, a strong example of collaboration and compromise in selecting and developing an historic site for the Jefferson National
Expansion Memorial—the St. Louis Arch. Although not completed
during Roosevelt's administration, Roosevelt did secure funding for
the project and was accused of embellishing the significance of St.
Louis in the process.[26]

The first assessments of the New Deal came from Roosevelt
and the New Dealers themselves. In addition to the publication
of Roosevelt's public papers, the number of memoirs written by
New Dealers is remarkable.[27] Not only did the leaders of the New
Deal publish their own books on political philosophy or solutions
to the economic problems at hand, but they also published books
and reports pertinent to their responsibilities in the New Deal. [28]
Their memoirs, edited diaries, and other works served as an important part of public memory.[29]

David Lilienthal's *TVA: Democracy on the March* (1944) demonstrated that little separated the recovery and relief efforts of the
Depression from the war effort. Lilienthal, who headed the Tennessee Valley Authority (TVA) from 1941-1946, described the promise of a public corporation in the example of the TVA, identifying
how public money and resources could be used to develop natural
resources for private and public gain. He wrote, "[t]he Tennessee

River had always been an idle giant and a destructive one. Today, after ten years of TVA's work, at last its boundless energy works for the people who live in this valley." So successful was the TVA, according to Lilienthal, that it could be a model for reconstruction following World War II. He recounted examples of the many international visitors who had come to learn the TVA's methods so that they might be applied in bettering their own countries following the war. After describing many of the TVA's economic benefits as "the people's dividend," Lilienthal wrote that "the war has added mightily to the list . . . when the full story of one industrially laggard valley's part in production for war can be revealed, it will rank as one of the miracles of American enterprise."[30] In Lilienthal's account, the New Deal efforts of the TVA not only improved the region's economy, but they also made the war effort possible and provided models for repairing a world devastated by war.

The fireside chats provided a practice of public memory during the war years. Roosevelt continued to use the fireside chats throughout the war and, without mentioning the New Deal, he consistently reminded the American public of New Deal priorities and treated the overseas and domestic fronts as one. The principle that economic security ensured political liberty animated the New Deal and is a commonplace in Roosevelt's wartime rhetoric. The "arsenal of democracy" fireside chat, in December of 1940, compared the crisis in Europe to the economic devastation of 1932 and Roosevelt's response in 1933: "We face this new crisis—this new threat to the security of our nation—with the same courage and realism."[31] Meeting the challenge of world war did not require losing the benefits of the New Deal. In a fireside chat on May 26, 1940, Roosevelt insisted that in preparing for war "there be no breakdown or cancellation of any of the great social gains which we have made in these past years."[32] The principle found full expression in Roosevelt's four freedoms and his belief that realizing these freedoms would ensure a durable peace.

Roosevelt introduced his "four freedoms" prior to the United States' entry into World War II. He first discussed the principles in a press conference in July of 1940. While preparing for the 1941 state of the union address, he dictated the section on the four freedoms to his speechwriters Samuel Rosenman and Robert Sherwood. With little revision it was included in the speech. The four freedoms—freedom of speech, freedom to worship, freedom from want, and freedom from fear—were understood by Roosevelt to extend from the Declaration of Independence and distinguish American democracy from what he called the "corporate state" evident in Germany, Italy, and Russia.[33]

The four freedoms mark an important continuity in Roosevelt's administration. Over time the tenets took on new meaning in the national historical consciousness and shaped public memory of the 1930s. The four freedoms were used by Roosevelt and Winston Churchill as the basis of the Atlantic Charter (August 14, 1941), and in the initial constitution of the United Nations, the United Nations Declaration (January 1942); they also appeared in the preamble to the United Nations' Universal Declaration of Human Rights (December 10, 1948).[34] The freedoms are memorialized in Four Freedoms Park in New York City. Proposed in 1973 and opened in October 2012, the park is located on Roosevelt Island, in the East River between Manhattan and Queens.[35]

The four freedoms have an international character and their use in the charters and institutions was prefigured in Woodrow Wilson's Fourteen Points and the League of Nations. But they were given a distinctly American articulation in the 1940s in the paintings of Norman Rockwell. Rockwell's paintings, especially *Freedom from Want,* have become iconic in American culture. According to Maureen Hart Hennessey and Anne Knutson, Rockwell considered painting the Four Freedoms after having been moved by the Atlantic Charter. In 1943, the paintings were used in a national tour and raised $132 million in a war loan drive.[36]

The double articulation of the four freedoms, as a general principle for domestic and international politics, influenced how the New Deal was characterized after the war. Alan Brinkley, who concluded that the New Deal and the war efforts created a "compensatory state" for the federal government, wrote that by 1945 the New Dealers "who did attempt to define a domestic agenda were people fired with enthusiasm for the vision of a full-employment economy, people who considered the New Deal's principal legacy the idea of effective use of fiscal policy and the expansion of social welfare and insuring progress."[37] During and following the war, the New Deal was often remembered more for its failures than its achievements. As Brinkley noted, the failed experiments of the New Deal, such as the National Recovery Administration (NRA), shaped the administration's efforts in war production and the possibilities for governmental action following the war.[38] The idea of a powerful state needed to be defined differently than the states the war was fought against and the totalitarian states that continued or emerged following the war.

Continuing debate over the government's role in economic and social matters shaped the legacy of the New Deal following the war. David Halberstam's *The Fifties* (1993) demonstrated how the specter of the New Deal was raised and how it animated American politics. With Thomas E. Dewey leading Harry S. Truman in the 1948 presidential election polls, Truman called Congress back into session during the summer to present legislation that would allow him to campaign against the Republicans as the anti–New Deal party.[39] While Truman won the election, the New Deal was already being associated with socialism and communism. The associations became stronger during the Cold War and animosity toward the New Deal strengthened after 1948. By the early 1950s the second Red Scare was underway. In managing the financial indiscretion that precipitated Richard Nixon's 1952 Checker's speech, a spokesperson for Nixon, then the Republican vice-presidential candidate, used the opportunity to promote himself as a candidate against the New Deal, which he characterized as a socialist program "full of Commies."[40] Dwight D. Eisenhower's road to the White House culminated with his election in 1952, but it actually began in 1949 when Dewey began recruiting him to run as the Republican nominee because Eisenhower had not taken a public position against the New Deal. Dewey believed that the economic and social politics of the New Deal needed to be reversed but could only be challenged by someone who had not already taken a stand against them.[41]

A decade after Roosevelt's death a more critical account of the New Deal emerged. In situating the New Deal in the larger framework of American history, two directions for understanding the New Deal dominated. Emphasizing continuity, the New Deal represented the completion of a Progressive Era reform program. Emphasizing rupture, the New Deal represented the extraordinary measures needed to rescue democracy and capitalism from the loose practices of the 1920s. In the early 1970s, William Leuchtenburg, one of the key writers on the period, identified what he believed to be the New Deal's enduring achievements. His list included making the presidency the directing agency of the government, improving central banking and establishing monetary policy, supporting workers, creating a new system of social rights, changing the face of the land, influencing the aesthetic sensibility of the nation, and becoming increasingly concerned with conserving the nation's land and resources.[42] The New Deal made Washington more powerful than Wall Street. It provided help to people instead of leaving them to rely on charity. It trumped individual and corporate liberty with the public good, and it guaranteed that individuals could count on the government in spite of corporate malfeasance and economic catastrophe. While many New Deal programs ended with the beginning of World War II, those that survived became contested largely as a result of the countervailing influence initiated with Ronald Reagan's presidency in 1980.

In his book *In The Shadow of FDR* (1993), Leuchtenburg explored the irony of Reagan patterning himself after Roosevelt while working to dismantle the federal government's influence in the economic and social life of the United States. While Reagan's administration reversed many governmental practices rooted in the New Deal, Reagan did not challenge the strong executive office Roosevelt created for the presidency. Reagan's challenge to the New Deal was based in deregulation. Funding cuts were made in agencies that had the ability to regulate business practice. Leuchtenburg demonstrated that Reagan denounced the New Deal while mimicking Roosevelt's leadership style. In July 1982, Reagan authorized the construction of the Franklin Delano Roosevelt Memorial; however, no money was appropriated for its construction. As Leuchtenburg noted, "[n]o expression of the baffling, labyrinthine relationship of Ronald Reagan and Franklin Roosevelt could have been more fitting."[43]

Roosevelt is one of only four presidents to be memorialized in the nation's capital. Memorials for George Washington, Abraham Lincoln, and Thomas Jefferson communicated principles, whereas the Roosevelt memorial communicated practices. The legacy carved in granite and molded in copper along the Tidal Basin depicts a president and a government willing to intervene when nothing seemed to work; it depicts a government that worked to maintain the promise of American life. Despite the ambivalence the nation demonstrated in memorializing Roosevelt and despite contemporary questions about whether the New Deal was the correct response to the Great Depression, the first and second rooms of the memorial commemorate the New Deal as, in Roosevelt's words, "the consistent development of our . . . efforts toward the saving and safeguarding of our national life."[44]

Memory studies are important for historiography because they highlight how societies select from the past what is useful to address a present circumstance. The 1930s provided a challenging number of economic, social, and political circumstances. In managing these challenges, the New Deal offered solutions that were both old and new. Roosevelt often presented the progressive solutions as traditional in character and made new the solutions that were old. New Deal programs initiated change in governmental practice but many of these new practices contributed to America's heritage by conserving the land, by improving national parks and guiding their appreciation, by creating memorials and other historic sites, and by embracing new communication and technology in a way that facilitated a national community. The New Deal provided repositories for memory in recording its activities and developing the National Archives. Rather than supersede local and regional histories, practices of memory in the New Deal linked particular experience with national experience.

NOTES

1. Michael Kammen, *Mystic Chords of Memory: The Transformation of Tradition in American Culture* (New York: Vintage, 1991), 445, 460.

2. William E. Leuchtenburg, *In the Shadow of FDR: From Harry Truman to Bill Clinton*, second edition (Ithaca: Cornell University Press, 1993).

3. See Gene Smith, *The Shattered Dream: Herbert Hoover and the Great Depression* (New York: Morrow, 1970).

4. William E. Leuchtenburg, *The FDR Years: On Roosevelt and His Legacy* (New York: Columbia University Press, 1995), 11.

5. Herbert Croly, *The Promise of American Life* (Norwood, MA: Norwood Press, 1909; reprint, 1989).

6. Douglas B. Craig, *Fireside Politics: Radio and Political Culture in the United States, 1920-1940* (Baltimore: Johns Hopkins University Press, 2000), 145.

7. Richard W. Steele, *Propaganda in an Open Society: The Roosevelt Administration and the Media, 1933-1941* (Westport, CT: Greenwood Press, 1985), 23-24.

8. Croly, *Promise of American Life*, 287.

9. Susan J. Douglas, *Listening In: Radio and the American Imagination* (Minneapolis: University of Minnesota Press, 2004), 23-24.

10. Robert J. Brown, *Manipulating the Ether: The Power of Broadcast Radio in Thirties America* (Jefferson, NC: McFarland, 1998), 123.

11. Ibid.

12. Samuel I. Rosenman, ed., *The Public Papers and Addresses of Franklin D. Roosevelt* (New York: Random House, 1938), 5:235.

13. See Kammen, *Mystic Chords of Memory*, 455-74. See also Christine Bold, *Writers, Plumbers, and Anarchists: The WPA Writers' Project in Massachusetts* (Amherst: University of Massachusetts Press, 2006).

14. T. H. Watkins, *The Great Depression: America in the 1930s* (New York: Little, Brown, 1993), 5-6.

15. Bob Clark, "FDR, Archivist: The Shaping of the National Archives," *Prologue* 38 (Winter 2006): 52-57.

16. Kammen, *Mystic Chords of Memory*, 474.

17. Eric Gugler, the memorial's architect, became friendly with the Roosevelts in the 1920s while working with Roosevelt on the design of a polio rehabilitation center in Warm Springs, Georgia. He later completed the expansion and update of the Executive Office Building at the White House in 1934. William B. Rhoads, "Franklin D. Roosevelt and Washington Architecture," *Records of the Columbia Historical Society, Washington, D.C.* 52 (1989): 162.

18. Benjamin Hufbauer, "The Roosevelt Presidential Library: A Shift in Commemoration," *American Studies* 42 (Fall 2001): 173-93. See Benjamin Hufbauer, *Presidential Temples: How Memorials and Libraries Shape Public Memory* (Lawrence: University Press of Kansas, 2005).

19. Anthony J. Badger, *FDR: The First Hundred Days* (New York: Hill and Wang, 2008), xii-xiii.

20. John Bodnar, *Remaking America: Public Memory, Commemoration, and Patriotism in the Twentieth Century* (Princeton: Princeton University Press, 1992), 178.

21. Ibid., 170.

22. Kammen, *Mystic Cords of Memory*, 467.

23. Ibid., 473.

24. Bodnar, *Remaking America*, 182.

25. Kammen, *Mystic Cords of Memory*, 471-72.

26. Bodnar, *Remaking America*, 190.

27. Prior to Roosevelt's administration addresses and papers from presidents were made available through private presses and memoirs. Roosevelt's public papers, however, were collected and published by the federal government. See *Public Papers and Addresses of Roosevelt*.

28. Robert E. Sherwood, *Roosevelt and Hopkins: An Intimate History* (New York: Harper and Brothers, 1948), xi.

29. Other significant memoirs and diaries from Roosevelt's administration include Frances Perkins, *The Roosevelt I Knew* (New York: Penguin Group, 1946); Elliot Roosevelt, *As He Saw It* (New York: Duell, Sloan, and Pearce, 1946); Eleanor Roosevelt, *This I Remember* (New York: Harper, 1949); Samuel I. Rosenman, *Working with Roosevelt* (New York: Harper, 1952); Harold Ickes, *The Secret Diary of Harold L. Ickes*, 3 vols. (New York: Simon and Schuster, 1953-1954); Raymond Moley, *The First New Deal* (New York: Harcourt, 1966); Rexford G. Tugwell, *The Brains Trust* (New York: Viking Press, 1968); and, Katie Louchheim, ed., *The Making of the New Deal: The Insiders Speak* (Cambridge: Harvard University Press, 1983).

30. David E. Lilienthal, *TVA: Democracy on the March* (New York: Harper and Brothers, 1944), 3, 35.

31. Franklin D. Roosevelt, *FDR's Fireside Chats*, eds. Russell D. Buhite and David W. Levy (New York: Penguin Books, 1993), 164.

32. Ibid., 159.

33. *Public Papers and Addresses of Roosevelt*, 10:281-83.

34. The Universal Declaration of Human Rights and information on the Atlantic Charter and United Nations Declaration are available at http://www.un.org/en/aboutun/history/charter_history.shtml

35. Information on Four Freedoms Park is available at http://www.fdrfourfreedomspark.org/

36. Maureen Hart Hennessey and Anne Knutson, *Norman Rockwell: Pictures for the American People* (New York: Harry N. Abrams, 1999), 100, 102.

37. Alan Brinkley, *Liberalism and Its Discontents* (Cambridge: Harvard University Press, 1998), 60-61.

38. Ibid., 87-88.

39. David Halberstam, *The Fifties* (New York: Fawcett Columbine, 1993), 8.

40. Ibid., 273.

41. Ibid., 4.

42. Leuchtenburg, *The FDR Years*, 236-82.

43. Leuchtenburg, *In the Shadow of FDR*, 235.

44. In addition to providing a general history of the Franklin Delano Roosevelt Memorial, Robert Dallek noted that the resistance to memorializing Roosevelt is consistent with a general American reluctance to create memorials for presidents in Washington, D.C. See Robert Dallek, "The Franklin D. Roosevelt Memorial, Washington, D.C.," in *American Places: Encounters with History*, ed. William E. Leuchtenburg (New York: Oxford University Press, 2000), 66-77. Roosevelt delivered this fireside chat on June 28, 1934. See Roosevelt, *FDR's Fireside Chats*, 47.

Bibliography

ARCHIVES

Franklin D. Roosevelt Presidential Library, Hyde Park, New York.

PRIMARY AND SECONDARY SOURCES

Adams, Jane, ed. *Fighting for the Farm: Rural America Transformed.* Philadelphia: University of Pennsylvania Press, 2003.

Agee, James, and Walker Evans. *Let Us Now Praise Famous Men: Three Tenant Families.* Boston: Houghton Mifflin, 1941.

"*AHR* Forum: The Debate Over the Constitutional Revolution of 1937." *American Historical Review* 110 (October 2005): 1046-1115.

Allen, Frederick Lewis. *The Lords of Creation.* New York: Harper and Brothers, 1935.

———. *Only Yesterday: An Informal History of the 1920s.* New York: Harper and Brothers, 1931.

———. *Since Yesterday: The 1930s in America.* New York: Harper and Brothers, 1939.

Allred, Jeff. *American Modernism and Depression Documentary.* New York: Oxford University Press, 2009.

Almunia, Miguel, Agustin Benetrix, Barry Eichengreen, Kevin H. O'Rourke, and Gisela Rua. "Lessons from the Great Depression." *Economic Policy* 25 (April 2010): 219-65.

Alperovitz, Gar. *Atomic Diplomacy.* New York: Vintage Books, 1965.

Amenta, Edwin. *When Movements Matter: The Townsend Plan and the Rise of Social Security.* Princeton: Princeton University Press, 2006.

American Liberty League. *The AAA and Our Form of Government: An Analysis of a Vicious Combination of Fascism, Socialism and Communism.* Washington, D.C.: American Liberty League, 1935.

Anderson, Kristi. *The Creation of a Democratic Majority, 1928-1936.* Chicago: University of Chicago Press, 1979.

Appleby, Joyce, Lynn Hunt, and Margaret Jacob. *Telling the Truth About History.* New York: W.W. Norton, 1994.

Arrington, Leonard. "Western Agriculture and the New Deal." *Agricultural History* 44 (October 1970): 337-53.

Auerbach, Jerold S. "New Deal, Old Deal, or Raw Deal: Some Thoughts on New Left Historiography." *The Journal of Southern History* 35 (February 1969): 18-30.

Badger, Anthony J. *FDR: The First Hundred Days.* New York: Hill and Wang, 2008.

———. *The New Deal: The Depression Years, 1933-1940.* New York: Hill and Wang, 1989. Reprint, Chicago: Ivan R. Dee, 2002.

Baldwin, Sidney. *Poverty and Politics: The Rise and Decline of the Farm Security Administration.* Chapel Hill: University of North Carolina Press, 1968.

Banks, Ann. *First-Person America.* New York: Alfred A. Knopf, 1980.

Beasley, Maurine H. *Eleanor Roosevelt: Transformative First Lady.* Lawrence: University Press of Kansas, 2010.

Béland, Daniel. *Social Security: History and Politics from the New Deal to the Privatization Debate.* Lawrence: University Press of Kansas, 2005.

Bennett, David. *Demagogues in the Depression: American Radicals and the Union Party, 1932-1936.* New Brunswick: Rutgers University Press, 1969.

Bentley, Joanne. *Hallie Flanagan: A Life in the American Theater.* New York: Knopf, 1988.

Berger, Samuel. *Dollar Harvest: The Story of the Farm Bureau.* Lexington, MA: Heath Lexington Books, 1971.

Bernstein, Barton J., ed. *Towards a New Past: Dissenting Essays in American History.* New York: Pantheon Books, 1968.

Bernstein, Irving. *A Caring Society: The New Deal, the Worker, and the Great Depression.* Boston: Houghton Mifflin, 1985.

———. *The Lean Years: A History of the American Worker, 1920-1933.* Boston: Houghton Mifflin, 1960.

———. *Turbulent Years: A History of the American Worker, 1933-1941.* Boston: Houghton Mifflin, 1970.

Best, Gary Dean. *Herbert Hoover: The Postpresidential Years, 1933-1964.* 2 vols. Stanford: Hoover Institution Press, 1983.

———. *Peddling Panaceas: Popular Economists in the New Deal Era.* New Brunswick: Transaction Publishers, 2005.

———. *Pride, Prejudice, and Politics: Roosevelt Versus Recovery, 1933-1938.* New York: Praeger, 1991.

Biles, Roger. *A New Deal for the American People.* DeKalb: Northern Illinois University Press, 1991.

Black, Conrad. *Franklin Delano Roosevelt: Champion of Freedom.* New York: Public Affairs, 2003.

Blinder, Alan S., and Mark Zandi. "How the Great Recession Was Brought to an End." (July 27, 2010): 1-22. Available at http://www.princeton. edu/~blinder/End-of-Great-Recession.pdf.

Bodnar, John. *Remaking America: Public Memory, Commemoration, and Patriotism in the Twentieth Century.* Princeton: Princeton University Press, 1992.

Bold, Christine. *The WPA Guides: Mapping America.* Jackson: University Press of Mississippi, 1999.

———. *Writers, Plumbers, and Anarchists: The WPA Writers' Project in Massachusetts.* Amherst: University of Massachusetts Press, 2006.

Bonnifield, Paul. *Dust Bowl.* Albuquerque: University of New Mexico Press, 1979.

Braeman, John. "The New Deal and the 'Broker State': A Review of the Recent Scholarly Literature." *Business History Review* 46 (Winter 1972): 409-29.

Braeman, John, Robert H. Bremner, and David Brody, eds. *The New Deal.* 2 vols. Columbus: Ohio State University Press, 1975.

Breisach, Ernst A. *American Progressive History: An Experiment in Modernization.* Chicago: University of Chicago Press, 1993.

Brinkley, Alan. *The End of Reform: New Deal Liberalism in Recession and War.* New York: Alfred A. Knopf, 1995.

———. *Liberalism and its Discontents.* Cambridge: Harvard University Press, 1998.

———. *Voices of Protest: Huey Long, Father Coughlin, and the Great Depression.* New York: Vintage Books, 1983.

Brody, David. "Labor and the Great Depression: The Interpretative Prospect." *Labor History* 13 (Spring 1972): 231-44.

Brooks, Van Wyck. "On Creating a Usable Past." *The Dial* 64 (April 11, 1918): 337-41.

Brown, Michael K. *Race, Money, and the Welfare State.* Ithaca: Cornell University Press, 1999.

Brown, Robert J. *Manipulating the Ether: The Power of Broadcast Radio in Thirties America.* Jefferson, NC: McFarland, 1998.

Brueggemann, John. "Racial Considerations and Social Policy in the 1930s: Economic Change and Political Opportunities." *Social Science History* 26 (2002): 139-77.

Buhite, Russell D. and David W. Levy, eds. *FDR's Fireside Chats.* Norman: University of Oklahoma Press, 1992. Reprint, New York: Penguin Books, 1993.

Burner, David. *The Politics of Provincialism: The Democratic Party in Transition, 1918-1932.* Cambridge: Harvard University Press, 1986.

Burns, James MacGregor. *Roosevelt: The Lion and the Fox.* New York: Harcourt, Brace, and World, 1956.

Campbell, Angus, et al. *The American Voter.* Chicago: The University Press of Chicago, 1976.

Campbell, Christiana McFadyen. *The Farm Bureau and the New Deal: A Study of Making of National Farm Policy, 1933-1940.* Urbana: University of Illinois Press, 1962.

Campbell, Lara. *Respectable Citizens: Gender, Family, and Unemployment in Ontario's Great Depression.* Toronto: University of Toronto Press, 2009.

Cannon, Brian. *Remaking the Agrarian Dream: New Deal Rural Resettlement in the Mountain West.* Albuquerque: University of New Mexico Press, 1996.

Carter, Ennis. *Posters for the People: The Art of the WPA.* Philadelphia: Quirk Books, 2008.

Clark, Bob. "FDR, Archivist: The Shaping of the National Archives." *Prologue* 38 (Winter 2006): 52-57.

Clayton, Virginia Tuttle, Elizabeth Stillinger, and Erika Lee Doss, eds. *Drawing on America's Past: Folk Art, Modernism, and the Index of American Design.* Washington, D.C.: National Gallery of Art, 2002.

Cochran, Bert. *Labor and Communism: The Conflict that Shaped America.* Princeton: Princeton University Press, 1977.

Cochrane, Willard Wesley. *The Development of American Agriculture: A Historical Analysis.* Minneapolis: University of Minnesota Press, 1993.

Cohen, Adam. *Nothing to Fear: FDR's Inner Circle and the Hundred Days that Created Modern America.* New York: Penguin, 2009.

Cohen, Lizabeth. *Making a New Deal: Industrial Workers in Chicago, 1919-1939.* Cambridge: Cambridge University Press, 1990.

Commager, Henry Steele. "Twelve Years of Roosevelt." *American Mercury* 40 (April 1945): 391-401.

Conkin, Paul. *The New Deal.* New York: Thomas Y. Crowell, 1967.

———. *Tomorrow a New World: The New Deal Communities Program.* Ithaca: Cornell University Press, 1959.

Conrad, David. *The Forgotten Farmers: The Story of Sharecroppers in the New Deal.* Urbana: University of Illinois Press, 1965.

Contreras, Belisario R. *Tradition and Innovation in New Deal Art.* London: Associated University Presses, 1983.

Cook, James W., Lawrence B. Glickman, and Michael O'Malley. *The Cultural Turn in U.S. History: Past, Present, and Future.* Chicago: University of Chicago Press, 2008.

Couch, Jim, and William Shughart II. *The Political Economy of the New Deal.* Northampton, MA: Edward Elgar, 1998.

Coughlin, Charles E. *A Series of Lectures on Social Justice.* 1935. Reprint, New York: DeCapo Press, 1971.

Couvares, Francis G., Martha Saxton, Gerald N. Grob, and George Athan Billias, eds. *Interpretations of American History: Patterns and Perspectives.* 2 vols. Seventh edition. New York: The Free Press, 2000.

Craig, Douglas B. *After Wilson: The Struggle for the Democratic Party, 1920-1934*. Chapel Hill: The University of North Carolina Press, 1992.

———. *Fireside Politics: Radio and Political Culture in the United States, 1920-1940*. Baltimore: Johns Hopkins University Press, 2000.

Croly, Herbert. *The Promise of American Life*. Norwood, MA: Norwood Press, 1909. Reprint 1989.

Crosby, Emilye. *A Little Taste of Freedom: The Black Freedom Struggle in Claiborne County, Mississippi*. Chapel Hill: University of North Carolina Press, 2005.

Cunfer, Geoff. *On the Great Plains: Agriculture and Environment*. College Station: Texas A&M Press, 2005.

Curtis, James. *Mind's Eye, Mind's Truth: FSA Photography Reconsidered*. Philadelphia: Temple University Press, 1989.

Cushman, Barry. *Rethinking the New Deal Court: The Structure of a Constitutional Revolution*. New York: Oxford University Press, 1998.

Cutler, Phoebe. *The Public Landscape of the New Deal*. New Haven: Yale University Press, 1985.

Dallek, Robert. *Franklin D. Roosevelt and American Foreign Policy, 1932-1945*. New York: Oxford University Press, 1979.

Daniel, Cletus. *Bitter Harvest: A History of California Farmworkers, 1870-1941*. Ithaca: Cornell University Press, 1981.

Davis, Anita Price. *New Deal Art in North Carolina*. Jefferson, NC: McFarland, 2009.

———. *New Deal Art in Virginia*. Jefferson, NC: McFarland, 2009.

Davis, Kenneth S. *FDR: The Beckoning of Destiny, 1882-1928*. New York: Putman, 1972.

———. *FDR: Into the Storm, 1937-1940*. New York: Random House, 1993.

———. *FDR: The New York Years, 1928-1933*. New York: Random House, 1985.

———. *FDR: The New Deal Years, 1933-1937*. New York: Random House, 1986.

———. *FDR: The War President, 1940-1943*. New York: Random House, 2000.

Day, David. *Reluctant Nation: Australia and the Allied Defeat of Japan 1942-1945*. New York: Oxford University Press, 1992.

Degler, Carl. "American Political Parties and the Rise of the City: An Interpretation," *Journal of American History* 51 (June 1964): 41-59.

Denning, Michael. *The Cultural Front: The Laboring of American Culture in the Twentieth Century*. New York: Verso, 1998.

Dickstein, Morris. *Dancing in the Dark: A Cultural History of the Great Depression*. New York: W.W. Norton, 2009.

Dixon, Marc. "Union Threat, Countermovement Organization, and Labor Policy in the United States, 1944-1960." *Social Problems* 57 (May 2010): 157-74.

Douglas, Susan J. *Listening In: Radio and the American Imagination.* Minneapolis: University of Minnesota Press, 2004.

Downey, Kirstin. *The Woman Behind the New Deal: The Life of Frances Perkins, FDR's Secretary of Labor and His Moral Conscience.* New York: Doubleday, 2009.

Dubofsky, Melvyn, ed. *Hard Work: The Making of Labor History.* Urbana: University of Illinois Press, 2000.

Dulles, Foster Rhea. *Labor in America: A History.* Third edition. New York: Thomas Y. Crowell, 1966.

Dunlap, Thomas R. "Wildlife, Science, and the National Parks, 1920-1940." *Pacific Historical Review* 59 (May 1990): 187-202.

Dunn, Susan. *Roosevelt's Purge: How FDR Fought to Change the Democratic Party.* Cambridge: The Belknap Press of Harvard University Press, 2010.

Dyson, Lowell. *Red Harvest: The Communist Party and American Farmers.* Lincoln: University of Nebraska Press, 1982.

Eden, Robert, ed. *The New Deal and Its Legacy: Critique and Reappraisal.* New York: Greenwood Press, 1989.

Egan, Timothy. *The Worst Hard Time: The Untold Story of Those Who Survived the Great American Dust Bowl.* Boston: Houghton Mifflin, 2006.

Fahlman, Betsy. *New Deal Art in Arizona.* Tucson: University of Arizona Press, 2009.

Farley, James. *Behind the Ballots: The Personal History of a Politician.* New York: Harcourt, Brace, 1938.

———. *Jim Farley's Story: The Roosevelt Years.* New York: McGraw Hill, 1948.

Fearon, Peter. *Kansas in the Great Depression: Work Relief, the Dole, and Rehabilitation.* Columbia: University of Missouri Press, 2007.

Ferguson, Karen. *Black Politics in New Deal Atlanta.* Chapel Hill: University of North Carolina Press, 2002.

Finegold, Kenneth. "From Agriculture to Adjustment: The Political Origins of New Deal Agricultural Policy." *Politics & Society* 11 (March 1982): 1-27.

Finegold, Kenneth, and Theda Skocpol. *State and Party in America's New Deal.* Madison: University of Wisconsin Press, 1995.

Fisher, Irving. *The Stock Market Crash—and After.* New York: The Macmillan Company, 1930.

Fitzgerald, Deborah. *Every Farm a Factory: The Industrial Ideal in American Agriculture.* New Haven: Yale University Press, 2003.

Flora, Peter, and Arnold Heidenheimer, eds. *The Development of Welfare States in Europe and America.* New Brunswick: Transaction Books, 1981.

Folsom, Burton. *New Deal or Raw Deal? How FDR's Economic Legacy Has Damaged America.* New York: Threshold Editions, 2008.

Foner, Eric, ed. *The New American History.* Philadelphia: Temple University Press, 1997.

————. *The Story of American Freedom.* New York: W.W. Norton, 1998.

Foner, Eric, and Lisa McGirr, eds. *American History Now.* Philadelphia: Temple University Press, 2011.

"Four Freedoms Park," available at http://www.fdrfourfreedomspark.org/

Fraser, Steve, and Gary Gerstle, eds. *The Rise and Fall of the New Deal Order, 1930-1980.* Princeton: Princeton University Press, 1989.

Freidel, Frank. *Franklin D. Roosevelt.* 4 vols. Boston: Little, Brown, 1952-1973.

Fried, Albert. *FDR and His Enemies.* New York: Palgrave, 1999.

Friedman, Lawrence M. *American Law in the Twentieth Century.* New Haven: Yale University Press, 2002.

Friedman, Milton. *Free to Choose: A Personal Statement.* New York: Harcourt, Brace, Jovanovich, 1980.

————. *Tyranny of the Status Quo.* San Diego: Harcourt, Brace, Jovanovich, 1984.

Friedman, Milton, and Anna Jacobson Schwartz. *A Monetary History of the United States, 1867-1960.* Princeton: Princeton University Press, 1936.

Fuertes, S. J. *When Public Housing Was Paradise: Building Community in Chicago.* Westport, CT: Greenwood, 2003.

Galarza, Ernesto. *Farm Workers and Agri-business in California, 1947-1960.* Notre Dame: Notre Dame University Press, 1977.

Galbraith, John Kenneth. *The Great Crash, 1929.* New York: Houghton Mifflin, 1954.

Garfinkel, Herbert. *When Negroes March: The March on Washington Movement in the Organizational Politics for FEPC.* New York: Atheneum, 1969.

Garraty, John A. "The New Deal, National Socialism, and the Great Depression." *The American Historical Review* 78 (October 1973): 907-44.

Gellman, Erik S., and Jarod Roll. "Owen Whitfield and the Gospel of the Working Class in New Deal America, 1936-1946." *The Journal of Southern History* 72 (May 2006): 303-48.

Genung, Albert Benjamin. *The Agricultural Depression Following World War I and Its Political Consequences: An Account of the Deflation Episode, 1921-1934.* Ithaca: Northeast Farm Foundation, 1954.

Ghirardo, Diane. *Building New Communities: New Deal America and Fascist Italy.* Princeton: Princeton University Press, 1989.

Gilbert, Jess. "Rural Sociology and Democratic Planning in the Third New Deal." *Agricultural History* 82 (Fall 2008): 421-38.

————. "Wisconsin Economists and New Deal Agricultural Policy: The Legacy of Progressive Professors." *The Wisconsin Magazine of History* 80 (Summer 1997): 280-312.

Gisolfi, Monica Richmond. "From Crop Lien to Contract Farming: The Roots of Agribusiness in the American South, 1929-1939." *Agricultural History* 80 (Spring 2006): 167-89.

Goldfield, Michael. "Worker Insurgency, Radical Organization, and New Deal Labor Legislation." *The American Political Science Review* 83 (December 1989): 1257-82.

Goldschmidt, Walter. *As You Sow*. New York: Harcourt, Brace, 1947.

Gonzalez-Perez, Margaret C. "A House Divided: Public Housing Policy in New Orleans." *Louisiana History* 44 (Autumn 2003): 443-61.

Gordon, Adam. "The Creation of Home Ownership: How New Deal Changes in Banking Regulation Simultaneously Made Homeownership Accessible to Whites and out of Reach for Blacks." *The Yale Law Journal* 115 (October 2005): 186-226.

Gordon, Colin. *New Deals: Business, Labor, and Politics in America, 1920-1935*. New York: Cambridge University Press, 1994.

———. "Rethinking the New Deal." *Columbia Law Review* 98 (December 1998): 2029-54.

Gordon, Linda. *Dorothea Lange: A Life Beyond Limits*. New York: W.W. Norton, 2009.

Gotham, Kevin Fox. "Racialization and the State: The Housing Act of 1934 and the Creation of the Federal Housing Administration." *Sociological Perspectives* 43 (Summer 2000): 291-317.

Gould, Lewis L. *Grand Old Party: A History of the Republicans*. New York: Random House, 2003.

Graham, Otis L. *An Encore for Reform: the Old Progressives and the New Deal*. New York: Oxford University Press, 1967.

Grant, Michael Johnston. *Down and Out on the Family Farm: Rural Rehabilitation in the Great Plains, 1929-1945*. Lincoln: University of Nebraska Press, 2002.

Grant, Nancy L. *TVA and Black Americans: Planning for the Status Quo*. Philadelphia: Temple University Press, 1990.

Greenberg, Clement. "Avant-Garde and Kitsch." *Partisan Review* 6 (Fall 1939): 34-49.

Gregg, Sara M. *Managing the Mountains: Land Use Planning, the New Deal, and the Creation of a Federal Landscape in Appalachia*. New Haven: Yale University Press, 2010.

Grieve, Victoria Marie. "Art as New Deal Experience: Progressive Aesthetics and the New Deal Federal Art." Ph.D. dissertation. George Washington University, 2004.

———. *The Federal Art Project and the Creation of Middlebrow Culture*. Chicago: University of Illinois Press, 2009.

Grubbs, Donald H. *Cry From Cotton: The Southern Tenant Farmers' Union and the New Deal*. Chapel Hill: University of North Carolina Press, 1971. Reprint, Fayetteville: University of Arkansas Press, 2000.

Hacker, Jacob S. *The Divided Welfare State: The Battle over Public and Private Social Benefits in the United States.* Cambridge: Cambridge University Press, 2002.

Hacker, Louis M. *The Shaping of the American Tradition.* New York: Columbia University Press, 1947.

Halberstam, David. *The Fifties.* New York: Fawcett Columbine, 1993.

Hamby, Alonzo L. *Liberalism and Its Challengers: FDR to Reagan.* New York: Oxford University Press, 1985.

———. "The New Deal: Avenues for Reconsideration." *Polity* 31 (Summer 1999): 665–81.

Hamilton, David E. "The Causes of the Banking Panic of 1930: Another View." *Journal of Southern History* 51 (November 1985): 581–608.

———. *From New Day to New Deal: American Farm Policy from Hoover to Roosevelt, 1928–1933.* Chapel Hill: University of North Carolina Press, 1991.

Hamilton, Dona Cooper, and Charles V. Hamilton. *The Dual Agenda: The African-American Struggle for Civil and Economic Equality.* New York: Columbia University Press, 1997.

Hapke, Laura. *Labor's Canvas: American Working-Class History and the WPA Art of the 1930s.* New York: Cambridge University Press, 2008.

Hariman, Robert, and John Louis Lucaites. *No Caption Needed: Iconic Photographs, Public Culture, and Liberal Democracy.* Chicago: University of Chicago Press, 2007.

Harris, Jonathan. *Federal Art and National Culture: The Politics of Identity in New Deal America.* New York: Cambridge University Press, 1995.

Hawley, Ellis W. *The New Deal and the Problem of Monopoly: A Study in Economic Ambivalence.* Princeton: Princeton University Press, 1966.

Hayes, Jack Irby, Jr. *South Carolina and the New Deal.* Columbia: University of South Carolina Press, 2001.

Hays, Samuel P. *Conservation and the Gospel of Efficiency: The Progressive Conservation Movement, 1890–1920.* Cambridge: Harvard University Press, 1959.

Hemingway, Andrew. *Artists on the Left: American Artists and the Communist Movement, 1926–1956.* New Haven: Yale University Press, 2002.

Henderson, Henry L., and David B. Woolner, eds. *FDR and the Environment.* New York: Palgrave Macmillan, 2005.

Hennessey, Maureen Hart, and Anne Knutson. *Norman Rockwell: Pictures for the American People.* New York: Harry N. Abrams, 1999.

Higgs, Robert. *Crisis and Leviathan: Critical Episodes in the Growth of American Government.* New York: Oxford University Press, 1987.

Hirsch, Jerrold. *Portrait of America: A Cultural History of the Federal Writers' Project.* Chapel Hill: University of North Carolina Press, 2003.

History of American Presidential Elections. 3 vols. New York: Chelsea House, 1971.

"History of the United Nations Charter," available at http://www.un.org/en/aboutun/history/charter_history.shtml

History of U.S. Political Parties. New York: Chelsea House, 1973.

Hoffman, Beatrix. "Health Care Reform and Social Movements in the United States." *American Journal of Public Health* 93 (January 2003): 75-85.

Hofstadter, Richard. *The Age of Reform: From Bryan to FDR.* New York: Knopf, 1955.

———. *The American Political Tradition: And the Men Who Made it.* New York: Vintage Books, 1948.

———. *The Progressive Historians: Turner, Beard, Parrington.* New York: Alfred A. Knopf, 1968.

Hoover, Herbert. *American Ideals Versus the New Deal.* New York: Charles Scribner's Sons, 1936.

———. *America's Way Forward.* New York: Charles Scribner's Sons, 1939.

———. *The Challenge to Liberty.* New York: Charles Scribner's Sons, 1934.

Horowitz, Ruth. *Political Ideologies of Organized Labor: The New Deal Era.* New Brunswick: Transaction Books, 1978.

Hufbauer, Benjamin. *Presidential Temples: How Memorials and Libraries Shape Public Memory.* Lawrence: University Press of Kansas, 2005.

———. "The Roosevelt Presidential Library: A Shift in Commemoration." *American Studies* 42 (Fall 2001): 173-93.

Hunt, D. Bradford. *Blueprint for Disaster: The Unraveling of Chicago Public Housing.* Chicago: University of Chicago Press, 2009.

Hurley, Jack F. *Portrait of a Decade.* Baton Rouge: Louisiana State University Press, 1972.

Hurt, R. Douglas. *Dust Bowl: An Agricultural and Social History.* Chicago: Nelson-Hall, 1981.

———. *Problems of Plenty: The American Farmer in the Twentieth Century.* Chicago: Ivan R. Dee, 2002.

Ickes, Harold. *The Autobiography of a Curmudgeon.* New York: Reynal and Hitchcock, 1943.

———. *Back to Work: The Story of PWA.* New York: The Macmillan Company, 1935.

———. *The Secret Diary of Harold L. Ickes.* 3 vols. New York: Simon and Schuster, 1953-1954.

Jackson, Charles. *Food and Drug Legislation in the New Deal.* Princeton: Princeton University Press, 1970.

Jackson, Kenneth T. *Crabgrass Frontier: The Suburbanization of the United States.* New York: Oxford University Press, 1985.

Jeffries, John W. "A 'Third New Deal'? Liberal Policy and the American State, 1937-1945." *Journal of Policy History* 8 (December 1996): 387-409.

Jenner, Robert E. *FDR's Republicans: Domestic Political Realignment and American Foreign Policy.* New York: Lexington Books, 2010.

Johnson, Charles S., Edwin Embree, and W. W. Alexander. *The Collapse of Cotton Tenancy: Summary of Field Studies and Statistical Surveys.* Chapel Hill: University of North Carolina Press, 1935.

Kammen, Michael. *Mystic Chords of Memory: The Transformation of Tradition in American Culture.* New York: Vintage, 1991.

Keller, Morton. *America's Three Regimes: A New Political History.* New York: Oxford University Press, 2007.

Kelley, Robin D. G. *Hammer and Hoe: Alabama Communists During the Great Depression.* Chapel Hill: University of North Carolina Press, 1990.

Kennedy, David M. *Freedom From Fear: The American People in Depression and War, 1929-1945.* New York: Oxford University Press, 1999.

———. "What the New Deal Did." *Political Science Quarterly* 124 (Summer 2009): 251-68.

Kennedy, Roger G. *When Art Worked: The New Deal, Art, and Democracy.* New York: Rizzoli, 2009.

Key, V. O. "A Theory of Critical Elections." *The Journal of Politics* 17 (February 1955): 3-18.

———. *The Responsible Electorate: Rationality in Presidential Voting, 1936-1960.* Cambridge: Harvard University Press, 1966.

Keynes, John Maynard. *The General Theory of Employment, Interest and Money.* London: Macmillan, 1936.

Kirby, John. *Black Americans in the Roosevelt Era: Liberalism and Race.* Knoxville: University of Tennessee Press, 1980.

Kirkendall, Richard S., ed. *The New Deal: The Historical Debate.* New York: John Wiley and Sons, 1973.

———. "The New Deal as Watershed: The Recent Literature." *The Journal of American History* 54 (March 1968): 839-52.

———. *Social Scientists and Farm Politics in the Age of Roosevelt.* Columbia: University of Missouri Press, 1966.

Klare, Karl E. "Judicial Deradicalization of the Wagner Act and the Origins of Modern Legal Consciousness, 1933-1941." *Minnesota Law Review* 62 (1978): 265-340.

Klehr, Harvey. *The Heyday of American Communism: The Depression Decade.* New York: Basic Books, 1984.

Klein, Jennifer. *For All These Rights: Business, Labor, and the Shaping of America's Public-Private Welfare State.* Princeton: Princeton University Press, 2003.

———. "New Deal Restoration: Individuals, Communities, and the Long Struggle for the Collective Good." *International Labor and Working Class History* 74 (Fall 2008): 42-48.

Klein, Maury. "The Stock Market Crash of 1929: A Review Article." *The Business History Review* 75 (Summer 2001): 325-51.

Kozol, Wendy. "Madonnas of the Fields: Photography, Gender, and 1930s Farm Relief." *Genders* 2 (Summer 1988): 1-23.

Krainz, Thomas A. *Delivering Aid: Implementing Progressive Era Welfare in the American West.* Albuquerque: University of New Mexico Press, 2005.

Langa, Helen. *Radical Art: Printmaking and the Left in 1930s New York.* Berkeley: University of California Press, 2004.

Lash, Joseph P. *Dealers and Dreamers: A New Look at the New Deal.* New York: Doubleday, 1988.

Lawson, Alan. *A Commonwealth of Hope: The New Deal Response to Crisis.* Baltimore: Johns Hopkins University Press, 2006.

Lee, Anthony. *Painting on the Left: Diego Rivera, Radical Politics, and San Francisco's Public Murals.* Berkeley: University of California Press, 1999.

Leff, Mark H. "Taxing the 'Forgotten Man': The Politics of Social Security Finance in the New Deal." *The Journal of American History* 70 (September 1983): 359-81.

Leighninger, Robert. *Building Louisiana: The Legacy of the Public Works Administration.* Oxford: University Press of Mississippi, 2007.

———. *Long-Range Public Investment: The Forgotten Legacy of the New Deal.* Columbia: University of South Carolina Press, 2007.

Leuchtenburg, William E., ed. *American Places: Encounters with History.* New York: Oxford University Press, 2000.

———. *The FDR Years: On Roosevelt and His Legacy.* New York: Columbia University Press, 1995.

———. *Franklin D. Roosevelt and the New Deal, 1933-1940.* New York: Harper and Row, 1963.

———. *In the Shadow of FDR: From Harry Truman to Bill Clinton.* Second edition. Ithaca: Cornell University Press, 1993.

———. *The Perils of Prosperity, 1914-1932.* Chicago: The University of Chicago Press, 1958.

———. *The White House Looks South: Franklin D. Roosevelt, Harry S. Truman, Lyndon B. Johnson.* Baton Rouge: Louisiana State University Press, 2005.

Levine, Lawrence W. *The Unpredictable Past: Explorations in American Cultural History.* New York: Oxford University Press, 1993.

Levine, Lawrence W., Cornelia R. Levine, and Michael Kazin, eds., *The Fireside Conversations: America Responds to FDR During the Great Depression.* Berkeley: University of California Press, 2010.

Levine, Rhonda. *Class Struggle in the New Deal: Industrial Labor, Industrial Capital, and the State.* Lawrence: University of Kansas Press, 1988.

Lewis, Michael E. "National Grasslands in the Dust Bowl." *Geographical Review* 79 (April 1989): 161-71.

Lewthwaite, Stephanie. "Race, Paternalism, and 'California Pastoral': Rural Rehabilitation and Mexican Labor in Greater Los Angeles." *Agricultural History* 81 (Winter 2007): 1-35.

Lichtenstein, Nelson. *Labor's War at Home: The CIO in World War II.* New York: Basic Books, 1995.

Lichtman, Allan J. *Prejudice and the Old Politics: The Presidential Election of 1928.* Chapel Hill: The University of North Carolina Press, 1979.

Lilienthal, David E. *TVA: Democracy on the March.* New York: Harper and Brothers, 1944.

Long, Huey P. *Every Man a King: The Autobiography of Huey P. Long.* New Orleans: National Book Company, 1933. Reprint, New York: Da Capo Press, 1996.

Lorence, James J. *The Unemployed People's Movement: Leftists, Liberals, and Labor in Georgia, 1929-1941.* Athens: University of Georgia Press, 2009.

Louchheim, Katie, ed. *The Making of the New Deal: The Insiders Speak.* Cambridge: Harvard University Press, 1983.

Louis, William Roger. *Imperialism at Bay 1941-1945: The United States and the Decolonization of the British Empire.* New York: Oxford University Press, 1977.

Lowitt, Richard. *The New Deal and the West.* Norman: University of Oklahoma Press, 1993.

Lubell, Samuel. *The Future of American Politics.* New York: Harper and Brothers, 1952.

Lukacs, John. *The Last European War: September 1939 to December 1941.* New Haven: Yale University Press, 2001.

Madsen, Jakob B. "Agricultural Crises and the International Transmission of the Great Depression." *Journal of Economic History* 2 (June 2001): 327-65.

Maher, Neil M. *Nature's New Deal: The Civilian Conservation Corps and the Roots of the American Environmental Movement.* New York: Oxford University Press, 2008.

Majka, Linda, and Theo J. Majka. *Farmworkers, Agribusiness, and the State.* Philadelphia: Temple University Press, 1982.

Maloney, C. J. *Back to the Land: Arthurdale, FDR's New Deal, and the Costs of Economic Planning.* Hoboken, NJ: Wiley and Sons, 2011.

Maney, Patrick J. *The Roosevelt Presence: A Biography of Franklin D. Roosevelt.* New York: Twayne, 1992.

Mangione, Jerre. *The Dream and the Deal: The Federal Writers' Project, 1935-1943.* New York: Avon Books, 1972.

Markowitz, Norman. *The Rise and Fall of the People's Century: Henry A. Wallace and American Liberalism.* New York: The Free Press, 1973.

Marling, Karal Ann. *Wall-to-Wall America: A Cultural History of Post Office Murals in the Great Depression.* Minneapolis: University of Minnesota Press, 1982.

Mathews, Jane De Hart. "Arts and the People: The New Deal Quest for a Cultural Democracy." *The Journal of American History* 62 (September 1975): 316-39.

——. *The Federal Theater, 1935-39: Plays, Relief, and Politics.* Princeton: Princeton University Press, 1967.

Matusow, Alan. *The Unraveling of America: A History of Liberalism in the 1960s.* New York: Harper and Row, 1984.

McCluskey, Audrey, and Elaine Smith, eds., *Mary McLeod Bethune: Building a Better World: Essays and Selected Documents.* Bloomington: Indiana University Press, 1999.

McConnell, Grant. *The Decline of Agrarian Democracy.* Berkeley: University of California Press, 1953.

McCoy, Donald R. *Landon of Kansas.* Lincoln: University of Nebraska Press, 1966.

McCraw, Thomas K. *Morgan Versus Lilienthal: The Feud Within the TVA.* Chicago: Loyola University Press, 1970.

McDonald, Michael J., and John Muldowny. *TVA and the Dispossessed: The Resettlement of Population in the Norris Dam Area.* Knoxville: University of Tennessee Press, 1982.

McElvaine, Robert S. *The Great Depression: America, 1929-1941.* New York: Times Books, 1984. Revised edition, 1993.

McGovern, James R. *And a Time for Hope.* Westport, CT: Praeger, 2000.

McKinzie, Richard D. *The New Deal for Artists.* Princeton: Princeton University Press, 1973.

McLerran, Jennifer. *A New Deal for Native Art: Indian Arts and Federal Policy, 1933-1943.* Tucson: University of Arizona Press, 2009.

McWilliams, Carey. *Factories in the Field: The Story of Migratory Farm Labor in California.* Boston: Little, Brown, 1939.

Mecklenburg, Virginia M. *The Public as Patron: A History of the Treasury Department Mural Program.* College Park: University of Maryland, 1979.

Meeks, Eric V. "Protecting the 'White Citizen Worker': Race, Labor, and Citizenship in South-Central Arizona, 1929-1945." *Journal of the Southwest* 48 (Spring 2006): 91-113.

Meier, August, and Elliott Rudwick. *Along the Color Line: Explorations in the Black Experience.* Urbana: University of Illinois Press, 1976. Reprint, 2002.

Melosh, Barbara. *Engendering Culture: Manhood and Womanhood in New Deal Public Art and Theater.* Washington, D.C.: Smithsonian Institution Press, 1991.

Meltzer, Milton. *Violins and Shovels: The WPA Arts Projects.* New York: Delacorte Press, 1976.

Mertz, Paul E. *New Deal Policy and Southern Rural Poverty.* Baton Rouge: Louisiana State University Press, 1978.

Mills, C. Wright. *The New Men of Power.* New York: Harcourt, Brace, 1948.

Milton, David. *The Politics of U.S. Labor: From the Great Depression to the New Deal.* New York: Monthly Review Press, 1982.

Mittelstadt, Jennifer. *From Welfare to Workfare: The Unintended Consequences of Liberal Reform, 1945-1965.* Chapel Hill: University of North Carolina Press, 2005.

Moehling, Carolyn M. "The American Welfare State and Family Structure: An Historical Perspective." *The Journal of Human Resources* 42 (Winter 2007): 117-55.

Moley, Raymond. *After Seven Years.* New York: Harper and Brothers, 1939.

———. *The First New Deal.* New York: Harcourt, 1966.

Molho, Anthony, and Gordon Wood, eds. *Imagined Histories: American Historians Interpret the Past.* Princeton: Princeton University Press, 1998.

Monroe, Gerald M. "The Artists' Union of New York." Ed.D. dissertation. New York University, 1971.

Moon, Henry. *A Balance of Power: The Negro Vote.* New York: Doubleday, 1948. Reprint, New York: Kraus Reprint, 1969.

Moreno, Paul D. *From Direct Action to Affirmative Action: Fair Employment Law and Policy, 1933-1972.* Baton Rouge: Louisiana State University Press, 1997.

Morgan, Arthur. *The Making of the TVA.* Buffalo: Prometheus Books, 1974.

Morgan, Iwan. "Jimmy Carter, Bill Clinton, and the New Democratic Economics." *The Historical Journal* 47 (November 2004): 1015-39.

Morris, Charles. *The Blue Eagle at Work: Reclaiming Democratic Rights in the American Workplace.* Ithaca: Cornell University Press, 2004.

Morrison, Minion K. C., ed. *African Americans and Political Participation.* Santa Barbara, CA: ABC-CLIO, 2003.

Myrdal, Gunnar. *An American Dilemma: The Negro Problem and American Democracy.* New York: Harper Brothers, 1944.

Nelson, Bruce. *Workers on the Waterfront: Seamen, Longshoremen, and Unionism in the 1930s.* Urbana: University of Illinois Press, 1988.

Noyes, Alexander Dana. *The Market Place: Reminiscences of a Financial Editor.* Boston: Little, Brown, 1938.

O'Connor, Francis V. *Art for the Millions; Essays from the 1930s by Artists and Administrators of the WPA Federal Art Project.* Greenwich, CT: New York Graphic Society, 1973.

———. *Federal Support for the Visual Arts: The New Deal and Now.* New York: New York Graphic Society, 1969.

———. *The New Deal Art Projects.* Washington, D.C.: Smithsonian Institution, 1972.

O'Connor, John, and Lorraine Brown. *Free, Adult, and Uncensored: The Living History of the FTP.* Washington, D.C.: New Republic Books, 1978.

Ottanelli, Fraser. *The Communist Party of the United States of America: From the Depression to World War II.* New Brunswick: Rutgers University Press, 1991.

Ottley, Roi. *"New World A-Coming": Inside Black America.* Boston: The Riverside Press, 1943.

Owen, A. L. Reisch. *Conservation under F.D.R.* New York: Praeger, 1983.

Paarlberg, Donald. *American Farm Policy: A Case Study of Centralized Decision-Making.* New York: J. Wiley, 1964.

Park, Marlene, and Gerald E. Markowitz. *Democratic Vistas: Post Offices and Public Art in the New Deal.* Philadelphia: Temple University Press, 1984.

Patel, Kiran Klaus. *Soldiers of Labor: Labor Service in Nazi Germany and New Deal America, 1933-1945.* New York: Cambridge University Press, 2005.

Patterson, Robert T. *The Great Boom and Panic: 1921-1929.* Chicago: Henry Regnery, 1965.

Paulsen, George E. *A Living Wage for the Forgotten Man: The Quest for Fair Labor Standards, 1933-1941.* London: Associated University Presses, 1995.

Penkower, Monty Noam. *The Federal Writers' Project: A Study in Government Patronage of the Arts.* Urbana: University of Illinois Press, 1976.

Perkins, Francis. *The Roosevelt I Knew.* New York: Penguin Group, 1946.

Perkins, Van. *Crisis in Agriculture: The Agricultural Adjustment Administration and the New Deal.* Berkeley: University of California Press, 1969.

Phillips, Sarah T. *This Land, This Nation: Conservation, Rural America, and the New Deal.* New York: Cambridge University Press, 2007.

———. "Lessons From the Dust Bowl: Dryland Agriculture and Soil Erosion in the United States and South Africa, 1900-1950." *Environmental History* 4 (April 1999): 245-66.

Phillips-Fein, Kim. *Invisible Hands: The Making of the Conservative Movement from the New Deal to Reagan.* New York: W.W. Norton, 2009.

Pimpare, Stephen. *A People's History of Poverty in America.* New York: The New Press, 2011.

Piven, Frances Fox, and Richard A. Cloward. *Poor People's Movements: Why They Succeed, How They Fail.* New York: Vintage Books, 1977.

Pollan, Michael. *Omnivore's Dilemma: A Natural History of Four Meals.* New York: Penguin Press, 2006.

———. *In Defense of Food: An Eater's Manifesto.* New York: Penguin Press, 2008.

Poole, Mary. *Segregated Origins of Social Security: African Americans and the Welfare State.* Chapel Hill: University of North Carolina Press, 2006.

Powell, Jim. *FDR's Folly: How Roosevelt and His New Deal Prolonged the Great Depression.* New York: Crown Forum, 2003.

Prindle, David F. "Voter Turnout, Critical Elections, and the New Deal Realignment." *Social Science History* 3 (Winter 1979): 144-70.

Pritchett, C. Herman. *The Tennessee Valley Authority: A Study in Public Administration.* Chapel Hill: University of North Carolina Press, 1943.

Purcell, Aaron D. *White Collar Radicals: TVA's Knoxville Fifteen, the New Deal, and the McCarthy Era.* Knoxville: University of Tennessee Press, 2009.

Quinn, Susan. *Furious Improvisation: How the WPA and a Cast of Thousands Made High Art out of Desperate Times.* New York: Walker, 2008.

Rabinowitz, Paula. *They Must Be Presented: The Politics of Documentary.* New York: Verso, 1994.

Radford, Gail. *From Tenements to the Taylor Homes: The Search for an Urban Housing Policy in Twentieth-Century America.* University Park: Pennsylvania State University Press, 2000.

———. *Modern Housing for America: Policy Struggles in the New Deal Era.* Chicago: University of Chicago Press, 1996.

Radosh, Ronald, and Murray N. Rothbard, eds. *A New History of Leviathan: Essays on the Rise of the American Corporate State.* New York: E.P. Dutton, 1972.

Raper, Arthur. *Preface to Peasantry: The Tale of Two Black Belt Counties.* Chapel Hill: University of North Carolina Press, 1936.

Rauch, Basil. *The History of the New Deal, 1933-1938.* New York: Creative Age Press, 1944.

Rauchway, Eric. *The Great Depression and the New Deal: A Very Short Introduction.* New York: Oxford University Press, 2008.

———. "New Deal Denialism." *Dissent* 57 (Winter 2010): 68-72.

Rawick, George, ed., *The American Slave: A Composite Autobiography.* 19 vols. Westport, CT: Greenwood Press, 1972-1979.

Reading, Don. "New Deal Activity and the States, 1933-1939." *Journal of Economic History* 33 (December 1973): 792-810.

Reagan, Patrick. *Designing a New America: The Origins of New Deal Planning, 1890-1943.* Amherst: University of Massachusetts Press, 1999.

Renshaw, Patrick. "Was There a Keynesian Economy in the USA between 1933 and 1945?" *Journal of Contemporary History* 34 (July 1999): 337-64.

Rhoads, William B. "Franklin D. Roosevelt and Washington Architecture." *Records of the Columbia Historical Society, Washington, D.C.* 52 (1989): 104-62.

Richburg, Donald. *My Hero: The Indiscreet Memoirs of an Eventful But Unheroic Life.* New York: Putnam, 1954.

Roberts, Michael. *The Great Recession: Profit Cycles, Economic Crisis, a Marxist View.* N.P.: Michael Roberts, 2009.

Rogers, Daniel. *Atlantic Crossings: Social Politics in a Progressive Age.* Cambridge: Harvard University Press, 1998.

Romer, Christina D. "The Great Crash and the Onset of the Great Depression." *Quarterly Journal of Economics* 105 (August 1990): 598-623.

Roosevelt, Eleanor. *This I Remember.* New York: Harper, 1949.

Roosevelt, Elliot. *As He Saw It.* New York: Duell, Sloan, and Pearce, 1946.

Roosevelt, Franklin D. *Whither Bound?* Boston: Houghton Mifflin, 1926.

———. *Looking Forward.* New York: John Day, 1933. Reprint, New York: Touchstone, 2009.

Rosen, Elliot A. *Hoover, Roosevelt, and the Brains Trust: From Depression to New Deal.* New York: Columbia University Press, 1977.

Rosenman, Samuel I., comp. *The Public Papers and Addresses of Franklin D. Roosevelt.* 13 vols. New York: Random House, 1938-1950.

———. *Working with Roosevelt.* New York: Harper, 1952.

Rosenzweig, Roy, ed. *Government and the Arts in Thirties America: A Guide to Oral Histories and Other Materials.* Fairfax, VA: George Mason University Press, 1986.

Rosenzweig, Roy, and Barbara Melosh. "Government and the Arts: Voices from the New Deal Era." *The Journal of American History* 77 (September 1990): 596-608.

Rothbard, Murray N. *America's Great Depression.* Princeton: Princeton University Press, 1963.

Rozwenc, Edwin C., ed. *The New Deal: Revolution or Evolution?* Lexington, MA: D.C. Heath, 1959.

Rundell, Walter, Jr. "Main Trends in U.S. Historiography Since the New Deal: Research Prospects in Oral History." *The Oral History Review* 4 (1976): 35-47.

Runte, Alfred. *National Parks: The American Experience.* Lincoln: University of Nebraska Press, 1979.

Rutkow, Eric. *American Canopy: Trees, Forests, and the Making of a Nation.* New York: Scribner, 2012.

Saab, A. Joan. *For the Millions: American Art and Culture between the Wars.* Philadelphia: University of Pennsylvania Press, 2004.

Salmond, John A. *The Civilian Conservation Corps, 1933-1942: A New Deal Case Study.* Durham, NC: Duke University Press, 1967.

Saloutos, Theodore. *The American Farmer and the New Deal.* Ames: Iowa State University Press, 1982.

Savage, Sean J. *Roosevelt: The Party Leader, 1932-1945.* Lexington: University Press of Kentucky, 1991.

Schivelbusch, Wolfgang. *Three New Deals: Reflections on Roosevelt's America, Mussolini's Italy, and Hitler's Germany, 1933-1939*. New York: Picador, 2006.

Schlesinger, Arthur M., Jr. *The Age of Jackson*. Boston: Little, Brown, 1946.

———. *The Age of Roosevelt*. 3 vols. Boston: Houghton Mifflin, 1957-1960.

———. *Cycles of American History*. Boston: Houghton Mifflin, 1986.

Schultz, Theodore. *Redirecting Farm Policy*. New York: Macmillan, 1943.

Schwarz, Jordan A. *The New Dealers: Power Politics in the Age of Roosevelt*. New York: Alfred A. Knopf, 1993.

Scroop, Daniel. *Mr. Democrat: Jim Farley, the New Deal, and the Making of Modern Politics*. Ann Arbor: The University of Michigan Press, 2006.

Shapiro, David. *Social Realism: Art as a Weapon*. New York: Frederick Ungar, 1973.

Sherwin, Martin. *A World Destroyed: The Atomic Bomb and the Grand Alliance*. New York: Knopf, 1975.

Sherwood, Robert E. *Roosevelt and Hopkins: An Intimate History*. New York: Harper and Brothers, 1948.

Shindo, Charles. *Dust Bowl Migrants in the American Imagination*. Lawrence: University of Kansas Press, 1997.

Shlaes, Amity. *The Forgotten Man: A New History of the Great Depression*. New York: Harper Perennial, 2007.

Shogan, Robert. *Backlash: The Killing of the New Deal*. Chicago: Ivan R. Dee, 2006.

Singleton, Jeff. *The American Dole: Unemployment Relief and the Welfare State in the Great Depression*. Westport, CT: Greenwood, 2000.

Sitkoff, Harvard, ed. *Fifty Years Later: The New Deal Evaluated*. Philadelphia: Temple University Press, 1985.

———. *A New Deal for Blacks: The Emergence of Civil Rights as a National Issue*. New York: Oxford University Press, 1978.

Sklaroff, Lauren Rebecca. *Black Culture and the New Deal: The Quest for Civil Rights in the Roosevelt Era*. Chapel Hill: University of North Carolina Press, 2009.

Skocpol, Theda, and Kenneth Finegold. "Explaining New Deal Labor Policy." *The American Political Science Review* 84 (December 1990): 1297-1315.

Smith, Gene. *The Shattered Dream: Herbert Hoover and the Great Depression*. New York: Morrow, 1970.

Smith, Jason Scott. *Building New Deal Liberalism: The Political Economy of Public Works, 1933-1956*. New York: Cambridge University Press, 2006.

Smith, Sharon. *Subterranean Fire: A History of Working Class Radicalism in the United States*. Chicago: Haymarket Books, 2006.

Sobel, Robert, *Herbert Hoover at the Onset of the Great Depression*. Philadelphia: Lippincott, 1975.

Solomon, Burt. *FDR v. The Constitution: The Court-Packing Fight and the Triumph of Democracy.* New York: Walker, 2009.

Steele, Richard W. *Propaganda in an Open Society: The Roosevelt Administration and the Media, 1933-1941.* Westport, CT: Greenwood Press, 1985.

Steinbeck, John. *The Grapes of Wrath.* New York: Viking Press, 1939.

Sternsher, Bernard. *Consensus, Conflict, and American Historians.* Bloomington: Indiana University Press, 1975.

Stock, Catherine McNicol, and Robert D. Johnston, eds. *The Countryside in the Age of the Modern State: Political Histories of Rural America.* Ithaca: Cornell University Press, 2001.

Stokes, Melvyn, ed. *The State of U.S. History.* New York: Berg, 2002.

Stott, William. *Documentary Expression and Thirties America.* New York: Oxford University Press, 1973.

Street, Richard Steven. *Beasts of the Field: A Narrative History of California Farmworkers, 1769-1913.* Palo Alto: Stanford University Press, 2004.

Sugrue, Thomas. *Land of Liberty: The Forgotten Struggle for Civil Rights in the North.* New York: Random House, 2008.

Sullivan, Patricia. *Days of Hope: Race and Democracy in the New Deal Era.* Chapel Hill: University of North Carolina Press, 1996.

——. *Lift Every Voice: The NAACP and the Making of the Civil Rights Movement.* New York: The New Press, 2009.

Sunstein, Cass. *The Second Bill of Rights: FDR's Unfinished Revolution and Why We Need It More than Ever.* New York: Basic Books, 2004.

Susman, Warren I. *Culture as History: The Transformation of American Society in the Twentieth Century.* New York: Pantheon Books, 1984.

Sutter, Paul. *Driven Wild: How the Fight against Automobiles Launched the Modern Wilderness Movement.* Seattle: University of Washington Press, 2002.

——. "Terra Incognita: The Neglected History of Interwar Environmental Thought and Politics." *Reviews in American History* 29 (June 2001): 289-97.

——. "What Gullies Mean: Georgia's 'Little Grand Canyon' and Southern Environmental History." *The Journal of Southern History* 76 (August 2010): 579-616.

Talbert, Roy, Jr. *FDR's Utopian: Arthur Morgan of the TVA.* Jackson: University of Mississippi Press, 1987.

Talbot, David. "Saving Holland." *Technology Review* 110 (July 2007): 50-56.

Taylor, David A. *Soul of a People: The WPA Writer's Project Uncovers Depression America.* Hoboken, NJ: Wiley, 2009.

Taylor, Gregory S. *The History of the North Carolina Communist Party.* Columbia: University of South Carolina Press, 2009.

Taylor, Nick. *American-Made: The Enduring Legacy of the WPA: When FDR Put the Nation to Work.* New York: Bantam, 2008.

Taylor, Paul. *Essays on Land, Water, and the Law in California.* New York: Arno Press, 1979.

Temin, Peter. *Did Monetary Forces Cause the Great Depression?* New York: Norton, 1976.

Trattner, Walter. *From Poor Law to Welfare State: A History of Social Welfare in America.* New York: Free Press, 1999.

Tugwell, Rexford. *The Brains Trust.* New York: Viking Press, 1968.

———. *The Democratic Roosevelt: A Biography of Franklin D. Roosevelt.* New York: Doubleday, 1957.

Tull, Charles. *Father Coughlin and the New Deal.* Syracuse: Syracuse University Press, 1965.

Unger, Irwin. "The 'New Left' and American History: Some Recent Trends in United States Historiography." *The American Historical Review* 72 (July 1967): 1237-63.

U.S. Congress. *Congressional Record.* 75th Congress, 3rd Sess., 1938. Vol. 83, pt. 2: 2305-306.

U.S. Senate. "A Bill to Provide for a Permanent Bureau of Fine Arts." March 1, 1938, 75th Congress, 3rd Session. Washington, D.C.: United States Government Printing Office, 1938.

Verba, Sidney, and Kay Lehman Schlozman. "Unemployment, Class Consciousness, and Radical Politics: What Didn't Happen in the Thirties." *The Journal of Politics* 39 (May 1977): 291-323.

Vermeer, Dura. "High and Dry Concept." *Technology Review* 110 (July 2007): 56.

Walker, Richard. *Conquest of Bread: 150 Years of Agribusiness in California.* New York: The New Press, 2004.

Wallace, Henry A. *America Must Choose: The Advantages and Disadvantages of Nationalism, of World Trade, and of a Planned Middle Course.* Boston: World Peace Foundation, 1934.

———. *New Frontiers.* New York: Reynal and Hitchcock, 1934.

Ward, Geoffrey C. *Before the Trumpet: Young Franklin Roosevelt, 1882-1905.* New York: Harper and Row, 1985.

———. *A First-Class Temperament: The Emergence of Franklin Roosevelt.* New York: Harper and Row, 1989.

Warren, Donald. *Radio Priest: Charles Coughlin, the Father of Hate Radio.* New York: The Free Press, 1996.

Warren, Frank. *Noble Abstractions: American Liberal Intellectuals and World War II.* Columbus: Ohio State University Press, 1999.

Warren, G. F. "The Agricultural Depression." *The Quarterly Journal of Economics* 38 (1924): 184-213.

Warren, Harris Gaylord. *Herbert Hoover and the Great Depression.* New York: Oxford University Press, 1959.

Watkins, T. H. *The Hungry Years: A Narrative History of the Great Depression in America*. New York: Henry Holt and Company, 1999.

——. *The Great Depression: America in the 1930s*. New York: Little, Brown, 1993.

Weaver, Audrey. "Declared For Equality in First Bid for Presidency, Held Fast to Policy." *Baltimore Afro-American*. April 14, 1945.

Weber, Karl, ed. *Food Inc.: How Industrial Food is Making Us Sicker, Fatter and Poorer*. New York: Public Affairs, 2009.

Weed, Clyde P. *The Nemesis of Reform: The Republican Party During the New Deal*. New York: Columbia University Press, 1994.

Weinberg, Gerhard L. *Visions of Victory: The Hopes of Eight World Leaders of World War II*. New York: Cambridge University Press, 2005.

Weisiger, Marsha. *Dreaming of Sheep in Navajo Country*. Seattle: University of Washington Press, 2009.

Weiss, Nancy J. *Farewell to the Party of Lincoln: Black Politics in the Age of FDR*. Princeton: Princeton University Press, 1983.

Whatley, Warren C. "Labor for the Picking: The New Deal in the South." *The Journal of Economic History* 43 (December 1983): 905-29.

Willkie, Wendell. *This is Wendell Willkie: A Collection of Speeches and Writings on Present-Day Issues*. New York: Dodd, Mead, 1940.

Whisnant, David. *Modernizing the Mountaineer: People, Power and Planning in Appalachia*. Knoxville: University of Tennessee Press, 1994.

White, Eugene Nelson. "A Reinterpretation of the Banking Crisis of 1930." *The Journal of Economic History* 44 (March 1984): 119-38.

——, ed. *Crashes and Panics: The Lessons From History*. Homewood, IL: Dow Jones-Irwin, 1990.

White, G. Edward. *The Constitution and the New Deal Court*. Cambridge: Harvard University Press, 2000.

White, Richard D., Jr. *Kingfish: The Reign of Huey P. Long*. New York: Random House, 2006.

Whitman, James Q. "Of Corporatism, Fascism, and the First New Deal." *The American Journal of Comparative Law* 39 (Autumn 1991): 747-78.

Williams, T. Harry. *Huey Long*. New York: Vintage Books, 1981.

Willis, H. Parker. "Who Caused the Panic of 1929?" *North American Review* 229 (February 1930): 174-83.

Wise, Gene. *American Historical Explanations: A Strategy for Grounded Inquiry*. Minneapolis: University of Minnesota Press, 1980.

Wolfskill, George. *The Revolt of the Conservatives: A History of the American Liberty League, 1934-1940*. Boston: Houghton Mifflin, 1962.

Wolters, Raymond. *Negroes and the Great Depression: The Problem of Economic Recovery*. Westport, CT: Greenwood, 1970.

Worster, Donald. *Dust Bowl: The Southern Plains in the 1930s.* New York: Oxford University Press, 1979.

———. *Rivers of Empire: Water, Aridity, and the Growth of the American West.* New York: Pantheon Books, 1985.

Wright, Gwendolyn. *Building the Dream: A Social History of Housing in America.* Boston: MIT Press, 1981. Reprint, New York: Pantheon Books, 1983.

Zeigler, Joseph Wesley. *Arts in Crisis: The National Endowment for the Arts Versus America.* Chicago: Chicago Review Press, 1994.

Zeigler, Robert. *American Workers, American Unions.* Baltimore: Johns Hopkins University Press, 1994.

Zhang, Aimin. *The Origins of the African-American Civil Rights Movement, 1865-1965.* New York: Routledge, 2002.

Zinn, Howard, ed. *New Deal Thought.* New York: Bobbs-Merrill, 1966. Reprint, Indianapolis: Hackett, 2003.

———. *A People's History of the United States: 1942-Present.* New York: Harper Collins, 2003.

Contributors

MICHAEL W. BARBERICH is a visiting assistant professor at the University at Albany, SUNY, where he teaches courses in presidential and political rhetoric, media communication, and the cultural history of radio broadcasting. He completed his PhD in rhetoric and communication at the University of Pittsburgh. His dissertation, "From the Frontier to the Fireside: Rhetoric and Public Memory in the Depression and the War," concerned the use of public memory in Roosevelt's fireside chats.

MICHAEL A. DAVIS is an associate professor of history at Liberty University, and the author of a forthcoming book on the wartime presidential campaign of 1944. He completed his PhD in history at the University of Arkansas. He lives in Lynchburg, Virginia, with his wife Holly and their three girls.

JENNIFER EGOLF teaches world history at Indiana University of Pennsylvania. She earned her PhD in history at the University of West Virginia. Her dissertation, "'Keep America American': Great Depression, Government Intervention, and Rural Conservative Response in Somerset County, Pennsylvania, 1922-1940," analyzed the ways in which New Deal programs, affecting farmers and the unemployed, created tension among rural Americans. Egolf co-edited *Culture, Class and Politics in Modern Appalachia: Essays in Honor of Ronald L. Lewis* (Morgantown: West Virginia University Press, 2009), which includes her chapter, "Radical Challenge and Conservative Triumph: The Struggle to Define American Identity in the Somerset County Coal Strike, 1922-1923." Her historical focus on twentieth-century United States includes specializations in labor, gender, and community.

TODD HOLMES is a postdoctoral fellow with the Bill Lane Center for the American West at Stanford University. He earned his PhD in history at Yale University and is the author of several publications, including the award-winning article, "The Economic Roots of Reaganism," in the *West-*

ern Historical Quarterly. His current book project uses the United Farm Workers Movement to examine shifts in party politics and political economy between the 1960s and 1980s.

PETER LUDDINGTON-FORONJY is an associate professor of history at Mt. San Jacinto Community College. He received his PhD in history at the University of California, Los Angeles. He is currently researching Franklin D. Roosevelt's role promoting economic interdependence in the international arena as both a means for preventing another global conflict and a vehicle for raising living standards throughout the world.

SHARON ANN MUSHER is an associate professor of history and director of the Master of Arts in American Studies at the Richard Stockton College of New Jersey. She earned a PhD in history from Columbia University. Musher has published articles and reviews in *American Quarterly, Journal of Interdisciplinary History, Jewish Journal of Sociology,* and *Women and Social Movements.* She has a forthcoming chapter on the WPA slave narratives in *The Oxford Handbook of the African American Slave Narrative* (New York: Oxford University Press), and her book, *A New Deal for Art,* is under contract with the University of Chicago Press.

STUART PATTERSON teaches a broad range of courses in the natural and social sciences and humanities at Shimer College in Chicago, Illinois. He earned a PhD in history from Emory University. His dissertation examined two New Deal "new towns" at Arthurdale, West Virginia, and Aberdeen Gardens, Virginia. Patterson's research explores themes in the culture and politics of the 1930s, including the myths and rituals of twentieth-century American life.

AARON D. PURCELL is a professor and director of special collections at Virginia Tech. He earned his PhD in history from the University of Tennessee and his Master's of library science from the University of Maryland, College Park. Purcell is the author of *White Collar Radicals: TVA's Knoxville Fifteen, the New Deal, and the McCarthy Era* (Knoxville: University of Tennessee Press, 2009), *Academic Archives: Managing the Next Generation of College and University Archives, Records, and Special Collections* (Chicago: Neal-Schuman, 2012), and *Arthur Morgan: A Progressive Vision for American Reform* (Knoxville: University of Tennessee Press, 2014). He is also the editor of *The Journal of East Tennessee History.*

DOUGLAS SHEFLIN is a PhD candidate and part-time instructor at the University of Colorado, Boulder. He studies modern American history with a focus on both environmental history and the history of the West. Sheflin's dissertation, "Conservation in Transition: The Colorado Plains through Dust, Rain, and War," deals with land use in southeast Colorado during the 1930s and 1940s, with a special focus on how residents responded to the Dust Bowl, New Deal reforms, and the onset of World War II.

GREGORY S. TAYLOR is a native of Rochester, New York. He earned a B.A. in history from Clemson University, an M.A. in history from The University of Alabama, and a PhD in history from The University of Mississippi. Taylor is the author of *The History of the North Carolina Communist Party* (Columbia: University of South Carolina Press, 2009), and *The Life and Lies of Paul Crouch: Communist, Opportunist, Cold War Snitch* (Gainesville: University Press of Florida, 2014). He serves as an associate professor of history at Chowan University in Murfreesboro, N.C.

GLORIA-YVONNE WILLIAMS received her PhD in history, gender, and women's studies from the University of Illinois at Chicago. Her dissertation, "A Passion for Social Equality: Mary McLeod Bethune's Race Woman Leadership and the New Deal," is a political biography that also focuses on the political friendship of Bethune and Eleanor Roosevelt. She has a chapter on Bethune in *The Economic Civil Rights Movement: African Americans and the Struggle for Economic Power,* ed. Michael Ezra (New York: Routledge, 2013). Her research and teaching interests include gender and ethnicity during the trans-Atlantic slave trade, transnational abolitionism in the nineteenth century, and women's social and political activism from the late nineteenth to the twentieth century.

Index